W9-CWT-535

DIMENSIONS OF LOVE

Other Books by the Author

MAN NEEDS GOD: An Interpretation of Biblical Faith

THE BEGINNING OF ETERNAL LIFE: The Dynamic Faith of Thomas Aquinas, Origins and Interpretation

DIMENSIONS OF FAITH: Yesterday and Today

THE ORIGIN AND EVOLUTION OF THE PRIESTHOOD: A Return to the Sources

THE HERESY OF MONASTICISM: The Christian Monks—Types and Anti-Types

COSMOS, MAN, GOD, MESSIAH: An Introduction to Religion

THE SCHOOL OF JESUS: An Overview of Christian Education Yesterday and Today

DIMENSIONS OF LOVE
East and West

James A. Mohler, S.J.

Doubleday & Company, Inc.

Garden City, New York

1975

Library of Congress Cataloging in Publication Data

Mohler, James A
    Dimensions of love: East and West.

    Bibliography
    Includes index.
        1. Love—History.   2. Love (Theology)—History.
    I. Title.
    BD436.M58   291.4
    ISBN 0-385-02473-8
    Library of Congress Catalog Card Number 74-9458

Grateful acknowledgment is given for permission to quote material from the following sources:

Sufism: An Account of the Mystics of Islam by A. J. Arberry, 1968, George Allen & Unwin, Ltd.; *On the Necessity of Loving God* by Bernard of Clairvaux, Terence Connoly, S.J., tr., published by Ave Maria Press; *A Literary History of the Arabs* by R. A. Nicholson, 1953, Cambridge University Press; *The Mathnawi* of Jalal al-Din Rumi, R. A. Nicholson, tr., 1934, Cambridge University Press; *The Pennants*, A. J. Arberry, tr., 1953, Cambridge University Press; from *The Collected Works of St. John of the Cross*, translated by Kieran Kavanaugh and Otilio Rodriguez. Copyright © 1964 by Washington Province of the Discalced Carmelites, Inc. Paperback edition published by ICS Publications, Washington, D.C., U.S.A.; *Buddhist Texts Through the Ages*,

Swami Prabhavananda, tr., 1968, Capricorn Books, G. P. Putnam Sons; *The Wisdom of China and India*, Lin Yutang, ed., 1942, Random House, Inc.; *The Zohar*, H. Sperling and M. Simon, trs., 1931, The Soncino Press, Ltd.; *The Sacred Books of Confucius*, C. and W. Chai, eds., 1965, University Books; *Mystical Poems of Rumi*, A. Arberry, tr., 1968, University of Chicago Press, courtesy of The Persian Heritage Series; *Narada's Way of Divine Love*, Swami Prabhavananda, tr., © 1971 by Vedanta Society of Southern California, published by Vedanta Press.

CONTENTS

      (Martin Luther, Wittenberg Sermons, March 9,
      1522)   275

         Communion of the Saints   276
         Faith and Love   284
         True Love vs. Crummy Love   287

XV.   O LIVING FLAME OF LOVE THAT TEN-
      DERLY WOUNDS MY SOUL IN ITS DEEP-
      EST CENTER (John of the Cross, *The Living
      Flame of Love*, 1)   291

         The Mystic Stream   291
         Teresa of Avila   294
         Teresa's Works of Love   298
         John of the Cross   307
         John's Works of Love   309

XVI. THE STATE OF LOVE CONSISTS IN A
      FLOWING OVER OF THE EGO-LIBIDO TO
      THE OBJECT (Sigmund Freud, *On Narcis-
      sism*, 121)   320

         Freud, Youth and Times   320
         Stages of Development   322
         Theories of Love   324
         Religious Love   332
         Response   337

XVII. EPILOGUE   341

         Varieties of Love   341
         Human Love Today   342
         Divine Love Today   347
         Conclusion   348

ILLUSTRATIONS

By Adrienne von Lates

1. "The *jen*-hearted man cannot be resisted by the multitude" (Mencius, 4a/7)

2. *Yin-yang*

3. "In every home there is a goddess of mercy" (Chinese proverb)

4. "Now always yours" (*Gita Govinda*)

5. "Ever climbing aloft" (Plato, *Symposium*, 211)

6. "She has loved much" (Luke 7/47)

7. "We are not yet wise and happy" (Augustine, *The Happy Life*, 4/35)

8. "The love of love itself" (De Rougemont, *Love in the Western World*, 46)

9. "The little butterfly has died with greatest joy at having found her rest" (Teresa of Avila, *The Interior Castle*, 7/3/1)

10. "The state of love consists in a flowing over of the ego-libido to the object" (Freud, *On Narcissism*, 121)

PRINCIPAL ABBREVIATIONS

ACW   *Ancient Christian Writers*, J. Quasten, et al., eds. (New York, Paulist/Newman)

DOB   *Dictionary of the Bible*, J. McKenzie (New York, Crowell-Collier)

FOC   *The Fathers of the Church*, R. Deferrari (Washington, D.C., Catholic University Press)

LCL   The Loeb Classical Library (Cambridge, Mass., Harvard University Press)

LW   *Luther's Works*, J. Pelikan and H. Lehmann, eds. (Philadelphia and St. Louis, Fortress Press)

NPNF   *A Select Library of the Nicene and Post-Nicene Fathers*, second series, P. Schaff and H. Wade, eds. (Grand Rapids, Eerdmans)

PL, PG   *Patrologiae Cursus Completus*, J.-P. Migne, ed. (Paris)

RMI   *Readings from the Mystics of Islam*, M. Smith, tr. (London, Luzac and Co.)

SE   *The Standard Edition of the Complete Psychological Works of Sigmund Freud,* S. Strachey and A. Freud, eds. (London, Hogarth)

WA   *M. Luthers Werke,* Weimar Edition

PROLOGUE

Love is a most popular subject. Probably more poems, plays, songs, novels have been written about love than about any other human experience. Why is man so intrigued by love? It is the very foundation of his relationships with his fellow man, as Confucius and Mencius teach us. Moreover, it is man's basic union with his god either through the Hindu *bhakti,* the Hebrew's marriage to Yahweh, or Christian and Moslem mysticism.

Love fired philosophers such as Plato and Aristotle, poets such as Homer and Ovid, teachers such as Jesus, Paul, Augustine, and Dionysius. Love inspired the medieval troubadours and modern psychiatrists. All sing of the need for love in man and his world or between man and his god. Sometimes the loves of the gods are celebrated in human love, as in the Hindu *shakti* yoga or the Jewish Kabbalah.

Our hope in this book is to gather together the many dimensions of love from different cultures, religions, and races to compare and contrast. It is not our main purpose to show influences, for example, whether Hindu love influenced Islamic traditions. Rather we wish to present the different views and let the reader make his own comparisons and parallels. Often cultures are so interwoven that it is difficult to ferret out ancestral lines. Of course, some trends are more evident, such as the Neo-Platonic stress in Augustine or the Islamic nuances in the troubadours.

Love is as important today as it ever has been. Millions of

marriages each year attest to the validity of male-female love. Increasing interest in Eastern and Western mysticism may reflect a new search for divine love. One of the questions we would like to pursue is the interrelationship between these two loves. Are they the same, or are they incompatible? Which is the greater? Can we have one without the other?

Love today, though popular as ever, is also in trouble, for we are in an age of free love. Some feel that today's sex without love is a reaction to the Victorian age's love without sex. Love can be a delight, but it also can be fleeting, can bring distress, sorrow, and suffering. This ambivalence of love we hope to follow through the ages.

There is much we can learn from the philosophers, teachers, mystics, troubadours, and even scientists of love, for they have battled with the same problems faced by today's lovers. Sometimes the same keen insights on love can be found in widely separated cultures. Perhaps this indicates that fundamentally man is the same, with similar love needs, human and divine, whether he lived thousands of years ago or today.

❧ I ❧

WHEN ALL THE PEOPLE IN THE WORLD LOVE EACH OTHER, THEN THE STRONG WILL NOT OVERPOWER THE WEAK

Mo Tzu

Confucius

It is appropriate to begin the discussion of love with the great Chinese teacher Master Kung, often called Confucius (6th–5th cent. B.C.). Perceiving that the China of his day was in a state of decay, he felt divinely called to teach morality.

Anarchy reigned, with 36 cases of regicide in 242 years and the emperor's court filled with concubines, wives, children, intrigue. For a while Confucius served as chief minister bringing a harsh peace. But he resigned when the emperor took up with some traveling dancing girls.

Confucius is a teacher of morality, one of the many great teachers honored in Chinese tradition. In a sense he is the founder of the great Chinese intellectual and cultural heritage. He taught poetry, history, music, and ritual to over three thousand students, free of charge. His teachings may be found in the *Ch'un Ch'iu* (*Spring and Autumn Annals*) and the *Lun Yu* (*Analects*).

For Confucius the secret to human morality lies in improved relationships between men. Confucius was accused by the Taoists and later by the modern Communists of favoring the upper ruling classes, especially in treating of the ideal relationship between the prince and the emperor. Taoists in particular say that overstress on ceremony and filial piety can lead to artificiality.

For Confucius, *jen* 仁 is the fundamental virtue of life. *Jen* combines man 亻 and two 二. Thus it is the essential relationship that should exist between two men. *Jen* is humaneness, humanity, and includes love, fellowship, charity, and kindness. To possess *jen* is to be truly human and to lack it is to be inhuman. *Jen* is the very foundation of Confucian ethics and politics.

One who practices *jen* is of the royal line, the lord's son, *chun-tzu* 君子, a prince and a true gentleman. He is the extreme opposite of the *hsiao jen* 小人, the small man.

Jen must begin in the home with fundamental family relationships: *hsiao* 孝, filial piety with the young son bearing up his old father, and *ti* 俤, fraternal love, and *hao* 好, good, those whom one loves, namely wife 女 and children 子.

Beginning with the family, *hsiao* and *ti* are to be extended to all men in social solidarity, implying allied virtues such as *chung* 忠, honesty and loyalty to oneself, and *shu* 恕, to forgive and feel compassion for others. Of course all the virtues are intertwined, though *jen* is more of the heart whereas *yi* 義, righteousness, is more of exterior conduct.

Ch'u Chai writes:

> *Jen* as the prime virtue of life leads the way in prompting us to positive efforts for the good of others. *Yi* follows as the highest principle embodied in the activities of mankind. *Li*, as the outward expression of moral sentiment and the standard of conduct, sheds light on *jen* and *yi* by bringing the whole conduct into harmony with reason and order, thus completing the foundation of Confucianism, to which all the humanistic principles and values are attributed.[1]

Jen is the central theme of Confucius' ethics and government. Humanity, humaneness are the bywords. That is, a man should be human to his fellow men. Only the true man has *jen*. The one who has no *jen* is inhuman and, therefore, not really a man at all. He is weak and despicable, *hsiao jen*. Confucius speaks of *jen* in the *Analects*. "It is only the man of *jen* who knows how to love and how to hate people" (4/3).[2]

If a *chun-tzu* (gentleman) departs from *jen*, he is unworthy of such a name. Not even for the space of a single meal should a *chun-tzu* act contrary to *jen*. In moments of hate, he cleaves to it. In times of difficulty he cleaves to it. (4/5).

When Chung Kung asked about *jen*, the Master said:

When abroad, behave as if you were meeting an honored guest. In employing the people, act as if you were officiating in the grand sacrifice. What you do not wish to yourself, do not do to others. Then neither in the country nor in the family will there be any resentment against you (12/2).

Not all, however, agreed with Confucius. For example, Mo Tzu (6th cent. B.C.) taught a universal love, because Heaven, *Tien* 天, loves all equally, a certain democracy that sometimes seemed to be missing in Confucius. Moreover, he reacted to Confucian love of music, fatalism, extravagance, and agnosticism. Also he felt that universal love is incompatible with war. Eventually Mo Tzu's teachings lost popularity. Perhaps they were too altruistic for the practical Chinese.

What is universal love?

It is to regard the state of others as one's own, the houses of others as one's own, the persons of others as one's self. When feudal lords love one another, there will be no more war. When heads of houses love one another, there will be no more mutual usurpation. When individuals love one another, there will be no more mutual injury. When ruler and ruled love each other, they will be gracious and loyal. When father and son love each other, they will be affectionate and filial. When elder and younger brothers love each other, they will be harmonious. When all the people in the world love one another, then the strong will not overpower the weak, the many will not oppress the few, the wealthy will not milk the poor, the honored will not disdain the humble, and the cunning will not deceive the simple. This is all due to mutual love that calamities, strifes, complaints, and hatred are prevented from arising. Therefore, the benevolent exalt it. . . . Whoever loves others is loved by others; whoever benefits others is benefited by others; whoever hates others is hated by others; whoever injures others is injured by them.[3]

The basis of Mo Tzu's universal human love is a divine universal love. Even Kung spoke of the *Tao*, or Way 道, as the Way of Heaven, *Tao Tien* 道天 . By and large, Heaven favors the good. Though Mo Tzu honored religious ceremony (*li*), he believed that it should not replace *jen*.

Tien, Heaven 天, drawn as a line over the head of a man was honored as a deity in the Chou dynasty (12th–3rd cent. B.C.), who felt that their revolt was justified by Heaven.

Mo Tzu teaches:

Now Heaven loves the whole world universally. Everything is prepared for the good of man. Even the tip of the hair is the work of Heaven. Substantial may be said of the benefits that are enjoyed by man. Yet there is no service in return, and they do not even know this to be unmagnanimous and unfortunate. This is why I say that the gentlemen understand only trifles and not things of importance.[4]

But the people do not appreciate the gifts of Heaven: sun, moon, stars; four seasons; snow, frost, rain, and dew to give grain, flax, and silk; hills, rivers, and valleys. Heaven appoints leaders to reward the good and punish the evil, to gather metal, wood, birds, and cultivate grain and flax and silk for the people. But man is ungrateful.

Though it eventually faded, for several centuries Mohism

was a successful rival of Confucianism. Zealous, frugal, and radical, whereas the Confucianists stressed culture, ceremony, and gentlemanliness.

Mencius

Master Meng or Mencius (4th cent. B.C.) studied with a disciple of Confucius' grandson. Although he was an admirer of Confucius, Mencius was more of an extrovert.

As his mentor, he placed a high value on *jen* 仁 but joined it with *yi* 義, righteousness, which is the counterpart of *jen* in one's external conduct.

Mencius founded his teachings on the basic goodness of human nature. It is human to be good and to love. Only the inhuman are evil and hate. What makes men bad is not their nature but the environment. Confucian etiquette and propriety improve the environment.

The cosmos follows the Law of Heaven, which man can perceive by looking within himself. This inwardness of Mencius shows similarities to Taoist mysticism.

It is by virtue of its innate quality that human nature can be considered good. This is why I say it is good. If it becomes evil, it is not the fault of its innate quality.

The sense of compassion is common to all of humanity (*jen*). The sense of shame constitutes righteousness (*yi*), the sense of respect constitutes propriety (*li*). The sense of righteousness constitutes wisdom (*chih*). (*The Book of Mencius*, 6a/6)

Men have these innate virtues in various degrees as they have discovered them or neglected them.

Is it possible for a man to lose *jen*? Yes, if he loses his good heart. Just as a tree is cut by an ax, so man by the inroads of the daily grind and occupations loses *jen* gradually and the nourishing influence of the night diminishes. Thus man gradually reverts to the animal status. But this does not mean that he never had *jen*. But rather that he had it and failed to cultivate it. (6a/8)

The proper relationships of man depend on his human nature.

> *Jen* in relating to father and son, *yi* in relation to sovereign and minister, *li* in relation to guest and host, *chih* in relation to men of worth and the sage in relation to the *Tao* of Heaven. All these relationships are submissive to fate, but their observance depends upon human nature. (1/7)

> To be a man (*jen*) is to show a heart of compassion and forgiveness, *shu* 恕, combining a womanly compliance with the higher impulses of the heart (*hsin*) 心.

> One who lacks a sense of compassion is not a man; one who lacks a sense of shame and dislike is not a man; one who lacks a sense of modesty and yielding is not a man; and that one who lacks a sense of right and wrong is not a man. The sense of compassion is the beginning of *yi*. The sense of modesty and yielding is the beginning of *li*. The sense of right and wrong is the beginning of wisdom (*chih*). Man has these four beginnings just as he has four limbs. (2a/6)

Later we will see the importance of compassion (*shu;* Sanskrit: *karuna*) in Chinese Buddhism.

Whereas the intellect and reason are the signs of humanity for the Greeks, the source of *jen* for the Chinese is the heart, *hsin* 心. We have already seen the centrality of the heart to the virtues of *chung* 忠, honesty, and *shu* 恕, compassion.

The man who loses his heart, loses *jen*. "The way to learning is nothing but the search for the lost heart." (6a/11) "The great man is he who has not lost his child's heart." (4b/12) The child's heart is naturally good, uncorrupted, open to others, filled with *jen*. But as one gets older, he tends to lose his innocence.

Mencius, as Confucius, sees the *chun-tzu* 君子, the lord's

son, a true gentleman, as the ideal of *jen*. "The *chun-tzu* in his heart upholds *jen* and *li*. *Jen* is the love due to men. *Li* is the respect due to men. He who loves men will certainly be loved by men. He who respects men will certainly be respected by men." (4b/28)

The *chun-tzu* is big-hearted, magnanimous. His opposite is the small man, a mean and despicable person, *hsiao jen*. This small person has little humanity. Of course, this does not refer to smallness of age or size, because a child has a magnanimous heart.

The *chun-tzu* never rests satisfied, for he is constantly anxious lest he fail in *jen*, lest he become a *hsiao jen*. This state of anxiety has been described as *yu-huan*. Thus the Confucian sage is dissatisfied when he fails to do a good act, when he fails to help each creature reach its destined fulfillment.

The Confucianist is conscious of his responsibility to his inner moral fiber. *Noblesse oblige*. For Mencius the anxious conscience feels the value of its own nature, the very foundation of moral goodness. Sin is dishonesty to this inner law of goodness.

As Confucius, Mencius is concerned with humane *jen* government. This is not ruling by force, but rather by good example. The *wang* 王, or king, is an example of *jen* to the people.

Some explain *wang* 王 with the vertical line representing the king, who connects the horizontal lines of Heaven, earth, and mankind. All three are connected by *jen*. Others see the calligraph as a string of the jade beads of the ruling class. At any rate, the *jen wang* is the opposite of the harsh feudal lord.

The king must act as a model of *jen* to his people. "If the sovereign is *jen*-hearted, all the people will be *jen*-hearted. If he is righteous, all will be righteous." (4b/5) And again: "Never has one become a king without winning the heart of the world." (4b/16) And: "There are cases when a single man devoid of *jen* has won a state. But there is not a single case where a man devoid of *jen* has ever won the world." (7b/13)

"Master Kung said, 'The *jen*-hearted man cannot be resisted by the multitude.' Thus if the sovereign of a state is fond of *jen*, he has no enemies in the world." (4a/7) But many rulers refuse to uphold humanity. This is like a man grabbing a red-hot iron rod without first wetting his hands. There is only one way to govern and that is by love, humanity, *jen*. This is the government of a true *wang* who joins Heaven and earth. The rule of the tyrant (*pa*) cannot endure.

1. "The *jen*-hearted man cannot be resisted by the multitude" (Mencius, 4a/7)

The *jen* of the ruler is shown by his practical concern for the people. The Chinese are practical people, so their *jen* is not just a theoretical virtue but must be shown in action. If the people are hungry, the *jen* ruler provides grain, guarding the seasons of farming and ecology, conserving the forests and planting mulberry bushes to provide silk for the aged. Respect for the aged (*hsiao*) is a sign of the *jen*-hearted ruler. "No ruler under whom the aged have silk to wear and meat to eat, and the common people suffer neither from hunger nor cold, has ever failed to be a [true] king [of the whole world]." (1a/3)

Jen government must be shown in action, fundamentally in land reform and conservation, dividing the land equally in the *ching tien* system. In a sense *jen* leadership ties in with the *Tao*, the Divine Way, the cosmic order, the natural way, the proper use of land, forests, and water. And the people, especially the old, must be cared for.

Kindness to the old is typical of the *jen* ruler. This is an extension of filial piety *hsiao* 孝 with the youth holding up the old man. This extends even further in the honoring of the dead. "When there is a sovereign in the world who serves the old well, all *jen*-hearted men will go to him." (7b/27)

The *jen*-hearted sovereign is the key to a *jen*-hearted state. "For this reason only he who abides by *jen* is fit to occupy a high position. When one who lacks *jen* occupies a high place, his evils will spread among the people." (4a/1)

Devoid of *jen*, the sovereign brings disgrace upon himself. "Now the sovereign who hates disgrace and yet acts contrary to *jen* is like one who hates damp and yet dwells on low ground." (2a/4)

Is the law of *jen* man-made or is it from Heaven? Confucius worshipped Heaven, *Tien* 天, though ethics and religion are not distinguished in his teachings. The Way of Heaven is the way of man, *tao* 道. *Jen* 仁, man's innate good nature, is from Heaven. It is the *jen*-hearted king, *wang* 王, who joins Heaven, earth, and man.

Indestructible and unchangeable, the Heavenly Law surpasses all. But although transcendent, it exists in the mind of the sage. Incarnate in the heart of man, the Law of Heaven constitutes man's basic humanity, his *jen*-heartedness. Is the Heavenly Law spoken from above? "No! Heaven does not speak, but makes its will known through man's conduct and his deeds." (5a/5)

As we have seen, Mencius is convinced of the goodness of man's nature, prompting him to do good acts for others. But these naturally good urges had to be cultivated to achieve *jen* and *yi*. Extending his heart to include others, one develops his spirit so that it fills all between Heaven and earth according to *tao* and *yi*.

The scholar pursues *jen* and *yi*. "Where should one's dwelling be? *Jen*. What should one's path be? *Yi*. When one lives in *jen* and follows *yi*, he occupies himself with what the great man should be occupied." (7a/33)

Jen and *yi* are gifts of Heaven along with loyalty, sincerity, and delight in goodness. If one uses them to acquire earthly honors, he will lose both. (6a/16)

Not all, of course, agreed with Mencius on the basic goodness of man. For example, Hsun Tzu (3rd cent. B.C.), living at the climax of the warring states, was convinced of man's evilness. Goodness must be acquired.

Later Confucian Schools

The teachings of the later Confucian schools was gathered in the *Li Chi*, the *Book of Rites*, an important part of which is the *Ta Hsueh* 大學. This teaches self-cultivation in the *Tao* of the Great Learning, uniting ethics and politics. This leads to the well-cultivated individual, the well-regulated family, the well-governed state, and finally a peaceful and harmonious world. The three guiding principles of the *Ta Hsueh* are: manifestation of illustrious virtues, loving the people, and rest in the highest good, the three main cords of ethical and political development. Eight minor wires include: investigation of things, extension of knowledge, sincerity of one's thoughts, rectification of one's heart, cultivation of one's person, regulation of one's family, governing of one's state, and insurance of world peace.

Jen or love is one of the three main cords of the *Ta Hsueh*. Thus King Wen. "As a sovereign, he rested in *jen;* as a minister, he rested in reverence; as a son, he rested in filial piety; as a father, he rested in kindness; in intercourse with the people, he rested in good faith." (3/11)[5]

There is an ascending order in the *Ta Hsueh*. Thus unless one can regulate his own life, rectifying his heart and extending his knowledge, he can never rule his family. And unless he can govern his family in love, how can he rule the state? "When one family practices *jen,* the whole state will abide by *jen*. When one family is prudent, the whole state will become prudent" and vice versa. (4/21)

"Happy be the lord—he is the parent of the people (*shih*). When the sovereign loves what the people love and hates what the people hate, then he is called the parent of the people." (3/25) The king shows *jen* and the people respond with *yi*. But "if the man who governs the state is devoted to the accumulation of wealth, he has no choice but to employ *hsiao jen*." As long as the *hsiao jen*, the small man, is employed in the state—disaster and injuries will be the result. (3/36)

In the *Chung Yung*, another part of the *Li Chi*, *ch'eng* 誠, sincerity, corresponds to *jen* 仁. This along with *chung yung* constitutes the *Tao* of Heaven and earth. The sincere man moves other men.

Hsiao Ching, the *Book of Filial Piety*, dates from the Han dynasty. According to the Confucian tradition, filial piety is not just in the family but in the whole life, political, social, etc. It begins in the home, but extends as *jen* to all men.

> The Master said, "One who loves one's parents does not dare to hate others. One who reveres one's parents does not dare to spurn others. When love and reverence are thus cherished in the service of one's parents, one's moral influence transforms the people and one becomes a pattern to all within the four seas. This is the filial piety of the son of Heaven." (ch. 2)

Hsiao Ching then describes the filial piety of the feudal princes, high officers, scholars, and the people.

Filial piety, *hsiao*, unites Heaven and earth. The Master said:

> Filial piety is the basic principle of Heaven, the ultimate standard of earth, and the norm of conduct for the people. Men ought to abide by the guiding principle of Heaven and earth as the pattern of their lives, so that by the brightness of Heaven and the benefits of earth they would be able

to keep all in the world in harmony and in unison. . . .
The early kings, knowing that their teachings could transform the people, made themselves an example of practicing
all-embracing love. Thereby the people do not neglect their
parents. (ch. 7)

The filial piety of the *chun-tzu,* the lord's son, spreads to all
men.

He need only teach filial piety and he will show reverence
due to all the fathers of the world. He need only teach
brotherly deference and thereby show reverence due to all
the elder brothers of the world. He need only teach the
duties of ministers and thereby show reverence due to all
the sovereigns of the world. In the *Shih* it is said, "The
princely man, cheerful and pleasant, is the father and mother
of the people! Without possessing the supreme virtue how
can he keep the people in harmony?" (ch. 13)

The *Li Chi,* the *Book of Rites,* contains the Confucian etiquette of social, political, ethical, and religious order known
as *li* 禮.

Confucianists see music as a unifying force in human relations. Whereas *li* 禮 separates and makes distinctions, music,
yueh 樂, unites and brings peace and harmony.

In spring all things burst forth, and in summer all things
grow. This is *jen.* In autumn all things consummate, and in
winter all things repose. This is *yi. Jen* is akin to music and
yi is like *li.* Music establishes union and harmony, and so
it accords with *shen* (spirits) and follows the pattern of
Heaven. *Li* maintains difference and distinction and so it
accords with *kuei* (ghosts) and follows the pattern of earth.
Therefore the sage creates music in response to Heaven and
institutes *li* to match earth. When *li* and music are distinct
and complete, Heaven and earth function in perfect order.
(p. 343)

Tung Chung-Shu (2nd cent. B.C.) a Neo-Confucianist, includes elements of Taoism in his *Ch'un Ch'iu Fan-lu.*

> As Heaven has its dual qualities of *yin* 陰 and *yang* 陽 the self has qualities of *tian* and *jen* 仁. As Heaven has restraints for *yin* and *yang*, the self has its confiner of feelings and desires. In this same sense, man is at one with the course of Heaven. (ch. 1)

Tung Chung-Shu taught a certain synergism. Thus man is born good but must try to improve himself. Heaven creates the seed of man's goodness but he must bring it to fruition. Man's nature is naturally good, reflecting the Taoist tradition. But he needs education to bring it to full bloom (Confucian).

Man is composed of *yang* and *yin*, male and female principles, just as Heaven and earth are. Man alone is capable of *jen* and *yi*, love and righteousness, uniting himself to Heaven.

We have seen some developments of Confucianism with the stress on *jen* 仁, humanity, manliness, love, which contrasts with the small man, *hsiao jen* 小人. *Jen* begins in the single person and extends to the family in *hsiao* and *ti*, filial piety and brotherly love. Then it projects itself to those outside and eventually to the whole world.

Now let us turn to a companion Chinese philosophy, Taoism and its teachings on love.

❧ II ❧

THE SAGE PUTS HIS OWN PERSON LAST AND YET IT IS FOUND IN THE FOREMOST PLACE

Tao Te Ching, 7

Tao

Though there were some vestiges of mysticism in Mencius, by and large the Confucian school was practical and activist. Taoism may have been a reaction to Confucianism with the feeling that the stress on *jen* and *li* could lead to artificiality and hypocrisy with too much emphasis on external deportment, ministers, etc. While the artificiality of Confucianism tends to bog down, the natural morality of Tao is creative.

One of the fundamental books of Taoism is the *Tao Te Ching*, attributed to Lao Tzu. Dating from the fourth century B.C., it is an anthology of brief passages. Lao Tzu means Old Teacher and may refer to a class of wandering teachers in the post-Kung period.

Some see in the *Tao Te Ching* a certain naturalistic quietism in the face of the fierce rulers of the Warring States.[1] Thus the Chinese saying: "The officials are like the wind, and the people grass. When the wind blows, the grass bends." Others see in the *Tao Te Ching* a work of genuine religious mysticism.

What is the *Tao*? In Master Kung it appears as the *Tao Tien*

道天, the Way of Heaven, a way of life that is sanctified by Heaven. The *Tao* of Lao Tzu seems to be a divine principle underlying and controlling the world. But it is a *Tao* that defies expression, definition, analysis, and words. This characteristic would also be *Tao*'s gift to Ch'an Buddhism.

The *Tao* is the First Principle which begets all creatures. Smart[2] compares it with the Great Mother goddess of many primitive peoples, the Eternal Feminine, passive, *yin*. Thus behind all the visible world and the invisible world is a supreme power, world soul, called *Tao*, indefinable, indescribable, in a sense nonexistent, source of all and eternal sustainer of creation.[3]

The perfect man is in complete agreement with *Tao*. He is not concerned with endless rituals and etiquette of the Confucianists, rather pursuing the natural way.

Indefinable in artificial scientific terms, *Tao*'s inherent nature is purity, tranquillity, rest, unity, and spirituality without any force, violence, or artificiality. Meekness, tenderness, poverty of spirit, and quietness, all are varieties of the essential emptiness of *Tao*. Only when the heart is empty is it open to the spirit of truth.

Wu-wei

Wu-wei 無為, nonaction, nonstriving, is a central theme of Taoism. Nature, the mother of all, acts through nonaction. Yet by its passivity it is creative. *Wu-wei* is perhaps better expressed as *Tao-wei*, action by the Spirit. The true man, *chen jen*, the perfect man, *chih jen*, is unworldly with suppressed desires and so identifies with the *Tao*, the inward Spirit. He will do nothing against nature or *Tao*.

Wu-wei also means a lack of dependence on artificiality or human strength, not clever, not relying on appearances or words, not tricky or demagogic. The disciple of *Tao* looks incompetent to the world because he is not trying to make an impression. No falsity or artificiality here. No, he lives by the spirit of *Tao*. *Wu-wei* seems so passive. Yet if man is passive, the *Tao* will act naturally. Heaven and earth were begotten by *wu*, the nonexistent, *Tao*, the Spirit. Parallels to *wu-wei* are: spontaneous, simple, pristine nature, absence of desire. "If we consider that action refers to deliberate, contrived, externally imposed efforts toward some personally desired end, then nonaction is a state of being from which actions freely flow."[4]

The *Tao Te Ching* says:

Tao invariably takes no action, and yet there is nothing left undone. If kings and barons can keep it; all things will transform spontaneously. If after transformation, they should desire to be active, I would restrain them with simplicity, which has no name. Simplicity, which has no name, is free of desires. Being free of desires, it is tranquil. And the world will be at peace of its own accord. (37)

This conquering of desires reminds us of the teachings of Gautama Buddha on the road to Nirvana.

The Book of Chuang Tzu (4th cent. B.C.) comments on *wu-wei*:

I look at what ordinary people find happiness in, what they all make a mad dash for, racing around as though they couldn't stop. They all say they're happy with it. I'm not happy with it and I'm not unhappy with it. In the end is there really happiness or isn't there?

I take inaction to be true happiness, but ordinary people think this is a bitter thing. I say highest happiness has no happiness, the highest praise has no praise. The world can't decide what is right and wrong and yet inaction can decide this. The highest happiness—keeping alive—only inaction gets you close to this.

Let me try to put it this way. The inaction of Heaven is its purity, the inaction of earth is its peace. So the two inactions combine and all things are transformed and brought to birth, wonderfully, mysteriously. There is no place they come out of. Mysteriously, wonderfully, they have no sign. Each thing minds its business and all grow out of inaction. So I say, Heaven and earth do nothing and there is nothing that is not done. Among men who can get hold of this inaction?[5]

Heaven and earth are passive and inactive, yet they produce all.

Closely allied with inaction, nature, and *Tao* is freedom from accretions of artificiality, *li*, and Confucianism. The true man, living on the basis of Heaven and earth, moves freely in virtue and harmony.

This includes a certain forgetfulness of others, live and let live, as the fishes are unmindful of each other, each going his own way. Yet this is not neglectfulness or carelessness or selfishness. "Forgetfulness is a state or condition in which all things live their own free lives unhindered and without interference."[6] Those following the natural way of *Tao* are not mindful of class, privilege, rank, *li*, etc. The perfect man, surrendering his spirit, is the only free man.

The sage seeks harmony with the *Tao*, the natural way. This prompts the Taoist to live close to nature. He is self-sufficient, not dependent in any way on the artificialities of life. His desire is only to have no desires.

In the political arena *wu-wei* means that the best government is the least government. Understandably Taoism was popular among the lower classes, whereas Confucianism appealed more to the higher levels of society. The Taoist is not a scholar in the Confucian sense, but more properly a mystic emptying his mind to better intuit the eternal *Tao* and unite himself with it.

The Three Jewels of Tao

The three jewels of *Tao* found in the *Tao Te Ching* are gentleness or mercy, economy, and not placing oneself ahead of others. Returning love for hate and humility for arrogance.

With that gentleness, I can be bold; with economy I can be liberal; not taking precedence over others, I can be a leader.

Nowadays they give up gentleness and are all for being bold, economy and are all for being liberal, the last place and seek the first. This is certain death.

Gentleness is sure to be victorious even in battle, and firmly to maintain its ground. Heaven will save its possessor, by his very gentleness protecting him.[7]

Water illustrates the humility of *Tao*, always placing oneself below others. Yet water, though seeking the lower places, is yet powerful. Men will drill deep wells to reach the humble stream. "The highest good is like water. Water gives life to the 10,000 things and does not strive. It flows in places men reject and so is like *Tao*." (8)[8]

Humility and self-effacement are the hallmarks of the Taoist.

Therefore, the sage holds in his embrace the one thing (humility) and manifests it all to the world. He is free from self-display, and therefore he shines; from self-assertion, and therefore he is distinguished; from self-boasting, and therefore his merit is acknowledged; from self-complacency, and therefore he acquires superiority. They do not quarrel, so no one quarrels with them. Therefore, the elders say, "Yield and overcome." Is that an empty saying? Be really whole and all things will come to you. (22)

Living for Others

Living for others is the key to successful Taoist living and it will be rewarded by the longevity for which he strives.

Heaven is long-enduring and earth continues long. The reason why Heaven and earth are able to endure and continue thus long is because they do not live of or for themselves. This is how they are able to continue and to endure. Therefore the sage puts his own person last and yet it is found in the foremost place. He treats his person as if it were foreign to him, and yet that person is preserved. Is it not because he has no personal and private ends that, therefore, such ends are realized? (7)

Putting oneself last is the secret of *Tao*. Humility is attractive, pride repels. Again the analogy of water is used.

That whereby the rivers and seas are able to receive the homage and tribute of all the valley streams is their skill in being lower than they—it is thus that they are the kings of them all. So it is that the sage wishing to be above men, puts himself by his words below them. And wishing to be before them, places his person behind them. (66)

Parallels can be found in later philosophers. "He who humbles himself shall be exalted." "The last shall be first."

Loving others and putting oneself last preclude war and aggression, for these are against *Tao*.

When you advise a ruler in the way of *Tao*, counsel him not to use force to conquer the universe. For this would only cause resistance. Thorn bushes spring up wherever the army has passed. Lean years follow in the wake of a great war. Just do what needs to be done. Never take advantage of power. (30)

Of course, one may fight of necessity, as in a defensive war, but not just to achieve mastery over another. Strength and power can only presage impending death. "Force is followed by loss of strength. This is not the way of *Tao*. That which goes against the *Tao* comes to an early end." (30)

And again:

Now arms, however beautiful, are instruments of evil omen, hateful, it may be said, to all creatures. Therefore, they who have the *Tao* do not wish to use them. (31)

The superior man ordinarily considers the left hand the most honorable place, but in time of war the right hand. Those sharp weapons are instruments of the superior man. He uses them only on the compulsion of necessity. Calm and repose are what he prizes. Victory [by force of arms] is to him undesirable. To consider this desirable would be to delight in the slaughter of men. And he who delights in the slaughter of men cannot get his will in the kingdom. (31)

In times of joy the left hand is the place of honor, in times of mourning the right hand. Thus the victor in battle who has killed many has his place on the right.

Universal love and kindness are the marks of a true sage.

The sage has no invariable mind of his own. He makes the mind of the people his mind. To those who are good [to me] I am good; and to those who are not good [to me] I am also good—and thus all get to be good. To those who are sincere [with me], I am sincere; and to those who are not sincere [with me], I am also sincere—and thus all get to be sincere. (49)

The *Tao* is the simple way not for the learned or clever. It is basically self-giving and self-forgetting as Heaven and earth are. "The sage does not accumulate [for himself]. The more that he expends for others, the more does he possess of his own. The more that he gives to others, the more does he have himself." (81) Simplicity, naturalness, selflessness, self-giving, humility, love, mark the *Tao*, the spirit of Heaven.

Though *Tao* is absolute and eternal, the world sees ceaseless changes and transformations. Two central themes in Chinese thought are *yin* and *yang* 陰陽. *Yang* is Heaven, active, masculine, light, while *yin* is earth, passive, feminine, and dark. Baird and Bloom[9] remark that *yin-yang* may have arisen from the early ceremonial confrontation of boys and girls preceding betrothal. Also weather changes reflect the *yin-yang* of nature, from the dark, cloudy, rainy, and cold (*yin*) to the bright, sunny, dry, and warm (*yang*). Some see the Confucianists as *yang*-like in their activity, while the Taoists pursue the passive mother of nature in *yin*.

2. *Yin-yang.*

As we have seen, Confucianism is a philosophy more of the upper classes, with ritual and etiquette, but Taoism appeals to the masses and soon absorbs elements of demonology, ancestor worship, and popular beliefs, with an elaborate pantheon, alchemy, and magic.

Taoism would meet and meld with Buddhism, exchanging themes and practices. It is the Taoist selflessness which paves the way for the success of the Chinese Mahayana Bodhisattva, whom we shall see in the following chapter.

~s III s~

WHEN HE (*BODHISATTVA*) EXERTS HIMSELF FOR THE GOOD OF OTHERS, HE SHOULD BE FILLED WITH LOVE AND LOVE ALONE WITHOUT ANY ADMIXTURE OF SELF-INTEREST

Arycura, Arya-Curas, Jataka-Mala, 4/24

Karuna

Karuna, selfless love and compassion with the suffering neighbor, plays a strong part in Buddhism, especially of the Mahayana variety. We see it beginning in Siddhartha Gautama's conversion and enlightenment in sixth-century-B.C. India. Impressed by the suffering of the world in sickness, old age, and death, he sought out the life of an ascetic in order to find the way to heal the wounds of the world.

Turning to meditation, Buddha found the defeat of suffering (*dukkha*) in nirvana, the squelching of desire (*tanha*), the root cause of suffering in the world. This is basically a personal struggle. Buddha resisted the temptation to remain in nirvana, and spent the rest of his life teaching his companions the way to enlightenment and the conquering of desire.

An important part of Buddha's eightfold path to nirvana is love and compassion for others. Return love for hate, taught Gautama.

If a man foolishly does me wrong, I will return to him the

protection of my ungrudging love. The more evil comes from him, the more good shall come from me. The fragrance of goodness always comes to me, and the harmful air of evil goes to him.

When someone abused him, Buddha replied: "Son, if a man declined to accept a present made to him, to whom would it belong?" To which the insulter responded: "In that case, it would belong to the man who offered it." So the abuse fell back on the abuser.[1]

The *Dhammapada*, an early Buddhist classic, describes compassion as the chief duty of the *bhikkhu* (monk). "Let him be perfect in his duties. Then in the fulness of delight he will make an end to suffering." (25) Controlling desires, the *bhikkhu* makes war on his own evil tendencies. Forgoing sexual pleasure (*kama*), by his compassion (*karuna*) he attacks the suffering of others.

Karuna is the positive side of *ahimsa*, not harming, the traditional Buddhist doctrine going back to the monk-king Asoka (3rd cent. B.C.). *Ahimsa*, coming in both Buddhism and Jainism, may have been a reaction to the violence and sufferings of the times. Some see it as a rejection of the bloody Vedic sacrifices. The practice soon spread to Hinduism, where it is seen as an expression of solidarity in *Atman*. Thus if each self is identical with every other self, he who harms another really harms himself. And he who helps others really is helping himself. (*Bhagavad-Gita*, 13/28, 5/25)

Ahimsa is also taught by Tiruvalluvar in his *Kural* (10th cent. A.D.). In part one, *Aram* (*Dharma*) he writes: "Even when another has injured him in his hate, the man who is pure in heart returns not the injury." (312) And: "The greatest virtue is non-killing; killing brings in its train every other evil." (321)[2]

Although *ahimsa* is basically "non-killing," it can also include vegetarianism, harmlessness, passive resistance, and pacifism. Its positive thrust includes *karuna* (understanding the needs of others), *daya* (tender sympathy), and *maitri* (welfare).

It is in Mahayana Buddhism that self-giving love of the *bhikkhu* comes into full bloom in the *bodhisattva*. Beginning in India, Mahayana Buddhism spread to China, Korea, and Japan. Mahayana means the greater vehicle—that is, a broader way of salvation including laymen and not limited to monks as in the Theravada branch.

Mahayana Buddhists were dissatisfied with some of the narrower doctrines of early Buddhism. For example, the belief that nirvana is extinction, and also the salvation of a few vis-à-vis the Mahayana principle of the salvation of all by the *bodhisattvas* (Buddhas-to-be), who, although they have tasted nirvana, nevertheless forgo its delights and submit to rebirth in order to save the world.

Prayer and devotion to the personal Buddha is characteristic of Mahayana, and an overall kindness to life in all forms. For example, in the *Suranyama Sutra* (1st cent. A.D.), the lord Buddha advises the assembled *bhikkhus* never to wear silk or leather because it means the taking of life. Even if one drinks milk or eats cheese, he deprives young calves of their sustenance.

> So all *bhikkhus* must be careful to live in all sincerity, refraining from even the appearance of unkindness to other life. It is such true-hearted *bhikkhus* who will attain a true emancipation. Even in one's speech and especially in one's teaching, one must practice kindness, for no teaching that is unkind can be the true teaching of Buddha. Unkindness is the murderer of the life of wisdom.[3]

The Bodhisattva

The *bodhisattva* of Mahayana Buddhism is one who has given his life for others. In lieu of a self-centered seeking of nirvana, he is wholly dedicated to the salvation of others.

Moreover, the *bodhisattva* should make use of all transformations to help creatures, whether as disciples, laymen, kings, lords, even harlots, adulterers, thieves, butchers, etc., so as to mix with all kinds of people in order to help them to salvation.

Karuna 悲, compassion, sympathy, and kindness, is the hallmark of the *bodhisattva*. Sometimes it is called *mahakaruna*, the height of compassion, 大悲.

For example, the *Ashtasahasrika* (1st cent. B.C.) (12/402–04) describes the compassion of a *bodhisattva*. "He becomes endowed with that kind of wise insight which allows him to see all beings as on the way to their slaughter. Great compassion thereby takes hold of him." The *bodhisattva* is anxious for the salvation of all those whose *karma* is leading them to hell, those who have had unfortunate rebirths, those who are about to be killed, those enveloped in false views, or who have lost a favorable rebirth.

He radiates a great friendliness and compassion over all those things and gives attention to them, thinking: "I shall become a savior to all those beings. I shall release them from their sufferings."[4]

Just as the heroic man does not abandon his family in the forest despite personal dangers, "so it is with the *bodhisattva* who is full of pity and concerned with the welfare of all beings, who dwell in friendliness, compassion, sympathetic joy and even-mindness."[5]

Mahayana Buddhism so stresses *karuna* that it seems to downplay wisdom. Whereas in early Mahayana altruism is one means of attaining enlightenment, in later times it seems to be a good in itself. Even placing the *bodhisattvas* who are on the road to enlightenment ahead of the buddhas, those already enlightened.[6]

The *bodhisattva* is raised to a high level early in the person of Manjukri and later in Avalokitesvara.

Avalokitesvara absorbs all the virtues, powers, functions and prerogatives of the other *bodhisattvas*. Because he is the Lord of Mercy, he occupies the supreme position in the universe and reigns without a rival. *Karuna* (mercy, love, pity, compassion) and its personification Avalokitesvara are all one. This is the last word and the consummation of Mahayana.[7]

Later in Chinese Mahayana Buddhism *karuna* is personified in the goddess of mercy Kuan-yin, the Chinese misinterpretation of the Sanskrit Avalokitesvara, and in the Japanese Kannon-In. Beginning as a male, he soon becomes a mother goddess of mercy.

Avalokitesvara can be translated as the "Lord who sees, or looks down," "the Lord of View," "the Lord of Compassionate Glances," "the Lord who sees the World with Pity." He regards with compassion all beings suffering from the evils of existence.[8]

Avalokitesvara is the chief minister in Amitabha's paradise and can be seen as an emanation of Buddha himself. Kuan-yin is often found in the Chinese Mahayana trinity along with Amitabha and Mahasthamaprapta, the personification of wisdom.

Here it might be good to make some mention of *bhakti*, which plays such a strong role in Mahayana Buddhism along with shrines, statues, and personifications of *bodhisattva* virtues. Mahayana lives of Buddha became more elaborate and supernatural. Thus the *Mahavastu* (1st cent. A.D.), in which adoration of the Buddha brings nirvana and the ten stages or *bhumis* through which the *bodhisattva* must progress. *Lalitavistara* describes the incarnation of the divine pre-existing Buddha. And the *Lotus Sutra* is also important.

Bhakti reaches its peak in the adoration of the Amitabha, the ruler of the Western Paradise. Entrance into Heaven can be gained by prayer to the Amitabha and he shares his infinite merits with the *bodhisattva*. So in lieu of the Theravada nirvana pursuit are the gifts which the gracious and merciful

Amitabha bestows on those who follow the way of love and devotion. We shall see more of *bhakti* love in the next chapter.

Avalokitesvara, Amitabha's chief minister of paradise and personification of his mercy, gives relief in the purgatory of *avici* and *pretas*, liberating them into the paradise of Sukhavati.

He helps all those in need. If they are hungry, he provides rain for the crops. If naked, he gives clothing; if sick, health; etc. He is the father and mother of all and, as we have seen, becomes the mother of mercy in Chinese and Japanese Mahayana Buddhism, perhaps because compassion is seen as a more feminine virtue.

Avalokitesvara's apotheosis culminates with his identification with the Spirit of the Universe and achieving the attributes of Brahman and Icvara. He has ten thousand arms and a million eyes. The sun and moon are from his eyes. Gods come from his shoulders and heart. And he has innumerable pores in which the faithful can be reborn.

Buddha for Others

How does one become a *bodhisattva?* The *bodhisattva* begins by thinking of and desiring to become a buddha for the welfare of others. He makes vows and his future greatness is foretold by a living buddha. Later literature stresses the preparation for *bodhisattva*-hood by faith, worship, prayer, etc.

In the *Mahavastu* (1/133–34) the *bodhisattva* ideal is clarified.

They are men of successful achievements, and are ready to come to the assistance of others and help those in distress. They do not become enervated by prosperity, and do not lose composure in adversity. They are skilled in uprooting the vices of mean men. They are unswerving in clothing the nakedness of others. They are anxious not to blight the maturing of their *karma,* and they acquire the roots of virtue by keeping themselves aloof from passion, hatred and folly.

They are skilled in bringing solace to those in trouble and misfortune. They do not hesitate to render all kinds of service. In all matters they are untiring in their purpose.[9]

Besides concern for his own salvation, and one might say even surpassing or excluding concern for his own salvation, the *bodhisattva* desires the safety of those around him, those immersed in sense pleasures of pride, sin, ingratitude, falsehood, and degeneracy. "Reflecting on the sad state of things, one should resolve to become a *bodhisattva* in order to help and save all creatures. Such pity, mercy, love and compassion are at the very root of the thought of enlightenment."[10]

The prayer of the *bodhisattva* according to the *Bodhisattva Bhumi* (4th cent. A.D.) (6a/2.2–3.1): "O, may I obtain supreme and perfect enlightenment, promote the good of all beings, and establish them in the final and complete nirvana and in the Buddha knowledge." By his act of self-giving, the *bodhisattva* transcends past sins and *karma*. Having crossed the stream of transmigration, he now helps all the other beings to cross. Liberated himself, he now liberates others.

Besides the thirty-seven *dharmas*, practices and principles of conduct—e.g., avoiding the *kamas* (sense pleasures) and practicing ascetics (*dhuta-gunas*)—the *bodhisattva* must apply himself in the *paramitas*, perfections or virtues such as *dana* (self-giving) and *karuna* (compassion).

Perhaps there may have been a Taoist influence in the humility and self-giving of Chinese Mahayana Buddhism, not to mention the meditations of Ch'an Buddhism. In many ways *Tao* and Mahayana walk along the same road.

By his *karuna* the *bodhisattva* resolves to undergo torments and torture if necessary to lead all men to enlightenment. He is selfless, not caring for his own happiness, but only for that of others. He loves all things as a mother loves her only child. And his love for all even surpasses his love of self and family.

Liberation and knowledge are superfluous if one has *karuna*.

"Of what use are knowledge and salvation or ascetic practices (matted hair and besmearing the body with ashes) to the man whose heart melts with pity for all living creatures?"[11]

Karuna can be seen from two points of view. First, seeing the equality of oneself with others, and second, substituting oneself for others. There is no more I and thou for the *bodhisattva*, for he feels the joys and sorrows of others as if they were his own. Not only this, but he is willing to go a step further and exchange his happy life for the miseries of others, lifting up the poor and injured. The two golden rules of Mahayana are: to treat others as yourself and to treat others as they would like you to.

Mahakaruna

The *tathagata*'s or buddha's great love (*mahakaruna*) of all beings never ceases till all are led to nirvana, and he postpones his own *samadhi* till this happens, refusing to enter nirvana while there is still suffering in the world.

The *mahakaruna* of the *tathagata* for all of creation is best seen in his abstinence from eating flesh. Thus it is written in the *Lankavatara Sutra* (8/244),[12] "These meat-eaters thus abandoning their desire for [its] taste will seek the *dharma* for their food and enjoyment, and regarding all beings with love as if they were an only child, will cherish great compassion towards them."

Man has a solidarity with the animals through reincarnation. "How can the *bodhisattva* Mahasattva 大士, who desires to approach all living beings as if they were himself and to practice the Buddha truths, eat the flesh of any living being that is of the same nature as himself?" (8/246) The meat-eaters literally terrify the poor living beasts, who fear for their lives. Those who eat the flesh of other beings are reborn as carnivorous animals. (8/257) This is basically the *ahimsa*, not harming, so strong in Eastern traditions of Jainism and Buddhism. It is not just a negative state, but a positive love of all living creatures, 不害.

The *Sikshasamuccaya* of Santideva (7th cent. A.D.) describes well the great compassion of the *bodhisattva*.

I take upon myself the burden of all suffering. I am resolved to do so. I will endure it. I do not turn or run away, do not tremble, am not terrified nor afraid, do not turn back or despond. And why? At all costs I must bear the burdens of all beings in that I do not follow my own inclinations. I have made the vow to save all beings. All beings must I set free. The whole world of living things I must rescue—from the terrors of birth, of old age, of sickness, of death and rebirth, of all kinds of moral offence, of all states of woe, of the whole cycle of birth and death, of the jungle of false views, of the loss of the wholesome *dharmas* of the concomitants of ignorance—from all these terrors I must resolve all beings.[13]

The *bodhisattva* assumes the pains and burdens that are crushing creatures. He gives himself away as a pawn that the world may be delivered from pain and suffering.

The whole life of the *bodhisattva* is self-giving says the *Pancavimsahasrika* (263–64).

I give, that one receives. This is the gift. I renounce all my possessions without stint. I act as one who knows the Buddha. I practice the perfection of giving. I, having made this gift into the common property of all beings, dedicate it to supreme enlightenment, and that without apprehending anything. By means of this gift and its fruit may all beings in this very life be at their ease, and may they one day enter nirvana.[14]

One can also make his self-gift without considering either himself, the recipient, or the gift, but dedicating the gift to supreme enlightenment.

Of course, Gautama Buddha himself is the model of *ma-*

hakaruna. The *Upasaka Sila Sutra* (24/1036) says: "My children, the enlightened one, because he saw mankind drowning in the great sea of birth, death and sorrow and longed to save them, for this reason he was moved to pity."[15]

He saw them straying on false paths, wallowing in the mire of the five lusts, fettered to wealth, wives, and children, doing evil with hand, heart, and tongue, afraid of birth, old age, and death, yet continuing to pursue them, consumed by fires of pain and sorrow, subjected to cruel tyrants and kings and suffering many ills, living in time of wars, killing and wounding each other and their hatred condemning them to endless retribution. For all of this Buddha was moved to pity.

Some had heard Buddha preach and had not received it. Others were overattached to their wealth. Still others slaved in the fields and businesses yet won only bitterness. For all of these Buddha was moved to pity. Buddha had led the way by his compassionate example. Now the *bodhisattva* must follow.

Although earlier Mahayana texts speak of *svartha,* an egoistic interest in the *bodhisattva,* along with the *parartha* or altruistic, in time *parartha* dominated as the true spirit of Mahayana.

> The *bodhisattva* should not think of self at all, when he exerts himself for the good of others. He should be filled with love and love alone, without any admixture of self-interest, however sublime and spiritual it may be. His mind must be overwhelmed and saturated with the feeling of pity for others, that it is not possible for him to think of his own enlightenment at the same time. . . . "By the Merit of my sacrifice, may I use my body in my future lives for the good of all creatures." (*Arya-curas Jataka-Mala,* 4/24) (6th cent. B.C.)

When the *bodhisattva* identifies himself with others, *svartha* and *parartha* are the same. Thus in the highest synthesis egotism and altruism are merged in perfect love.[16]

Many *dana* stories of the self-giving of the *bodhisattvas* dot the *sutras*. For example, King Civi, who distributes his wealth to the people and then wounds his body to feed the insects with his blood and donates his flesh to feed the hungry vultures. Yet his body is restored whole again (*Satiadhisthana*). Another time King Civi gives his eyes to a blind priest.

Jnanavati, the daughter of King Jnanabala, gives her flesh and blood in order to provide medicine for a sick monk. Yet in all these stories the *bodhisattva* suffers no pain even though he lose his eyes, ears, etc. For he is so filled with pity and love that he feels nothing.

The *bodhisattva* can give up his limbs and even his life for others. But can he transfer his merit (*punya*) to others, since merit and demerit are personal? The old Buddhist doctrine in the Pali Canon taught that merit is personal and nontransferable, since the inequalities of men are due to their own fault.

But gradually they came to recognize the possibility of a transfer of merit, e.g., in the *Ramayana*. An awareness of the vast suffering in India led to a greater sense of social solidarity along with a more social view of *karuna* and the idea of vast places of torture for the sinners lost favor. Thus in Mahayana a *bodhisattva* could cancel a sinner's merit by giving him some of his merit and thus release him from purgatory.

Love is the supreme law of Mahayana, not vindictive *karma*. "But the doctrine of *parinamana* did not grow in the arid soil of logic and metaphysics. It sprang from the heart of the Indian people, who could not tolerate the idea of suffering of any description."[17] Thus the *bodhisattva* shares his merit with others to ease their pain and sufferings, to save them from fear and lead them to peace.

Santideva writes in his *Bodhicaryavatara* (7th cent. A.D.) of his *bodhisattva*-hood.

Through this auspicious work of mine may all people become adorned with the practice of enlightenment. May all those in all the directions who are pained by ills of body and mind win through my merits oceans of happiness and joy.

Through all the changes of transmigration may their happiness never wane. Unceasingly may the world win the happiness of the *bodhisattva*.

Whatever hells there are in the universes, may all the goings in them rejoice in the happiness and joy of the happy universe, Sukhavati.

May those pained by cold become warm and those pained by heat become cool through the oceans of water shed by the great rain clouds of the *bodhisattvas*. . . .

May there be health for the sick, may prisoners be released from all bonds; may the weak become strong, may beings become kind to one another.

May all the directions become auspicious for all that travel on the road; and may the purpose for which they journey be successful.

May those who have embarked on a ship or mounted a car, succeed in their wishes. May they reach their family in peace and take their pleasure in their kinsfolk.

May those who have lost their way in the forest light upon a caravan. May they go without fatigue, and not in fear of robbers or tigers.

To those who are asleep, intoxicated or careless, in stress of sickness or in the jungle, to orphans, children or aged persons, may the gods give protection. . . .

As the career of Manjusri is to accomplish the weal of all beings within the bounds of the firmament in the ten directions, even so may be my career.

As long as abides the region of space, as long as the world abides, so long may be my abiding to destroy the pains of the world.

Whatever pain there is in the world, may it all ripen in me; and may the world be made happy by the merits of all the *bodhisattvas*.

The medicine, the one medicine for the pains of the world, the maker of all weal and happiness, endowed with gain and honor, may it long abide.[18]

Among the many virtues of the *bodhisattva*, including the revering and saluting of the buddhas, confession of sin, etc., is the salient quality of "transferring to others the merit of his good deeds."

As we have seen, the compassion of the *bodhisattva* is personified in the Amitabha and Avalokitesvara or Kuan-yin, the goddess of mercy. Devotion to both is great in Mahayana Buddhism as the following Chinese proverb relates.

The foundation of Buddhism is compassion, its door is convenience. In every home there is a goddess of mercy. In every place there is an Amitabha Buddha.

3. "In every home there is a goddess of mercy" (Chinese proverb)

Provide conveniences to others at all times; accumulate merits of all kinds.

To save one human life is better than to build a seven-storey pagoda. To do one good deed is better than to build a nine-storey pagoda.[19]

And Amitabha is sung in Masses for the Dead.

As gleaming moonlight plays upon 1000 waters at the same time, Thy great compassion does not pass by a single creature.

Steadily and quietly sails the great ship of compassion across the sea of sorrow.

You are the great physician for a sick and impure world in pity giving the invitation to the Paradise of the West.[20]

The *bodhisattva*, then, models his life on the compassionate Amitabha in every way and especially in self-giving. He lives for others and in so doing becomes a buddha.

As selfless, loving Mahayana Buddhism began in India before moving northwards, now let us see some other Indian love themes—namely, *kama, bhakti,* and *shakti.*

ᴥᶬ IV ᶬᵛ

THOSE WHO DESIRE TO TRANSCEND
ALL LIMITATIONS AND BONDAGES
MUST ACCEPT SUPREME LOVE AS
THE HIGHEST GOAL

Narada, Way of Divine Love, *33*

Kama

The Hindu householder balances three factors: *dharma*—religious obligation; *artha*—economics and politics; and *kama*—sense life. Sex for the Hindus, as for many other cultures, takes on a sacramental aspect, the union of matter and energy.

Kama for the Hindus is a legitimate subject for study along with *dharma* and *artha*. For example, Vatsyayana (1st cent. A.D.) wrote the *Kama Sutra,* which does not limit itself to sex pleasure but deals with the whole range of male-female life: education, courtship, marriage. Also it covers customs from different sections of India and different classes of people.

Vatsyayana takes a scientific approach to *kama,* but he does not recommend pleasure for its own sake. Moreover, one should study not just *kama* but also *dharma* and *artha,* and also the sixty-four auxiliary arts, including singing, dancing, music, writing, drama, gardening, sports, cosmetics, etiquette.

Vatsyayana's ideal is the *nagarika,* the city dweller, a man of culture and leisure. So he writes of elegant furnishings, apartments for the ladies, lutes, books, garden, dress, toilet, cosmetics, social life, picnics, etc. The female counterpart of the *nagarika* is the *nayika*, maidens, twice-married women, and courtesans.

For the average Hindu the renunciation of the *sannyasi* came only at the end of his life after he had passed through the first three stages of student, householder, and detached participant in worldly affairs. But those specially called can pass from the student life of the *bramacarin* to the *sannyasi* class, bypassing the middle two and forgoing *kama* for future rewards, *moksha*, nirvana, or whatever.

Kama is primarily for the householder.

He should acquire learning in his childhood, in his youth and middle age he should attend to *artha* and *kama* and in his old age he should perform *dharma*, and thus seek to gain *moksha*, that is, release from further transmigration. (*Kama Sutra*, 1/2/65)[1]

This is the ordinary course of the average Hindu layman. Those called especially to bypass *kama* are holy men, monks, etc.

But what is *kama?*

Kama is the enjoyment of appropriate objects by the five senses of hearing, feeling, seeing, tasting and smelling assisted by the mind together with the soul. The ingredient in this is a peculiar contact between the organ of sense and its object. And the consciousness of pleasure which arises from that contact is called *kama*. (1/2/65)

So *kama* is sensual pleasure and not necessarily sexual in nature, although it often has this meaning. In general, *kama* was looked upon as the lowest of the big three—*dharma, artha,* and *kama*. Exceptions are kings, for whom *artha* takes precedence, and prostitutes, who specialize in *kama*.

Vatsyayana lists four kinds of love in his *sutra*. Love acquired by continual habit; love from imagination; "the love which is mutual on both sides, and proved to be true. When each looks upon the other as his or her very own, such is called love resulting from belief by the learned; and love from the perception of external objects." (2/1/92)

Proper methodology in hugging and kissing should be learned.

On the occasion of the first congress, kissing and the other things mentioned above should be done moderately. They should not be continued for a long time and should be done alternately. On subsequent occasions, however, the reverse of all this may take place and moderation will not be necessary. They may continue for a long time, and for the purpose of kindling love, they may be all done at the same time. (2/3/96)

And again:

Whatever the things done by one of the lovers to the other, the same should be returned by the other. That is, if the woman kisses him, he should kiss her in return. (2/3/98)

Pain and pleasure are united in scratching, biting, and striking.

Kama should be approached gradually to remind the bride and groom that marriage is not just a *kama* license, but a relationship sanctioned by and contributing to the community.[2] Thus for the first three days of marriage sexual abstinence should be exercised, with husband and wife sleeping on the floor and eating unseasoned foods. The next seven days they dine, bathe, and play together. And on the tenth night he begins to build up her confidence.

A man acting according to the inclination of a girl should try to gain her over so that she may love him and place her confidence in him. A man does not succeed either by implicitly following the inclination of a girl, or by wholly opposing her. And he should therefore adopt a middle course. He who knows how to make himself beloved by women, as well as to increase their honor and create confidence in them, this man becomes an object of their love. One should neither avoid the bashful girl nor force the timid. (3/2/130–31)

In wooing the girl, the man should spend some time with her, playing games, trying to please her, giving her gifts, and talking with her in a private place. And the girl, in turn, shows her love. She gets flustered when he looks at her or asks her a question. She shows off her legs on some pretext or other. And she delights in his presence, which she seeks to prolong. She confides in her lover's friends and is kind to his servants. She is always dressed and made up properly to please him. She wears his gifts and sends presents to him by a female friend.

A man who has seen and perceived the feelings of the girl towards him, and who has noticed the outward signs and movements by which those feelings are expressed, should do everything in his power to effect union with her. (3/3/135)

But even though the girl loves him very much, she should never make the first move. And when he does approach her, she should be reluctant.

It is only, moreover, when she is certain that she is truly loved and that her lover is indeed devoted to her, and will not change his mind, that she should then give herself up to him, and persuade him to marry her quickly. . . . Of all the lovers of a girl, he only is her true husband who possesses the qualities that are liked by her, and such a husband only enjoys real superiority over her because he is the husband of love. (3/4/138–39)

Part Four of the *Kama Sutra* is the conduct of the wife, her relations with her husband's family, relatives, and strangers.

The wife, whether she be a woman of noble family, or a virgin, widow remarried, or a concubine, should lead a chaste life, devoted to her husband, and doing everything for his welfare. Women acting thus acquire *dharma, artha* and *kama,* obtain a higher position, and generally keep their husbands devoted to them. (4/1/146)

When is it allowed for a man to take the wife of another? When it is a question of life and death for him. As he passes through the degrees of love: love of the eye, attachment of the mind, constant reflection, restriction of sleep, emaciation of the body, turning away from objects of enjoyment, removal of shame, madness, fainting, death.

A woman's love differs from a man's, for she loves without regard to right or wrong. And she does not try to win him for a particular purpose. His first overtures are resisted.

Even if a man begins to love, he conquers his feelings out of morality and wisdom. Sometimes he makes an attempt to win the object of his affection, and when he fails, he leaves her alone. Whatever the cause of a woman's rejection of her lover —affection for her husband, difference in rank, bashfulness, distrust, etc.—he should try to remove the cause.

Successful lovers are men versed in the science of love, good storytellers, present givers, good talkers, men who have not loved other women, who are desirable, neighbors, friends, lovers of sex, picnics, parties, liberal, well dressed, and who surpass the women's own husbands.

The woman easily won is she who stands at the door of her house, who stares, who looks sideways at you, who hates her husband, is lonely, childless, the wife of an actor, widow, poor woman, slighted woman, lazy, jealous, old, etc.

A clever man, depending on his own ability, and observing carefully the ideas and thoughts of women and removing the causes of their turning away from men, is generally successful with them. (5/2/153)

Vatsyayana treats of many other facets of *kama,* including polygamy, the use of the go-between, love of a courtesan, plus the intricate ways and means of love. But *kama* can be

used for selfish ends. So Vatsyayana warns at the end of his
sutra: "An intelligent and prudent person, attending to
dharma and *artha* and attending to *kama* also without becoming a slave to his passions, obtains success in everything he may
undertake." (7/2/220)

The *Kama Sutra* has had a great impact on Hindu literature,
sculpture, and painting and for millennia has been the sex and
marriage manual of India.

Tiruvalluvar also wrote of *kama* in his *Kural*. In the first part,
Aram (*Dharma*), he sees *kama* as the foundation of the home.
"If love abounds in the home and righteousness does prevail,
the home is perfect and its end is all fulfilled." (45)[3]

Love is self-propagating. "Those that love not, live only for
themselves; as to those that love, they will give their very
bones for helping others." (72) It was to taste love that the
soul is reborn again. Without love, man is just skin and bones.
(80)

In Part Three of the *Kural*, called *Inbam* (*Kama*), Tiruvalluvar sees two *kamas*. The first, *kalavu*, is a secret spontaneous
love (*Gandharva* Marriage), a prelude to the binding married
love, *karpu*.

Of *kalavu* he writes: "She looked, and then she bowed. That
was the watering of the young plant of love that was springing
up between us." (1093) "Joyous to the loving pair is the embrace that allows not even air to come between." (1108) Separation is unbearable. "It is as life when she is near; but it is as
very death when she leaves my side." (1124)

Karpu is married love with its pangs of separation and joys
of reunion. "What the rain is to all the world, that is the tenderness of the beloved to her that loves." (1192) Lovers' quarrels heighten delight.

It is the one who yields first who is the winner in lovers'
quarrels; you cannot see it indeed at the hour of reconciliation. . . . Sulkiness is the charm of love, and the charm of
that again is the sweet embrace at its close. (1327, 1330)

But, though *kama* is good, he who restrains his desire is really free. "When he has conquered utterly desire, anger and delusion, all suffering ceases for man." (360) And again: "It is those who have conquered their desire that are called the liberated ones." (365)

The Laws of Manu, dating perhaps from the second century A.D. and dependent on the earlier *Manava Dharma Sutra*, spell out *kama* customs for the householder. After his celibate student days, the young Hindu takes a wife of equal caste, but of different *gotra* (3/4), avoiding the undesirable.[4]

There are eight different marriage rites according to caste. For example, the gift of a daughter to a sacrificing priest is called the *Daiva* rite. "The voluntary union of a maiden and her lover one must know [to be] the *Gandharva* rite [*kalavu*] which springs from desire and has sexual intercourse for its purpose." (3/32) Forcible abduction is called *Rakshasa* and seduction, the lowest type, is *Pisakas*.

> Let the husband approach his wife in due season, being constantly satisfied with her [alone]. He may also, being intent on pleasing her, approach her with a desire for conjugal union [on any day] excepting the Parvans. (3/45)

The virtuous husband limits his *kama*. "He who avoids women on the six forbidden nights and on eight others is [equal in chastity to] a student, in which order he may live." (3/50)

Finally (3/60): "In that family where the husband is pleased with his wife and the wife with her husband, happiness will assuredly be lasting."

In Chapters 5 and 9, Manu's Laws list the duties of husband and wife. Male chauvinism and female dependency are the orders of the day. "Though destitute of virtue, or seeking pleasure [elsewhere], or devoid of good qualities, [yet] a husband must be constantly worshipped as a god by a faithful wife." (5/154)

Yet the godlike husband is not self-sufficient. He needs his wife and family. "He only is a perfect man who consists [of

three persons united], his wife, himself, and his offspring."
(9/45) In the *Vedas* and *Brahmanas* the husband is one with
his wife.

Manu also tells the reasons for divorce. "For one year let a
husband bear with a wife who hates him; but after [the lapse
of] a year let him deprive her of her property and cease to co-
habit with her." (9/77) And: "A barren wife may be super-
seded in the eighth year." (9/81)

But on the female side, a maid should not allow herself to
be presented to an evil man. (9/89) And if her father fails to
give her in a good marriage, after three years she can seek her
own man. (9/90–91) The age gap between groom and bride is
much greater than in Western practice. (30/12, 24/8)

"The husband receives his wife from the gods. [He does
not wed her according to his own will.] Doing what is agreeable to the gods, he must always support her [while she is]
faithful." (9/94) And: " 'Let mutual fidelity continue until
death.' This may be considered as the summary of the highest
law for husband and wife." (9/101)

Though *kama* is important to the householder, we also see a
certain sexual restraint in Indian tradition. It is most proper
to the student, wanderer, and ascetic. But even in marriage
we see restraint praised. Continence (*brahmacharya*) is one
of the "accessories" of yoga by which "the light of wisdom
reaches up to discriminate knowledge."[5] Continence for the
yogi has its origins in *ahimsa* (not harming). By his restraint
of the power of generation the Brahmana renders his *ahimsa*
purer and purer, says Vyasa. Vachaspati adds: "The desire of
seeing and speaking to women and embracing them as seats
of Cupid is also incontinence. . . . Other tendencies towards
that are also to be checked."

Tapas is a word used often to express the hot and volatile
but self-contained sexual heat and energy. The gods reside in
one in such a state and he can do anything.[6]

We have seen much of *kama*, human sexual love. But what is
its relationship to *bhakti*, disinterested, selfless divine love?

Though *kama* is important to the householder, the very *Kama Sutra, Kural,* and Laws of Manu imply that it can be fleeting and unstable. It has to be won and can be easily lost.

Bhakti, on the other hand, is a stable gift of God. And it would seem that it cannot be gained in its highest level of divine union unless earthly *kama* pleasures are curtailed, or perhaps outlived. Although the yogis forgo the normal course of *artha, kama,* and *dharma* in their pursuit of *moksha,* generally the world-rejection of the liberated man is not that of the innocent. "His knowledge is the outcome of doubts conquered, pleasures tasted, sorrows experienced, love shared, and conceptualization surpassed."[7]

Moksha is an expanding of limits, a transcending of finitude, not only a release from suffering, sorrow, and evil of the world, but also an openness to union with the transcendent and self-realization and fulfillment (*marga*) through *jnana, karma,* yoga, or *bhakti.*

Early Bhakti

Early in the Vedic hymns we find a loving faith in the gods called *sraddha.* And in the *Upanishads* man's union with Atman-Brahman is compared to the love between husband and wife. Thus *Brhad-aranyaka Upanishad* (4/3/21):

As a man when in the embrace of his beloved wife knows nothing without or within, so the person in the embrace of the intelligent self knows nothing without or within. That verily is his form in which his desire is fulfilled, in which the self is his desire, in which he is without desire, free from any sorrow.[8]

In this embrace all distinctions are lost—father, mother, world, gods, *Vedas,* etc.

The same *Upanishad* sees procreation as a sacred *soma* rite, with the woman's body as a sacrificial altar and fire (6/2/5,

6/4/3), a concept more fully developed later in the Tantric tradition.

Divine *bhakti* love grew strong in the epic period with its great heroes Rama and Krishna. *Bhakti* devotion and love seemed to appeal more to simple folk than the priestly rites and distinctions of the Brahmans or the esoteric intellectual practices of the yogis.

What is *bhakti?* It comes from the Sanskrit word *bhaj,* meaning to share or participate.[9] It is used of persons sharing all, including mind and heart, in love. It embraces all the nuances of interpersonal relationships of loyalty, service, reverence, devotion, and love. Dhavamony writes:

> The best description of *bhakti* includes interpersonal participation and communion between god and man in mutual love and surrender. The god of *bhakti* is gracious and compassionate towards all. But he is especially benevolent to those who love him. And he takes every initiative to commune with them through love. *Bhakti,* on man's side, is the loving response to god, on whom he acknowledges his utter dependence for gaining liberation from the cycle of rebirth.[10]

What is the relationship between man's *bhakti* union with God and his selfless love of his fellow man, the sharing and love between husband and wife, father and son, student and teacher? Human love is a weak image of that between God and man. Sometimes, rather than flowing from divine *bhakti,* human love seems to be a necessary presupposition.

In the Vedic era (1500–900 B.C.) *bhaj* means to share in the sacrificial rites. It points to a love and devotion to God in the *Svetas Vatara.*

In epics such as the *Mahabharata* and *Ramayana, bhakti* can mean either secular or religious love. But in the *Bhagavad-Gita* it is only divine love. *Kama,* on the other hand, is interested human, male-female sexual love, as we have seen.

Bhakti is love and devotion to a personal god with little mention of ritualism, asceticism, or apologetics. Dhavamony comments: "The object of *bhakti* is the personal god of a concrete nature, endowed with attributes. He is regarded as affectionate protector or master."[11]

As the Vedic gods declined, more personal folk gods grew. For example, Vishnu, an early minor Vedic sun god, appeared as Rama and Krishna. And Shiva, an early god of destruction, grew in importance. Also Shivite gods and goddesses—non-Vedic, Dravidian, non-Aryan, or pre-Aryan.

And along with the personal gods came personal devotion and love, *bhakti*, a road to salvation, and *moksha*, a release from the human condition of *karma* and *samsara*.

We find *bhakti* in the *Bhagavad-Gita* (2nd cent. B.C.–2nd cent. A.D.), which is a small part of the *Mahabharata* and shows an *Upanishad* influence. Here the lord Krishna is the guru or teacher of Arjuna, leading him to higher levels of enlightenment through yoga. A detachment from the lower self of desires, passions, etc., and an attachment to the higher self.

There are many types of yoga: *karma* (action), *jnana* (wisdom), *raja* (a cessation of mental modifications), and *bhakti* (devotion and love). We are here more interested in *bhakti* yoga.

In Chapter 11 (44) of the *Gita* the relationship between the lord Krishna and Arjuna is described as that between lover and beloved. Thus Arjuna cries:

> You are the Supreme Lord, to be worshiped by every being. Thus I fall down to offer you my respects and ask your mercy. Please tolerate the wrongs that I have done to you and bear with me as a father with his son, or a friend with his friend, or a lover with his beloved son.[12]

In Chapter 12, the *Gita* seems to synthesize the more abstract and introspective voice of the *Upanishads* with the dualistic man-god relationship of folk religion. Thus when Arjuna asks Krishna who is more learned in yoga, those who honor him or those who worship the imperishable and unmanifested

Brahman, Krishna replies: "He whose mind is fixed on my personal form, always engaged in worshiping me with a great and transcendental faith, is considered by me to be most perfect." (2)

But those who worship the unmanifested, impersonal Truth by controlling the senses, well disposed to all and seeking the welfare of all, will finally achieve union with Krishna also. But they take the indirect route. *Bhakti* is the direct road to oneness with Krishna.

The one who is a friend to all, humble, equanimous, "who is always satisfied and engaged in devotional service with determination and whose mind and intelligence are in agreement with me—he is very dear to me." (12/14)

It is through the yoga of freedom and renunciation that one reaches Krishna. "Having become Brahman, tranquil in the Self, he neither grieves nor desires. Regarding all beings as equal, he attains supreme devotion (*mat-bhaktim*) to me." (18/54) "By devotion (*bhaktya*) he knows me, what my measure is and what I am essentially. Then having known me essentially, he enters forth into me." (18/55) This is the height of *bhakti* devotion, love, belief in Krishna, going to him, uniting oneself to him.

When this higher *bhakti* is there, one can go ahead without fear of being interested only in the fruit of his action. He now acts in a spirit of sacrifice without any hope of reward, but only out of love for the divine.[13]

Higher *bhakti* gives a complete insight into Reality by which the lover is united perfectly with the divine, linking his *dharma* with the divine so that what he does is essentially a divine act unattached and free as only God can be.

Besides Krishna *bhakti*, there is devotion to other gods. For example, we see Rama *bhakti* in the *Ramayana*. And Buddha *bhakti*, with its statues, *stupas, sutras*, and devotion, we saw in the previous chapter. Devotion to Shiva and his Shakti we will pursue later.

Bhakti hymns were also sung by the Alvars, wandering troubadours of southern India (7th–8th cent.), chanting to Vishnu in the Tamil tongue.

But strong Hindu monist traditions still resisted the popular *bhakti* dualism of man and God. Thus Sankara (8th cent.) said that *bhakti* was useful only in the beginning stages of *sadhana*. It is only *jnana* (wisdom) that can bring man to *moksha*. In response, Tamil philosophers and theologians (*acharyas*) such as Ramanuja (11th cent.) got to work to bolster up the intellectual side of Vaishnavism.

Medieval Bhakti

In medieval times *bhakti* grew strong—repeating God's name, performing rituals, fixing one's mind on a divine avatar, and a gradual increase of awareness of God's presence within.

A famous medieval *bhakti sutra* is Narada's *Way of Divine Love*.[14] Narada was an ancient figure mentioned in the *Upanishads* and the *Srimad Bhagavatam*. He saw his real self as divine. The greatest remedy for evil is to surrender the fruits of *karma* to the lord.

> Work which we perform as service to the lord creates love and devotion in us. This love and devotion, in turn, bring wisdom; and at last, guided by this wisdom, we surrender ourselves to the Lord of Love and meditate upon him. Thus it is that I attained to wisdom and love. (3)

As Narada meditated on love of the lord, he saw him seated in his heart.

Narada died and returned several times as a guru of divine love to the people. "Wherever I go, I play on my *vina* and sing the praises of the lord, and the Lord of Love is ever manifest in my heart. Those who hear my song in praise of the lord find peace and freedom." (4)

Narada taught many aphorisms of divine love. The second reads: "*Bhakti* is intense love for This." Notice that he does not use the names of personal gods as Krishna or Rama. Rather a divine Reality is found in our hearts. There is no definition of God. Rather he is experienced.

Bhakti is in two steps. The first is *gauni bhakti*, the path of devotion which leads to the experience of *para bhakti*, an intense love for God. In highest *bhakti* the subject and object are one. This is why perfect men (avatars) are worshipped.

There are two stages of spiritual experience (*samadhi*). The first is *savikalpa*, a vision of the chosen ideal or an aspect of God, and inexpressible bliss. But there is still a sense of separation from God. *Nirvikalpa* is a higher stage of *samadhi* in which the lover and the beloved are one. God is experienced as impersonal, immanent, and transcendent intense love (*prema*). One's ego is completely dissolved. Now he loves the lord for love's sake. He knows no fear and has no rival beloved.

Sri Chaitanya cried out: "O you, who steal the hearts of your devotees, do with me what you will—for you are my heart's beloved, you and you alone." One becomes what he loves and shares immortal bliss, sweetness and joy. He becomes free, immortal, perfect.

Narada comments (5): "On attaining That a man does not desire anything else. He grieves no more, is free from hatred and jealousy. He does not take pleasure in the vanities of life, and he loses all eagerness to gain anything for himself." And again: "The devotee may first become intoxicated with bliss. Then having realized That, he becomes inert and silent and takes his delight in Atman."

There have been many descriptions of *bhakti*, from worship to praising the name of God, to taking delight in Atman.

Narada gives his portrait of *bhakti*. "When all thoughts, all words, and all deeds are given up to the lord, and when the least forgetfulness of God makes one intensely miserable, then love has begun." Complete surrender and constant recollection of God.

Bhakti is greater than *karma, jnana,* and yoga (*raja* yoga), the three paths of union through action, wisdom, and meditation. *Bhakti* is the ultimate end of the spiritual life. All paths lead to it. It avoids egotism and loves humility.

How is supreme love attained? (35-37) By renouncing sense pleasure (*kama*), by uninterrupted and constant worship of God, hearing and singing the glory of the lord, even while engaged in the ordinary activities of life.

> The principal means of attaining *bhakti* is the grace of a great soul, because it is hard to recognize such a one. But if a man receives his grace, the effect is infallible. Through the grace of God alone an aspirant obtains the grace of a great soul. (38-40)

The great soul, the great guru in union with the Brahman, serves as a vehicle of God's grace. Brahman dwells within his devotees. True, God loves all, but his devotees alone experience his overwhelming love.

But one has to work to obtain *bhakti*, avoiding evil company, giving up attachment to earthly pleasures, living in solitude and dependence on the lord. Removing all self-love and even rites and ceremonies, he can attain supreme love of God.

This supreme love of God is an inexpressible inner experience. "When a man attains this supreme love, he sees his Beloved everywhere, he hears of him everywhere, he talks only of him, and thinks of him only." (55) This supreme love transcends ordinary forms of divine love, that is, devotion to God out of distress, to obtain unfilled earthly desires or to seek knowledge.

There are five types of love relationships with God: *shanta*, or peaceful; *dasya*, as a servant or child of God; *sakhya*, as a friend in equality; *vatsaylya*, loving God as a helpless babe; and finally in *kanta* or *madhura*, God is our husband. This is the highest form of love, the spiritual marriage spoken of by the mystics. Swami Prabhavan writes: "We are all women, there is but one man, that is our beloved." (144) Sri Ramakrishna says that bliss from loving God as our beloved is like sex pleasure enjoyed in every pore of our body. But it is eternal and infinite, not transitory as *kama*.

Narada sums it up:

> The highest class of devotees are those who have one-pointed love for God, and for love's sake only. When devotees talk of God, their voices choke, tears flow from their eyes, their hair stands erect in ecstasy. (67–68)

This supreme love manifests itself in many ways (82). The lover may chant and praise the lord or love his enchanting beauty, worship with all his heart, meditate on his presence constantly, love him as a servant, friend, child, or beloved; surrender to him completely. He loves to be completely absorbed in him and paradoxically loves to feel the pangs of separation.

Krishna *bhakti* is one of the most popular forms. In medieval times this was expressed in love stories about Krishna and the *gopi* shepherd girls. For example, the *Srimad Bhagavatam* or *Bhagavata Purana*.

In Book Three we read of the sage Kapila's teaching on divine love.

> Our senses, O mother, draw us to things because we love the world. If we direct our knowledge to God, we find divine knowledge and absolute freedom. But there are souls who find such great joy in love and in the service of the lord that they may have no concern for their own salvation. Even so divine love ultimately brings freedom to them also.
>
> Those who love God as dearly as themselves; those who have affection for him as for their children, those who trust him as their beloved companion, and reverence him as the teacher of teachers; those who love him as their dear friend, and worship him as God—theirs is eternal life.[15]

In the *Bhagavata*, Krishna is the personification of love. To Yasoda he is the God of Love, to the shepherd boys a beloved companion, and to the *gopis* friend and lover.

The *gopis* are drawn to Sri Krishna in love. When he tries

to send them home to their husbands and children where they can meditate on him for salvation, they reply:

> O cruel lover, we desire to serve only you. You know the scriptural truths, and you advise us to serve our husbands and children. So let it be. We shall abide by your teaching. Since you are in all and are all, by serving you we shall serve them. (10/5)

Krishna divides himself among the *gopis* so that each can feel his divine love. "Truly it can be said that those who meditate on the divine love of Sri Krishna, and upon the sweet relationship between him and the shepherd girls, become free from lust and sensuality." (10/5)

Swami Vivek comments:

> Oh for one, one kiss of those lips. One who has been kissed by you—his thirst for you increases forever, all his sorrows vanish. And he forgets love for everything else but for you and you alone. . . .
>
> Ay, forget first the love of gold and name and fame and for this little trumpery world of ours. Then, only then, will you understand the love of the *gopis*, too holy to be attempted without giving up everything, too sacred to be conceived until the soul has become perfectly pure. People with ideas of sex, and of money, and of fame, bubbling up every minute in their hearts, daring to criticize or interpret the love of the *gopis*. (200)

In order to partake in the disinterested *bhakti* love of Krishna, one must forsake all selfish love of *kama* or *artha*. As Krishna instructs his disciple Uddhava: "I bring my peace and infinite happiness to those who forsake all other pleasures for my sake. The shepherd girls love me more than anything else in this world, and they love me for love's sake only." (10/7)

And Uddhava to the shepherd girls:

> How blessed are you to have surrendered yourselves com-

pletely and wholeheartedly to Bhagavan Sri Krishna, the God of Love. . . . Fortunate indeed are you who were born with all-consuming love and devotion and have renounced everything for the love of your dear Krishna. O happy ones, who enjoy the bliss of divine love, I am blessed and purified by coming into your presence. (10/7)

Krishna really has never left his lovers, for he resides in them united with the self and revealed through yoga and meditation. There are many means of attaining the highest good—love, duty, self-control, truth, sacrifice, gifts, austerity, charity, vows, morality.

But, of all I could name, verily love is the highest: love and devotion that make one forgetful of everything else, love that unites the lover with me. What ineffable joy does one find through love of me, the blissful Self! Once that joy is realized, all earthly pleasures fade into nothingness. (11/8)

The whole world seems filled with bliss.

Not by yoga, philosophy, or deeds or study or discipline and quelling of desires is Krishna attained. "Those only who have pure love for me find me easily. I, the Self dear to the devotee, am attainable by love and devotion. Devotion to me purifies even the lowliest of the low. Without love for me, virtues and learning are unfruitful." (11/8) Love purifies, melts the heart, brings bliss, tears, laughs, etc. All evil is melted away. "By thinking of objects of sense, one becomes attached to them. By meditating on me, and dwelling on thoughts of me, one experiences increasing love for me and at last is merged in me." (11/8)

Wherever there is manifested fullness of life, there is Krishna —in power, beauty, fame, prosperity, modesty, sacrifice, concord, fortune, strength, fortitude, or knowledge. "To him who is endowed with love for me, O Uddhava, belongs the fulness of life." (11/10)

Those who still have desires and are attached to work must

follow the yoga of work. So work until your heart becomes tranquil and free of desires. The yoga of work frees the mind from evil desires and purifies the heart. "In the pure heart arise true wisdom and true love for me . . . for the yogi who loves me and whose heart is one with mine, there remains nothing to be attained." (10/13)

Uddhava sums up the God of Love: "O, friend of all. . . . The Self of all, you fulfill the desires of those who take refuge in you. Knowing how you love your lovers, who could resist loving you?" (10/21)

The influence of the *Bhagavata Purana* was strong in the North. The Krishna of the *Bhagavata Purana* is a *gopi*-lover rather than a destroyer of tyrants as in the *Gita*. Organ comments. "*Bhakti* shifted from man's response of gratitude for the freely offered grace of God to the erotic love enjoyed as archetypal of the man-god relationship."[16]

Radha, Krishna's favorite *gopi*, was popular in Bengal, where her love for Krishna, her paramour, is paradigmatic of the human soul's longing for God.

> Secret, illicit sex love rather than the love within marriage was selected because the elements of risking discovery, of planning for trysts, and of uniting for pleasure, rather than the fulfillment of marriage vows made this form of love emotionally like the unfathomable communion of man and God.[17]

As Radha gives herself completely to Krishna, so man offers himself to God. The extramarital loves of Krishna and Radha may also reflect the sexual mores of the time.

Bengali Vaishnavas sing their *madhurya-bhava* lyrics in which Krishna is the divine lover, while the troubadour identifies with Radha or one of the other *gopis*. There are two main types of love hymns: *vipralambha*, in which the lovers are in painful separation, and *sambhoga*, the joyful union. Separation and union are contained in each other, for even in union there remains the fear of separation.[18]

Separation songs are: *purva-raga*, in which erotic desire is aroused by sight or description; *mana*, in which the girl is offended by her beloved's interest in other rivals; *premavaicittya*, in which satisfaction and the pain of longing are joined; and *pravasa*, the suffering caused by the beloved's departure to a distant country.

Jayadeva, court poet of King Laksmanasena, wrote his *Gita Govinda* (*Cowherd in Song*) (12th cent.), chanting of Krishna's love for Radha, their separation and reconciliation. Thus Krishna speaks to his sweetheart.

O woman with desire, place on this patch of flower-strewn floor
    your lotus foot,
And let your foot through beauty win,
To me who am the Lord of all, O be attached, now always
    yours.
O follow me, my little Radha.
O Lovely Woman, give me now the nectar of your lips, infuse
    new life into this slave of yours, so dead,
This slave, whose heart is placed in you, whose body burned
    in separation, this slave denied the pleasure of your love.[19]

4. "Now always yours" (*Gita Govinda*)

Vidyapati, a fourteenth-century Bihar poet, sings of the beautiful Radha.

> Each day the breasts of Radha swelled,
> Her hips grew shapely, her waist more slender.
> Love's secrets stole upon her eyes.
> Startled her childhood sought escape,
> Her plum-like breasts grew large,
> Harder and crisper, aching for love.
> Krishna soon saw her as she bathed
> Her filmy dress still clinging to her breasts,
> Her tangled tresses falling on her heart,
> A golden image swathed in yak's tail plumes.
> Says Vidyapati: O wonder of women,
> Only a handsome man can long for her.[20]

The eternal question in poetry of this type: Is it religious or secular or both? Perhaps the answer lies in the eyes of the beholder.

Meantime Ramananda was teaching *bhakti* salvation in Benares, spreading *Bhagavata* throughout northern India. His disciple Kabir inspired the Sikh syncresis of Islam and Hinduism.

Caitanya (15th cent.) sought religious reform in Bengal, based on the *Bhagavata Purana.* For Caitanya, Krishna is an *avatarin,* God himself, rather than an avatar, or an incarnation of God. *Bhakti* for Caitanya is *moksha,* release, vision of God. "*Bhakti* is *prema*-love, a love that is more than a sexual love, although the joyous submission of sexual intercourse between devoted lovers is held by Caitanya to be the paradigm and symbol of the love between man and God."[21] Caitanya pictured himself as Radha longing for her Krishna. This led to some excesses among his followers, who considered him to be the incarnation of Radha. Others saw in him the union of Radha and Krishna.

Shiva and Shakti

We have seen Vaishnava *bhakti* in early and medieval India. A second popular form of *bhakti* is Shaiva, devotion to Shiva. Shiva may have evolved from the Vedic god Rudra, malevolent storm deity who was called Shiva, the auspicious one, in the hope of his mercy.

In the Hindu trinity, Brahma, Vishnu, and Shiva, Shiva is the most active, posing as Nataraja the dancer. Furthermore, he is strong and energetic with his bull, Nandi, and his Shakti, Parvati, in her many guises, for example, Kali, inspiring fear. Shiva also appears as the androgynous *ardhanarisvana*, Shiva and Parvati in eternal union.

The Shaiva cults are less well organized than the Vaishnava. Yet Shiva is worshipped as a personal god, and sixty-three poet-saints (*Adiyars* or *Nayanmars*), the Shaiva complements to the Vaishnava *Alvars*, sing his praises (2nd–9th cent.).

Two main Shaiva sects are the Lingayata or Virashaivism in southern India and Kashmir Shaivism in the North. The former worship Shiva's *linga*, while the latter are more idealistic and monistic, avoiding extremes of the South. But both seek loving surrender to Shiva in order to break the endless round of *samsara*.

Famous Tamil Shaivite mystics are Campantar (7th cent. A.D.), Cuntarar (9th cent.), and Manikkavacakar (9th cent.). Campantar writes that God loves his devotees with the love of a father, mother, master, and spouse. "You are my mother, my father. You are gracious. Your devotee's mind longs to show love to you who are the object of the Vedic inquiry. Five persons [the senses] dwelling in my body prevent me from uniting to you." (1452)[22] *Bhakti* for Campantar is the complete surrender of the whole person to God as his servant. He alone is the protector. (1136)

Bhakti fructifies into a deeper realization of God, freeing the devotee and uniting him to God in supreme bliss. "You, desirous of [supreme] bliss, praise the golden abode of our friend at Anniyur to become divine." (290)[23] Cuntarar sees *bhakti* as a gift of God so the devotee may melt in love for God, dispelling darkness and kneeling at his feet in bliss. (1457) Just as the secular lover, so the *bhakti* lover constantly pursues his beloved.

The higher experience of love is sweet as sugar or honey, precious as a jewel, succulent as fruit, dear as a friend and husband. Cuntarar, as many of the mystics, considered himself a woman in love with her husband God, and finding the separation unbearable, lies awake at night and grows thin from lack of appetite.

> The *bhaktas* make love to you, revel in bliss. They praise and worship you with fragrant flowers and never fail to do all in their power [to show you love]. It is not fair to doubt [their sincerity]. . . . [On my part] I will never forget you . . . take possession of me.[24]

There is mutual penetration of God and the devotee. God penetrates the heart of the *bhakta* and is so united that he becomes the *bhakta*. (62)

Manikkavacakar, the last of the Tamil Shaivite poet-mystics, wrote *Tiruvacakam* as part of a revival of Hinduism against inroads of Buddhism and Jainism.

Manikkavacakar teaches that God indwells in all creatures out of love for men and his love is perfect and strong. God's *bhakti* is a free gift to man. "Grant me the grace of melting in ceaseless love for you." (31/3)[25] "I desire nothing else but intense love for you." (32/4) "I long to sing your praise, while all my being sinks and melts in love. I long to unite with you in order to leave falsehood aside, you who are true to the genuine devotees." (5/100)[26]

Even though a sinner, Manikkavacakar cries out to God. Love joins him to God in a mystic union. "He came and while my soul dissolved in love he made me his own." (5/29)[27] Like many mystics, he compares divine union with marital love.

> Wearing the flowery "Cassia" wreath, I will join myself to Shiva's mighty arms. And joining, I will cling to him lost in ecstasy. Then shrinking will I melt with love of his rosy lips. I will seek him, and seeking I will meditate on his feet." (8/17)[28]

Bhakti for these Shaivite mystics is not just a means of salvation, but salvation itself, union with God in love, stripped of self. The mutual compenetration of Cuntarar. First of all, one must be completely humble with wholehearted surrender to God, finally achieving a union not unlike that of conjugal love.

Bhakti can have many levels, from external preparation in the temple, singing, etc., where the devotee is like a servant to Shiva. In the second stage the devotee offers flowers, fruit invoking God's presence as a son loves his parents. The third stage is the love between friends, loving meditation on God as intelligence, purifying the soul. And the fourth level of *bhakti* is the union of lovers, realizing fully the nondifference between knower, known, and knowing, united completely with Shiva.

The mystics frequently used conjugal love to illustrate their abiding love of Shiva. Thus the lover or *bhakta* is like a love-sick woman. Especially in the Tantric era this parallel was practiced in the worship of Shiva and Shakti.

Tamil sources such as the *Shaiva-Agamas* say that Shiva by his Shakti creates, maintains, dissolves, obscures truth, frees souls. Here Shakti seems to be the personification of Shiva's energy, acting on souls and all matter in an immanent manner. Meykanta (*Sivanopatam*, 2/4) writes that God is inseparable from his Shakti as sun and sunlight. Arulnanti (*Cittiyar*, 2/77) says Shiva begets Shakti and Shakti begets Shiva. Both together in love union produce the world and souls. Yet both remain chaste. Is this an unselfish *bhakti* love among the gods? Shakti seems to be God's immanent presence much like the

Shekhinah in Jewish tradition. Arulnanti (*Cittiyar*, 2/5–6) describes this divine immanence as "the presence in every soul of God's power (Shakti) on which each soul's activity and change radically depend as on an instrumental cause." God operates and cooperates in souls through his Shakti.[29]

As God performs various functions in the world, his Shakti assumes different forms and names. Even Brahma the creator and Vishnu the preserver can act only through Shiva's Shakti, for of themselves they cannot rise above the plane of *prakrti*.

Hara's Shakti is in the form of grace and love. Thus there is no Shiva but for the supreme grace and love. And without Shiva there is no Shakti. As the sun dispels darkness with its rays, so God removes the illusions of souls and grants them final bliss (*Cittiyar*, 5/9).

Shiva's union with Shakti is celebrated by Tantric Hinduism and Buddhism. Tantra (system) is a synthesis of yoga and *bhakti*, stressing sex. For the last four or five hundred years Tantra worship has been strong in India. Today two-thirds of Hindu religion and one-third of Hindu medicine are Tantric.[30] Because of its sexiness Tantra has often been labeled trivial, corrupt, obscene, licentious. For example, Indian prostitutes are often called Tantric women.

Tantric ideas are found early. Thus the *Rig Veda* speaks of embracing the *deva* sexually. (10/43/1) Moreover, each Vedic *deva* has a spouse (Shakti) personifying his energy. Shakti brings divine energy and power to man and makes God more approachable.

Shiva, the chief god of Tantra, has 1,008 Shaktis: Kali, Durga, Bhairavi, etc., as partners to his 1,008 names. Shakti is energy personified, the power to act according to nature. Thus the Shakti of fire is to burn. In Tantra, Shakti is personal, Caitanya (Pure Consciousness), or Para Shakti (Supreme Being of Power).

While right-handed Tantra sacrificed animals, the popular left-handed Tantra celebrates sexual intercourse as the origin of life. It is called left-handed because Shakti sits on Shiva's left hand. Their hierogamy is celebrated in ritual, literature, and art.

Organ notes[31] that energetic Tantra grew strong in times of need. For example, the ninth-century resistance to Sankara's lethargic philosophy and the nineteenth- and twentieth-century struggle for Bengali independence. Shakti is celebrated annually at the end of the dreary monsoon season and the beginning of the fall growing time.

Many facets contributed to the evolution of Tantra. Vestiges are seen in the *Vedas* and *Upanishads*. Moreover, Shakti worship is found in the *Mahabharta* (4/6) and philosophical *Sankhya*.

Vaishnavism had Tantric elements, as we have seen in the loves of Krishna and Radha. Radha is the fullness of the lord's joy and energy.

Bengali Vaishnavism teaches the Radha-Krishna theme. Thus Caitanya becomes Radha in her love of Krishna. And poets such as Jayaveda imagined themselves *gopis* peeking in on the divine lovers, while the Vaishnava Sahajiya cult felt that man could best partake in Krishna love by extramarital coitus (*parakiya*).

Organ says: "Illegal coitus was regarded as man's most exciting experience and hence as a fitting approximation of the overpowering joy of the immediate relations between God and man. In the intimacy of sexual love, the devotee is Radha submitting herself to her divine lover."[32]

Tantric *sadhana*, as described in the *Agamas* and *Nigamas*, is the recovery of a lost identity, the union of Shiva and Shakti, God's Wisdom and Power. And the human body is a microcosm with the outward energy directed inwardly.

In Kundalini yoga, the serpent Kundalini is coaxed up from her lair in the perineum to rise through the *nadi* channels, releasing her physical and psychic energy to the *chakras*. Thus the powers of the macrocosm are united to the microcosm and the joyous union of Shiva and Shakti is celebrated in each human being.

A controversial type of Tantra is the *Pancha Makaras*, practicing the five *M*'s (wine, meat, fish, cereal, and sex). It was popular in left-handed Tantra. Its devotees claim to reach a state of *kaula*, beyond morality. If one reaches this ultra-moral state, he can do things that ordinarily would be forbidden to mortals. Some defend the illicit loves of the gods in this manner. Others see in this Tantra a rejection of the ascetical side of Hinduism with its abstinence, fasting, and sexual continence, stressing rather the goodness of nature, worshipping the Great Mother and defying earlier restraints.

Tantra believes that *bhaya*, sensual bliss, should be a type of yoga and a way to enlightenment. This is pictured in temple sculptures in various acrobatic sexual positions. Is the purpose of Tantric intercourse purely sexual pleasure (*kama*)? At least initially human intercourse was seen as a parallel to the divine hierogamy, the union of the two souls in coitus approximating the divine yoke. In fact, Hindu mythology portrays Shiva as the enemy of Kama, whom he destroys for tempting his wife Shakti while Shiva is in meditation.

In the beginning, the Shakti union of man and woman commemorating the marriage of Shiva and Shakti under controlled conditions, was probably far from erotic in nature. Rather it was a type of yoga in which the intertwined couples were to remain virgin and restrained, just as Shiva and Shakti are virgin in their love embrace. *Coincidentia oppositorum*. The male consort withholds his seed, uniting it with his mind and breath. Here perhaps is the creative virginity found in many pantheons and imitated on the human level in many forms.

There were likely abuses in the Tantric *shakti* yoga rituals, but the initial purpose seems to have been religious, that is, commemorating and even recapitulating the divine union of Shiva and Shakti. In a sense the human union of man and woman not only recapitulates the divine, but even may bring it about.

Semen retention in *shakti* yoga is linked closely with mind control.

The moment of suspense affected by simultaneous breath and seminal control in conjunction with the Shakti or *mudra*, seems to effect suspension of the distracting mental functions —that is to say—of all the discursive functions of the mind, cognitive, conative and volitional. . . . Entasy is reached when the mind succeeds in surrendering temporarily at first, but in increasing spans of time, all object-thought, and in concentrating on the non-discursive, interiorized object of his meditating which is variously described in anthropomorphic terms as the *Istam* (Tibetan *yiddam*), the chosen deity, or in absolutist, speculative terms as the case may be.[33]

The devotee tries to unite the three jewels of breath, mind, and semen in his individuality (*yuganaddha*).

Shakti yoga is a division of *laya* yoga, in which one concentrates on the feminine or negative aspect of the universe, embracing spiritual forces of the Cosmic Mind. Shakti is personified as the mother goddess, while Shiva is the male or positive pole of the divine dyad, paralleling the *yin-yang* of Taoism and the *yum-yab* of Lamaism. Shakti finds analogies in Sophia of the Gnostics, Shekhinah of the Jews, Prajna of the *Prajna Paramita*, all personifications of the feminine aspect of the deity.

How does *shakti* yoga compare with *bhakti* yoga? Evans-Wentz writes: "Whereas in Bhakti Yoga one-pointedness of mind is attained through yogic concentration on divine love as Bhakti, in Shakti Yoga a result yogically equivalent comes from yogic concentration on divine power as Shakti."[34]

We have seen three major love themes in Hinduism: *kama*, interested sensual love; *bhakti*, disinterested love of God; and *shakti*, imitating the love embrace of Shiva and Shakti in creative restraint.

Let us now turn to see how some Western philosophers and mystics described love. How much the West was influenced by the East is hard to say. Some feel that Hindu or Buddhist inspirations may be seen in the Greek philosophers, in John's Gospel, and in mystics such as Evagrius and the Islamic Sufis. There are similarities, but much more needs to be explored before we can discover definite lines of ancestry in Eastern thought.

We will begin our Western love tour with Plato, the Greek philosopher, who in many ways is the father of Western mysticism.

❧ V ❧

LOVE IS OF IMMORTALITY

Plato, Symposium, *207*

Mythos and Logos

Plato is a pioneer in the Western philosophy of love. His doctrine of salvation is based at least partially on the Orphic mysteries in which Zagreus or Dionysius, the son of Zeus, is
destroyed and consumed by the Titans. When Zeus, in turn,
killed the Titans, the human race rose up from their ashes. Thus
man's nature is twofold, Titanic and evil and Zagreic and divine. Man is earthly but with a spark of Heaven which constantly seeks to escape into the world of the divine.

Another myth which influences Plato's views on love is that
of the god Eros, who is part human and part divine. In his
Symposium, Plato describes Eros as the son of Poros and Penia,
resourceful initiative and need. Penia came begging to the feast
honoring the birth of Aphrodite. When Poros, drunk with nectar, went out into the garden to sleep it off, Penia lay down
beside him and conceived Eros. Conceived on the birthday of
the beautiful Aphrodite, Eros is to be beauty-oriented.

Taking after Mama, Eros is poor, homeless, and in need. But
he takes after Daddy, too—love of beauty and good, brave, im-
petuous, high-strung, seeking wisdom and truth, a master of
witchcraft and artful speech. Eros stands midway between
morality and immorality, waxing and waning, wisdom and ig-

norance, but his major direction is love of the beautiful and good.

Plato uses both *mythos* and *logos* to explain love, although Eros lies more in the realm of myth. Eros is the basis of Plato's salvation and his forms lead up to it.

Plato has two worlds—the world of forms and the sense world. Man recognizes the reflection of the forms in the sense world and is drawn to union with them through Eros. As A. Nygren writes: "Eros is man's conversion from the sensible to the super-sensible; it is the upward movement of the soul; it is a real force, driving the soul upwards to seek the world of forms."[1] Eros unites the two worlds.

Although Plato's Eros has a beginning in carnal love, "Plato's whole endeavor is to show the way to escape from the world of sense. And he does this best to prevent the Eros which he has in mind from being confused with ordinary sensual love."[2]

Symposium

Though Plato's love theme is central to his thought, as it is in the minds of his students, it is in his *Symposium* and *Phaedrus* dialogues that he treats it at greater length.

At the Symposium, the customary banquet of the Greek philosophical societies (416 B.C.), besides the master, Socrates, and the host, Agathon, are disciples Aristodemus, Eryximachus, Pausanias, Phaedrus, and others. It is Eryximachus who proposes the theme of discussion, namely, Eros, the god of love so neglected by the poets, and usually taking a back seat to Aphrodite.

Phaedrus begins by showing from mythology that the gods approve of true love which inspires justice and valor. But Pausanias objects that all loves should not be treated equally. As Aphrodite, the goddess of love, is twofold, so there are two loves, heavenly and popular.

Popular love has as its objects women as well as boys, and

the body more than the soul—witless people. Heavenly love, however, is of the male, the elder of the younger who has reached the age of wisdom. "For I conceive that those who begin to love them at this age are prepared to be always with them and share all with them as long as life shall last." (181)[3]

Pederasty (*pais erastēs*), the lover or friend of young people, particularly boys, the love of master for his disciple, is the very basis of Greek *paideia*.[4] But as Phaedrus and others have taught, this is not a fleshly thing, the attraction of young and shapely limbs, but rather the mutual love of two souls who beget wisdom in their dialogues. Moreover, it is not an ephemeral love based on quickly waning beauty, but enduring.

Pederasty can be either noble or evil, echoing Athenian and Spartan practices.

By "wicked" we mean that popular lover, who craves the body rather than the soul. As he himself is not in love with what abides, he himself is not abiding. As soon as the bloom of the body he so loved begins to fade, he "flutters off and is gone," leaving all his speeches and promises dishonored. Whereas the lover of a nature that is worthy abides throughout life, as being fused into one with the abiding. (183)

Pederasty reaches its height when it is coupled with philosophy or the love of wisdom.

Let us compare the two rules—one dealing with the passion for boys, and the other with the love of wisdom and all virtuous ways. By this we shall see if we are to conclude it a good thing that a favorite should gratify his lover. . . . The elder of his plenty contributing to intellectual and all other excellence, the younger in his paucity acquiring education (*eis paideusin*), and all learned arts. Only then, at the meeting of these two principles in one place, only then and there, and in no other case, can it befall that a favorite may indulge his lover. (184)

This is the heavenly love that is felt in *paideia* and the mutual seeking of wisdom.

This is the love that belongs to the Heavenly Goddess, heavenly itself and precious in both public and private life. For this compels lover and beloved alike to feel a zealous concern for their own virtue. But lovers of the other sort belong to the other Goddess, the Popular. (185)

The physician Eryximachus supplements Pausanias' remarks about the two loves with his medical observations. Moreover, the two loves are found not only in men, but also in creatures.

The master physician is he who can distinguish between nobler and baser loves and can effect such alteration that the one passion is replaced by others. And he will be deemed a good practitioner who is expert in producing Love where it ought to flourish, but exists not, and in removing it from where it should not be. Indeed, he must be able to make friends and happy lovers of the keenest opponents in the body. (186)

The physician is concerned with love, for much illness is due to misplaced love. He must apply his potions and remedies to bring love into proper alignment.

Eryximachus concludes about man's twofold love:

Well ordered men, and the less regular only so far as to bring them to better order, should be indulged in this Love. And this is the sort we should preserve. This is the noble, the heavenly love, sprung from the Heavenly Muse. But the Popular Love comes from Queen of Various Song. In applying him we must proceed with all caution that no debauchery be implanted with the reaping of his pleasure. . . . Thus in music and medicine and every other affair whether human or divine, one must be on the watch as far as may be for either sort of love; for both are there. (187)

All divination, the intercourse between the gods and men, is concerned only with the preservation or the cure of love.

Aristophanes takes another tack to explain love as man's seeking after his primordial integrity. Thus he says that men were originally of three types—male, female, and androgynous. They were spherical with four hands and feet, two faces, etc. But then they were ambitious and conspired against the gods. Zeus punished them by splitting them in two. Henceforth each one strives to be united to his better half. Those whose origin was androgynous seek a bisexual union, whereas those split from male or female spheres seek their own kind.

Love is the god who brings this about. He fully deserves our hymns for not only in the present does he bestow the priceless boon of bringing us to our very own, but he also supplies this excellent hope for the future, that if we will supply the gods with reverent duty, he will restore us to our ancient life and heal and help us unto the happiness of the blest. (193)

Love, the most beautiful, blissful, youngest, best of the gods, causes these excellences among men. He is the healer and physician of souls.

He it is who casts alienation out, draws intimacy in. He brings us together in all such friendly gatherings as at present. At feasts and dances and oblations he makes himself our leader. Politeness contriving, moroseness outdriving; kind giver of amity, giving no enmity; gracious, benign; a marvel to the wise, a delight to the gods; coveted of such as share him not, treasured of such as good share have got, father of luxury, tenderness, elegance, graces, longing and yearning; careful of the good, careless of the bad, in toil and fear, in drink and discourse, our trustiest helmsman, boatswain, champion, deliverer; ornament of all gods and men; leader fairest and best, whom one should follow, joining tunefully in the burden of his song, wherewith he enchants the thought of every good man. (197)

Eros (love) is a longing implying a need, taking after his mother, Penia. Love is a middle stage between having and not having, pointing upwards, desiring the heavenly forms. He is a mediator between man and the divine life, drawing the imperfect towards the perfect, and the mortal towards immortality. Love is divine in the sense that it brings men to the gods. Gods do not feel love since they lack nothing. (200–01) So Eros is the way of man to the divine and not the way of the gods to men.

Next Socrates tells his disciples of love as described by the Mantinean woman Diotima. She claims that love is neither bad nor good, ugly nor beautiful, but somewhere in between. Because it lacks good and beautiful things, it desires them. But the gods are totally good and beautiful and so lack nothing. (202)

But if love is not a god, what is he? Neither mortal nor divine, he is a spirit (*daimōnion*) in between, a messenger or angel between the gods and men, son of Poros and Penia, poor and wanting, yet desiring the good and beautiful. (203)

Love and wisdom are closely related, for both search for beauty. "Love must needs be a friend of wisdom and, as such, must be between wise and ignorant." (204) For whereas his father is wise and resourceful, his mother is ignorant and resourceless.

Love is also egocentric, set on the acquisition of beautiful things which will make him happy (*eudaimōn*).

Love is creative.

Hence it is that when the pregnant approaches the beautiful it becomes not only gracious but also exhilarate, that it flows over with begetting and bringing forth. . . . Therefore when a person is big and teeming-ripe, he feels himself in sore flutter for the beautiful because its possessor can relieve him of his heavy pangs. (206)

Love, then, is not of the beautiful, but of engendering and

begetting upon the beautiful. And it is a love of begetting immortality.

Because this is something ever-existent and immortal in our mortal life. From what has been admitted we must yearn for immortality no less than for good, since love loves good to be one's own forever. And hence it necessarily follows that love is of immortality. (207)

It is the search for immortality that lies behind generation and love. "So do not wonder if everything naturally values its own offshoot, since all are beset by this eagerness and this love with a view to immortality." (208) This love of immortality in one's offspring some modern authors would identify with narcissism.

But other men, pregnant of soul and mind, seek a higher immortality—artists, teachers, lawyers, writers, etc. This is the secret of the union of souls rather than bodies, bringing about spiritual children rather than bodily.

What are these things that are brought forth which exceed mortal offspring? Prudence and virtue in general by the poets and craftsmen—justice and sobriety. One pregnant with these divine things seeks a fair disciple in body and soul in order to educate him and bring forth immortal offspring.

Equally too with him he shares the nurturing of what is begotten so that men in this condition enjoy a far fuller community with each other than that which came with children, and a far surer friendship, since the children of their union are fairer and more deathless. (209)

Witness the eternal classical children of Homer, Hesiod, and Plato. Indeed, their natural children, if any, are unknown.

This spiritual begetting is the very basis of pedagogy, for between master and disciple are begotten deathless wisdom and virtue, a begetting which surpasses that of natural parents. Thus in many cultures the master is the new father of his disciples, superseding the natural parenthood of mother and father.

True love leads upwards to true beauty, whereas false love pulls down. The lower beauties of earth should lead up to the highest beauty.

5. "Ever climbing aloft" (Plato, *Symposium*, 211)

Beginning from obvious beauties he must for the sake of that highest beauty be ever climbing aloft, as on the rungs of a ladder, from one to two and from two to all beautiful bodies. From personal beauty he proceeds to beautiful observances, from observances to beautiful learning, from learning at last to that particular study which is concerned with the beautiful itself and that alone. So that in the end he comes to know the essence of Beauty. (211)

And when at last he beholds beauty, it will outshine gold, fine clothing, beautiful boys, and when he sees the Divine Beauty, he will breed not illusions but true example of virtue. "So when he has begotten a true virtue and has reared it up he is destined to win the friendship of Heaven. He above all men is immortal." (212) Here perhaps is the philosophical basis of creative celibacy of the philosophers, teachers, monks, clergy, etc.

But what is the place of sexual love in Plato's erology? D. Morgan feels that Plato is ambivalent towards sex.[5] *Phaedo* and parts of the *Republic* reflect an ascetical Plato, turning away from earthly pleasures for those of Heaven. But in the *Symposium* and *Phaedrus* there is a continuity of love growth between that of the imperfect world of beautiful bodies and the perfect world of forms. But in neither case is sex exalted. It is either avoided or seen as a lesser pursuit of beauty which is a mere reflection of Divine Beauty.

Lysis

Lysis is a dialogue between the boy Lysis and his friend Menexenus on friendship (*philia*). Some say that Plato uses the word *philia* here to downplay the sexual aspects of Eros. Is the loved person a friend even though he does not reciprocate love? All love is of the good and cannot be of the bad, for even wicked men can only love good men.

But can the self-sufficient good man have friends?

How can we say that the good will be friends to the good at all, when neither in absence do they long for one another —for they are sufficient for themselves even when apart—nor in presence have they need of one another? (215)

Can like befriend like? No, for opposites attract. "Only that which is neither good nor bad proves to be friendly to the good and to that only." (217) Thus the sick man is a friend of the doctor. A friend in need is a friend indeed.

It is impossible for a totally bad person to be a friend of the good. "For we say that, in the soul and in the body and everywhere, just that which is neither good nor bad, but has the presence of bad, is thereby friend of the good." (218) What is loved may be the good and beautiful, but it is loved because of the presence of some evil in the subject. (219) Desire is possible only if some good is wanting.

But with all their discussion of friendship Lysis and Menexenus do not succeed in defining it. (223) Perhaps like love it is more easily experienced than explained.

Republic

The *Republic*, too, has some of Plato's insights on love. In describing the ideal state he speaks of two types of love: one loves the good itself while the other loves good things. The former is the philosophical nature. "It is ever enamored of the kind of knowledge which reveals to them something of that essence which is eternal, and is not wandering between the two poles of generation and decay." (6/485)

All culture either in music, gymnastics, or literature is a love of the beautiful. Plato grades lovers according to the object of their love. The lover of wisdom, the philosopher, is the highest. (5/475)

How about the *philotheamones*, the show lovers? Are they as good as the philosophers? No serious debates on the essences of life for them, but only choruses and Dionysiac festivals. Those who practice and frequent the minor arts are by no means to be ranked with the lovers of wisdom. "But they do bear a certain likeness to philosophers." (475) The former hunger only for the individual event which shows beauty and order and not beauty and order itself.

The true philosopher is one for whom the truth is the spectacle of which he is enamored. "The true lover of knowledge must, from childhood up, be most of all a striver after truth in every form." (6/485)

When one's desires incline strongly to any one thing, they are weakened for other things, as a stream diverted into another channel.

So, when man's desires have been taught to flow in the

channel of learning and all that sort of thing, they will be concerned, I presume, with the pleasures of the soul in itself, and will be indifferent to those of which the body is the instrument, if the man is a true and not a sham philosopher. (485)

Such a one will be temperate and not greedy for money. No narrowness, bragging, or pettiness here.

Of course, a forgetful soul can't be a philosopher, since a philosopher must have a good memory, quick apprehension, and be magnificent, gracious, friendly, truthful, just, brave, sober. (487) "When men of this sort are perfected by education and maturity, would you not entrust the state solely to them?"

The *philotheamones* only look at present events, having no passion for the essence of each thing, for the good. It may be true that in the case of the just and honorable, many would prefer the semblance without the reality in action, possession, and opinion. "Yet when it comes to the good nobody is content with the possession of the appearance but all men seek the reality, and the semblance satisfies no one here." (505)

Plato frequently distinguishes between good things of ephemeral interest which the *philotheamones* delight in and the good of philosophers, "the self beautiful and good that is only and merely good."

Without the good there would be no good objects of knowledge and love. Knowledge and truth reflect good just as light and vision depend on the sun. The good is to the mind what the sun is to the eye; man's happiness can only be found in the apprehension of the good itself. Only here can his love be sated.

What place do love and marriage have in Plato's ideal Republic? Of the three classes of people there—namely, the *phylakes* (rulers), *epikouroi* (military assistants), and *demos*— Plato is concerned primarily with the eugenics of the upper two leader classes.

Thus marriage partners are eugenically selected by an inner committee of *phylakes*. (5/460a) But ordinary Greek marriage customs seem to have prevailed in the *demos*. But even here marriage is not for pleasure, but for society. Though the temporary marriages of the upper classes are eugenic and utilitarian in order to create an elite leadership, those above and below the procreative age seem to be freer in sexual matters.

Exclusive male-female love would always present a problem to strict communism. H. Rankin comments:

> Eros as a powerful *nosos*, or disease, could fall upon any individual member of any class, and the individual concerned would be expected to cope with it as best he might within the context of the mores of his class. A phylax would be expected to strive and win in the struggle with Eros. Personal happiness was not part of the socially approved aim of the phylax. [419a–421c] Less would be expected of members of the lowest class. In all cases, however, erotic choices would encounter obstacles.[6]

In a word, Eros is to be used for the Republic and not for individual pleasure.

Phaedrus

This dialogue between Socrates and Phaedrus is a chief source of Plato's teaching on love. They are discussing Lysias' speech about love. Lysias' thesis is that favors should be granted to a non-lover rather than to a lover. He seems to be proposing a sensual gratification, but without being carried away by erotic emotion. The objectivity of sensual gratification is seen as prudence, a virtue (*aretē*), rather than love (eros). Against this objective, rational view of pleasure, the erotic appears as irrational and sick. The Sophists repudiated such erotic excesses.[7] Lovers freely admit that they are mad.

Phaedrus reads Lysias' speech (*logos erōtikos*).

And if you were to choose the best from among your lovers, your choice would be limited to a few; whereas it would be made from a great number, if you choose the most congenial from non-lovers. So that you would have a better chance in choosing among many, of finding the one most worthy of your affection. (231)

Lysias portrays desire without love, craving for pleasure without capacity for emotion—similar to the Sophists and later Stoics, who valued life without passion (*sōphrosunē*). Lysias' love doctrine—maximum pleasure with minimum complications—seems to have been popular with the youth of Plato's day.

Socrates then observes that he who is ruled by desire and pleasure will try to make his beloved as pleasing to himself as possible. One of unsound mind may take pleasure only in him who is weaker and who does not rival or challenge him. (239) So the lover tries to keep his beloved ignorant and dependent on him for everything.

Also his love of the body will keep his beloved effeminate. Moreover, he wants his beloved to be bereft of family and property in order to be all the more dependent on him. (239–40) Thus the lover is not only harmful to his beloved but disagreeable to live with as well. Can the old lover be anything but disgusting to the young beloved? And when his love ceases, he is then false to his former beloved. "These things, dear boy, you must bear in mind, and you must know that the fondness of the lover is not a matter of good will, but of the appetite which he wishes to satisfy. 'Just as the wolf loves the lamb, so the lover adores his beloved.'" (241)

The non-lover possesses all the advantages that are opposed to the disadvantages of the lover. (242)

But Socrates begins to feel bad both about his speech and that of Lysias. "If love is, as indeed he is, something divine, he can be nothing evil. But the two speeches just now said that he was evil, so then they sinned against love." (242)

Socrates then recants what was said in the previous speeches, for they were speaking of love as lowly gobs who had never experienced generous love.

Socrates then attacks the view that the non-lover is to be preferred over the lover, the sane over the insane. Indeed, many blessings come through madness (mania). "The greatest of blessings come to us through madness when it is sent as a gift of the gods." (244)

First of all there is prophecy as seen at Delphi, Dodona, and the Sibyl. Indeed, prophecy is called the manic art. There is also a cathartic mania by purification and sacred rites, releasing from evil and danger. And a third type of madness is that of the Muses inspiring poetry and song.

Love, too, is a divine gift of madness. Socrates argues against those who hold that the right approach to sensual gratification is that of reasoned objectivity. Rather love is a madness given to all for their greater happiness.

The human soul is like a pair of winged horses, one lusty and the other right-willed, and a charioteer. Striving for beauty, the charioteer and the right-willed horse try to master the lusty one.

The soul that has seen the most beauty will become a lover and a follower of the Muses, rising up to the heights. He who has seen less will dwell in the king, statesman, athlete, prophet, poet, artisan, sophist, or tyrant. (248)

And therefore it is just that the mind of the philosopher only has wings, for he is always, so far as he is able, in communion through memory with those things, the communion with which causes god to be divine. Now a man who employs such memories rightly is always being initiated into perfect mysteries and he alone becomes truly perfect. But since he separates himself from human interests and turns his attention toward the divine, he is rebuked by the vulgar who consider him mad and do not know that he is inspired (*enthousiazōn*). (249)

This is the fourth type of mania, he who, seeing the beauty of earth, remembers the true beauty and, feeling his wings grow, wants to take to flight. But since he cannot yet do so, he gazes longingly upwards, neglecting the things of earth. He who has this enthusiastic divine madness is called a lover.

Plato does not say that everyone in erotic mania is divinely inspired. But he may be. "The price is a surrender of his autonomy. He must throw himself open to god, rather than lock the doors of his soul by choosing sensual pleasure alone."[8]

And in this encounter with beauty, he is taken out of himself. He is beside himself.

The earthly physical lover is shaken to his depths by the encounter with beauty, which is to say, once again with something earthly, physical, apparent to the senses. But in that overpowering emotion he is carried out of the dimensions of here and now, becomes unborn and imperishable, and his emotion cannot be satisfied with anything else than the Whole, the totality of being, truth, goodness and beauty.[9]

The winged soul can ascend to the gods. This is realized in the shock of ecstatic enthusiasm at the sight of beauty and the recollection of a beauty which exceeds the gratification of anything here below.

Sensuous beauty is sometimes called ravishing, for it can rob one of his calm security, his reason and self-possession, replacing them with ferment, unrest, and helplessness.

But there is a difference between lust and love. The lusters know what they want. They have their wits about them. "But lust is not love. The object of desire is, strictly speaking, not loved. Rather that person is loved for whom something is desired."[10] The lover is moved by the sight of his beloved—beauty. Much of what is ordinarily called love is really lust.

The sight of beauty alone evokes memories and yearning, so that one who is deeply moved by beauty wishes to leave the orbit of ordinary human concerns.

But not all recognize beauty as a reflection of Absolute

Beauty, but rather as beasts seek lust and begetting, even pursuing pleasure against nature.

But he who is newly initiated, who beheld many of those realities, when he sees a god-like face or form which is a good image of Beauty, shudders at first, and something of the old awe comes over him. Then, as he gazes, he reveres the beautiful one as a god, and if he did not fear to be thought stark mad, he would offer sacrifice to his beloved as to an idol or a god. (250)

Beauty makes the wings of his soul grow so that he can fly to the home of the gods whence his soul has come. Both lovers and philosophers can only be filled by divine satiation.

That about which I am speaking is called Love by men, but when you hear what the gods call it, perhaps because of your youth you will laugh. . . . "Mortals call him winged Love, but the immortals call him the Winged One, because he must needs grow wings." (252)

Pieper comments:

Love insofar as it is real *ekstasis*, a stepping stone out of the narrow circle of the self-concerned ego, a frenzy, mania, is capable of carrying aloft with it even the heaviest burden for it remembers the holy things it once contemplated.[11]

Socrates shows four different varieties or abuses of love. First there is the love of the masses who seek only raw pleasure. Second, the rational and sophisticated approach to sensuality, unencumbered by the witlessness or obligations of true love. The third love gives up enjoyment and when this lover dies, he flies to the heavenly sphere to sit at the banquet of the gods.

Fourth, there is a love between lust and continence, a madly amorous passion, a ravishing ecstasy. When these lovers die, they will not have the full-fledged wings but budding ones. "They are not winged to be sure, but their wings have begun to grow, so that the madness of love brings them no small reward." Once they have started their upward flight, they will never again pass through darkness. (256)

But the calculated affection of the non-lover, the reasoned search for pleasure, will beget only the narrowness that the common people see as virtue. It will bring only wandering to the soul for nine thousand years on earth, ending up as a fool below the earth. (257)

Thus Socrates concludes his recantation of earlier remarks offensive to the divine Eros, defending the thesis that the sophisticated affection of the non-lover is to be preferred to the mad ravishment of the true lover.

Though Plato rejects the identification of lust and love, he teaches the nearness of the two, with erotic love of beauty giving wing to the soul to fly back to the abode of the gods.

Based on his primordial recollection of true beauty, the soul of the lover is never satisfied till it returns and the true lover sees in his earthly love a reflection of Divine Beauty.

Though love starts in the human senses, it is a rising thing, flying to beauty, creative, seeking immortality not so much in earthly children as in immortal wisdom.

The height of earthly love is seen by Plato not in male-female union but rather in the love of the academy or philosophical fraternity, master and disciple, the pederasty of Greek *paideia*. But this attraction and love is toward beauty of soul and the mutual generation of eternal wisdom—rather than fleshly desires.

Later Plato and Aristotle

Whereas earlier (*Symposium* and *Republic*) Plato had taught that the human psyche derives its energy and motion from the love of the good, later (*Phaedrus, Timaeus,* and *Laws*) the psyche is a self-generating motion.[12] But if the psyche is self-motion, how can the good be the cause of motion? Also the psyche as self-motion hardly explains the problem of evil.

In *Laws* (10) Plato speaks of two kinds of psyche, that of self-generating circular motion and the rectilinear motion of bodily and irrational parts of the psyche. But in the *Timaeus* (70b) the irrational psyches are so housed within us that one has no excuse for not keeping them under our intelligence.

But the identification of psyche as self-caused motion

leads Plato to a fantastically physical description of the role of intelligence and good in the dynamics of events. But such a description necessarily put an end to the hope that the world could be explained with any clarity as the product of love.[13]

Aristotle did away with Plato's later changes and re-established the love theme as found in the *Phaedo*. "What Aristotle did was to abandon the notion of self-motion in favor of a system based once more on the desire for good."[14]

Aristotle, as Eryximachus, sees love as the sole cause of all events in the world. Thus the Prime Mover of the universe is the best and most beautiful thing of all and causes everything to move by being the object of its love. "The final cause, then, produces motion as being loved, but all other things move by being moved." (*Metaphysics*, 1072b)

Aristotle, then, abandons Plato's idea of the psyche as self-motion.

A man's psyche, therefore, might be the ultimate source of the motion which originated within him. But the psyche moves not because it is itself in motion, but because it is the pattern of full realization which the whole man, or the real man within the man strives inevitably to achieve.[15]

The divine intelligence as pure motionless form is perfection desired by and moving the universe as a whole.

There seems to be a direct development from middle Plato to Aristotle's teleology, skipping the more physical version of the later Plato.

Like Plato, Aristotle sees friendship and love as closely related, describing three types of friendship in his *Eudemian Ethics*. (7, chs. 1 and 2) There are useful friendships between unlikes, pleasureful friendships desiring apparent good, and excellent friendships desiring real good.[16]

Friendship is really a kind of self-love because the friend is the alter ego.

And if as the virtuous man is to himself, he is to his friend also (for his friend is another self): if all this be true, as his own being is desirable for each man, so, or almost so, is that of his friend. . . . and this will be realized in their living together and sharing in discussion and thought. (Nic. Eth. 9, 10, 1170b)

Aristotle follows the later Plato in using *philia* for true friendship and eros for excess pleasure.

One cannot be a friend (*philos*) to many people in the sense of having friendship of the perfect type with them, just as one cannot be in love with many people at once. (For love [*erōs*] is a sort of an excess feeling, and it is the nature of such only to be felt towards one person.) (Nic. Eth. 8, 6, 1158a)

Aristotle sees correctly that the communism proposed by Plato for his Republic militates against true friendship. (*Politics*, 2, 1262b)

Aristotle re-establishes final causality, giving back to love its primary role in the universe. However, he prefers teleological terms to love talk, though he uses eros in his description of the First Mover and the universe in his *Metaphysics*. The beautiful and good are objects moving desire to love and motion. The Prime Mover causes motion by being the object of love. Moreover, this prime mover is God. (12, 7, 1072b)

Form causes motion. Thus God, the eternal form and mover, causes the perpetual motion of the stars affecting seasons and cycles of birth and death. (*Generation and Corruption*, 2, 10)

But as one gets more towards the center of the universe

and farther from the First Mover, there is more confusion, pulled this way and that by various forms. But this does not worry Aristotle. For if the leader of the government is on course, it does not matter if the lower elements are distracted. (*Metaphysics*, 12, 10, 1075a)

For Aristotle, then, it is a final teleology or a cosmic love that moves the universe. Even the stars are moved by their attraction to highest beauty.

Both Plato's and Aristotle's love themes influenced later thought. Thus Middle and Neo-Platonism and mysticism perfected Plato's ascending love, while Aristotle's god-centered teleology would stimulate medieval scholastic theology of love.

❧ VI ❧

YOU SHALL LOVE THE LORD YOUR GOD WITH ALL YOUR HEART, AND WITH ALL YOUR SOUL, AND WITH ALL YOUR MIGHT

Deuteronomy, 6/5

We have seen love themes in Eastern religions and in the Greek philosophers with a pre-eminence of divine love. Now let us turn to Palestine to see the love relationship between the Hebrews and their God Yahweh.

Yahweh and Israel

Love is the essential relationship between Yahweh and Israel. This is frequently shown in the anthropomorphism of husband and wife, the ancient hierogamy. In the marriage analogy the initiative comes from the man. Thus Yahweh loves Israel first.

Creation is his first act of love and, in a sense, his self-love, for he creates in his own image. God loves the world insofar as it is good and reflects himself. In other cultures the hierogamy of father sky and earth mother generate creatures. But in Hebrew tradition the Father creates alone, though in later times his Shekhinah, or divine Presence, takes on the appearance of a goddess and consort of Yahweh. We shall see more of this in Chapter XIII.

Yahweh has a twofold love for his people, the Hebrews. The first is *ahab*, the love of election, while the second is *hesed*, his covenant love. Whereas *ahab* can be directed toward many love objects, persons, or things, *hesed* implies a covenant. Thus the blood brotherhood of David and Jonathan. (1 Sam 20/14–16)

And while the love of election is the choosing of the beloved, covenant love carries this out. Though divine love is expressed in anthropomorphic terms, there is a subordination of sex to the hierogamy.

It is as if from the beginnings of the Hebraic faith human passion was always taken up into a fully personalized relationship where feeling, emotional desire and fulfillment were not rejected, but where their meaning was found in a personal order which absorbed them into a larger pattern of devotion and loyalty.[1]

Deuteronomy

The Book of Deuteronomy specifies the covenant love between Israel and Yahweh. The covenant is a contract of love, a marriage vow. If Israel keeps the agreement, proving her abiding love of Yahweh, he will bless her. But if she is unfaithful, he will punish her.

For I am the Lord your God, a jealous God, visiting the iniquity of the fathers upon the children to the third and fourth generation of those who hate me, but showing steadfast love to thousands of those who love me and keep my commandments. (Dt 5/8–10)[2]

Yahweh is a jealous husband.[3] But jealousy is impossible without love. For how can the lover be jealous when his beloved is led astray, if he is not in love with her and her alone?

As a lover chooses his beloved from among many, so Yahweh selects Israel for his bride.

Hear, O Israel, the Lord our God is one Lord; and you shall love the Lord your God with all your heart, and with all your soul, and with all your might. And these words which I command you this day shall be upon your heart and you shall teach them diligently to your children. (Dt 6/4–7; 10/12–15)

This is the *shema,* the shibboleth of Judaism. Their love for Yahweh is to be wholehearted, undivided love, infatuation, with no other lover either god or man or riches.

The whole Torah is the love of God and man. No love of false gods will be tolerated and no hate, false love, deception, stealing is allowed. Even the Sabbath is based on love. One who loves his fellow men, his servants and beasts, will provide them with a day of rest.

The love covenant binds both God and man and the Lord will continue to show his *hesed* to those who keep their promise.

Know, therefore, that the Lord your God is God, the faithful God who keeps covenant and steadfast love with those who love him and keep his commandments to a thousand generations. . . . And because you hearken to these ordinances, and keep and do them, the Lord your God will keep with you the covenant and steadfast love which he swore to your fathers to keep. He will love you, bless you, and multiply you . . . (Dt 7/9–13)

As a continuing proof of his *hesed,* Yahweh will bless their families, land, grain, oil, cattle, health, and will destroy their enemies. (Dt 7/13–16; 11/13–15; 28/1–14) But hate and disobedience bring punishment and retribution. (Dt 28/15–68)

So the covenant is a love agreement between husband and wife. Israel agrees to observe the Torah, and Yahweh will bless her with his covenant love.

The mutual love of Israel and Yahweh is strong in the Deuteronomic and prophetic traditions, but perhaps less in evidence in later times when Yahweh's anthropomorphisms give way to intermediaries as his Name, Word, or Shekhinah. Thus one loves the Name of the Lord (Is 56/6) or his Shekhinah.

Greek love (*erōs*) implies a need and so it is not proper to the gods, who are entirely self-sufficient and indeed are more the objects than the subjects of love. But the constant parallels of divine and human love in Hebrew literature seem to indicate a love of desire or need. There is a loneliness in a man's life which his girl fills. Could the Biblical parallels attempt to show the Israelites that Yahweh chose them because he needed them and so he is disappointed and sad when he loses their love?

True, when God loves Israel, he really loves himself since he created Israel to his image, as a human husband picks a similar wife, or a wife who somehow reflects his ideal. But when Israel sins, she loses her divine image and her husband turns away.

Songs and Proverbs

The love of God is seen throughout the Bible, for example in the Psalms. The Lord loves those who are righteous like himself. (Ps 11/7) "He loves righteousness and justice; the earth is full of the steadfast love of the Lord." (Ps 33/5; 37/28) Love and election are one, for Yahweh never would have chosen Israel for his bride unless he loved her. (Ps 47/5; 87/2)

In Proverbs the Lord chastises those whom he loves. "My son, do not despise the Lord's discipline or be weary of his reproof. For the Lord reproves him whom he loves, as a father the son in whom he delights." (Prov 3/11–12) Chastisement— that is, correction—can be done only by a father who loves. For, in a sense, he loves his own ideal image in his beloved. And when this likeness is clouded by sin, he hopes to correct it in love. God's Wisdom is personified in Proverbs and is the object of love.

In Proverbs love and hate are opposites. Thus he who hates wisdom loves death. (Prov 8/36) And whereas hatred causes strife, love covers offenses. (Prov 10/12)

The Greatest Song is *the* love poem of the Bible. Attributed

to Solomon, it describes the love of the shepherd boy and his
Shulamite girl, typifying the affection between Yahweh and
Israel, human love reflecting the divine.

> O that you would kiss me with the
>   kisses of your mouth!
> For your love is better than wine,
>   your anointing oils are fragrant,
> Your name is oil poured out;
>   therefore the maidens love you.
> Draw me after you, let us make haste.
>   The king has brought me into his chambers.
> We will exult and rejoice in you;
>   We will exult your love more than wine;
>   Rightly do they love you. (1/1–4)

> I am the rose of Sharon,
>   a lily of the valleys.
> As a lily among brambles,
>   so is my love among maidens.
> As an apple tree among the trees
>   of the wood,
> so is my beloved among young men. (2/1–3)

>   O queenly maiden!
> Your rounded thighs are like jewels,
>   the work of a master hand.
> Your navel is a rounded bowl
>   that never lacks mixed wine.
> Your belly is a heap of wheat,
>   encircled with lilies.
> Your twin breasts are like two fawns,
>   twins of a gazelle. . . .
> How fair and pleasant you are,
>   O loved one, delectable maiden. (7/1–6)

The twenty-five lyric poems that comprise the Song of Solomon were probably sung at weddings. But generations of rabbis and mystics have seen in them reflections of the love that should abide between God and man. We will see more of this in later chapters.

Prophets

The Prophets also proclaim Yahweh's love for Israel. Thus Deutero-Isaiah (43/4-5): "Because you are precious in my eyes and honored, and I love you, I give men in return for you, peoples in exchange for your life. Fear not for I am with you."

The husband and unfaithful wife theme is popular in the Prophets. Though Israel is stripped naked and sent into the desert for her adultery, she is still the beloved of Yahweh.[4]

> For the Lord has called you like a wife forsaken and grieved in spirit, like a wife of youth when she is cast off, says your God. For a brief moment I forsook you, but with great compassion I will gather you. In overflowing wrath for a moment I hid my face from you. But with everlasting love I will have compassion on you, says the Lord, my redeemer. (Is 54/6-8)

For though the mountains depart and the hills are removed, Yahweh's steadfast love remains.

And again:

> You shall no more be termed Forsaken, and your land shall no more be termed Desolate. But you shall be called My Delight is in Her, and your land Married, for the Lord delights in you, and your land shall be married. For as a young man marries a virgin, so shall your sons marry you, and as a bridegroom rejoices over the bride, so shall your God rejoice over you. (Is 62/4-5)

Jeremiah, too, sings the song of love. Thus says the Lord: "I remember the devotion of your youth, your love as a bride,

how you followed me in the wilderness, in a land not sown."
(Jer 2/2) But Israel has been like a beast in heat, running after
the Baals. (Jer 2/23–24)

Yahweh punishes his errant bride because he still loves her.

You have polluted the land with your vile harlotry. Therefore
the showers have been withheld and the spring rain has not
come. Yet you have a harlot's brow. You refuse to be
ashamed. Have you not just now called to me, "My father,
you are the friend of my youth—will he be angry forever,
will he be indignant to the end?" Behold you have spoken.
But you have done all the evil you could. (Jer 3/2–5)

Ezekiel also chastises Israel's harlotry.

Thus says the Lord God, because your shame was laid bare
and your nakedness uncovered in your harlotries with your
lovers, and because of all your idols, and because of the
blood of your children that you gave to them, therefore, behold, I will gather all your lovers, with whom you took pleasure, all those you loved and all those you loathed. I will
gather them against you from every side and will uncover
your nakedness to them, that they may see all your nakedness. And I will judge you as women who break wedlock and
shed blood are judged, and bring upon you the blood of
wrath and jealousy. . . . I will make you stop playing the
harlot and you shall also give hire no more. (Ez 16/35–41)

But though she is cast out naked and despised, Yahweh will
seek her out again as his spouse. And ashamed of her adultery,
she will turn once again to him in perfect fidelity.

The unrequited love theme is also dominant in Hosea, who
compares his love for his harlot wife Gomer to Yahweh's abiding love for Israel.

For their mother has played the harlot; she that has conceived them has acted shamefully. For she said, "I will go
after my lovers, who give me my bread and my water, my
wool and my flax, my oil and my drink." (Hos 2/5)

But seeking her lovers in vain, she cries out: "I will go and return to my first husband, for it was better with me then than now." (2/7)

Hosea contrasts the false love of harlotry and adultery of Gomer (2/5) with his true and faithful love.

And in that day, says the Lord, you will call me "My husband" and no longer call me "My Baal." For I will remove the names of the Baals from your mouth and they shall be mentioned by name no more. . . . And I will betroth you to me in righteousness and justice in steadfast love, and in mercy, I will betroth you to me in faithfulness. And you shall know the Lord. (Hos 2/16–20)

The Lord persuaded Hosea to buy back Gomer as he had done his own faithless people. "And I said to her, 'You must dwell as mine for many days; you shall not play the harlot, or belong to another man; so will I also be to you.'" (3/3)

As Yahweh's *hesed* love is steadfast and faithful, so he desires that of Israel. But "your love is like a morning cloud, like the dew that goes away early. Therefore I have hewn them by the prophets, I have slain them by the words of my mouth, and my judgment goes forth as the light. For I desire steadfast love and not sacrifice, the knowledge of God, rather than burnt offerings." (6/4–6)

The abiding covenant love of God brings knowledge of him. For just as a wife knows her husband in marital love, so Israel can know Yahweh in her steadfast love.

Though Yahweh punishes Israel, sending her naked into the desert, turning his back on her, he still loves her. He is torn between just punishment and love for his errant bride. Perhaps in the desert she will mend her ways and find a new beginning as the faithful bride of Yahweh.

Yahweh will heal Israel. "I will heal their unfaithfulness. I will love them freely, for my anger has turned from them." (14/4)

Several questions come to mind concerning Yahweh's love

of Israel. First his love seems to be exclusively for Israel. But
how about the Nations? Is the Hebrew God the same as the
gods of other peoples? Are Baal, Yahweh, and Vishnu one and
the same?

God created the whole world in his image and likeness. And
he will smite and heal Egypt and Assyria as he does Israel.
"Blessed be Egypt my people, and Assyria the work of my
hands and Israel my heritage." (Is 19/25) Israel, though, is
God's special love. She is to be his priest to the world, an example and light to the Nations. (Is 49/6)

But what about the loving compassion of Yahweh? As we
have seen, the Greek philosophers felt that love was inappropri-
ate for the gods since it implies a need. Yahweh in the Hebrew
Bible is portrayed as loving and compassionate.

But how can God suffer with his people? Is he not almighty,
impassible, without any wants or needs? Is the love of Yahweh
a suffering love? He feels for his wayward people. He mourns
for his lost bride and is anxious for her return. And expresses
his compassion through angels, prophets, and his Messiah. If
the Hebrew Bible teaches us anything about Yahweh, it is that
he is not monolithic and unchangeable, for he can be angry
with his people, jealous and righteous and at the same time
loving and compassionate.

Human Love

We have seen much of divine love in Hebrew tradition. But
how about human love? As God loves the Israelites, so they
must love their fellow man, human love mirroring the divine.

Ahab, to love, can have many meanings in the Hebrew Bible.
Most frequently it is used of love between the sexes. For example, Shechem's love for Dinah. "He seized her and lay with
her and humbled her, and his soul was drawn to Dinah the
daughter of Jacob. He loved [ahab] the maiden and spoke tenderly to her." (Gen 34/2–3; also Ez 16/33–37 and Hos 2/7–15)

But love can mean something more than sexual affection. "Then Jacob brought her into his tent and took Rebekah and she became his wife. And he loved her." (Gen 24/67)

Human love is an emotional experience, a ravishing of the spirit. Thus the Greatest Song: "O that you would kiss me with the kisses of your mouth for your love is better than wine." (1/2)

Proverbs speaks of the proper love between husband and wife.

Let your fountain be blessed and rejoice in the wife of your youth, a lovely hind, a graceful doe. Let her affection fill you at all times with delight. Be infatuated at all times with love. (Pr 5/18–19)

Do not lose yourself with loose women.

Do not desire her beauty in your heart, and do not let her capture you with her eyelashes. For a harlot can be hired for a loaf of bread, but an adultress stalks a man's very life. Can a man carry fire in his bosom and his clothes not be burned? Or can one walk upon hot coals and his feet not be scorched? So is he who goes in to his neighbor's wife. None who touches her will go unpunished. (Prov 6/25–29)

Adultery can only exist where love is violated. It is the very essence of infidelity and illustrates Israel's rejection of Yahweh's love.

There are degrees of human love. "If a man has two wives, the one loved and the other disliked, and they have borne him children, both the loved and the disliked . . ." (Dt 21/15) This is basically the love of preference. Love is shown in the family between husband and wife, parents and children, mother-in-law and daughter-in-law. (Ruth 4/15) There is love between the king and his people. Thus David is loved by the Israelites.

Love also is between friends, even surpassing that which a man may have for a woman, reflecting a theme we have already seen in Plato. Thus David loves Jonathan. "Jonathan lies slain upon your high places. I am distressed for you, my brother Jonathan. Very pleasant have you been for me. Your love to me has been wonderful surpassing the love of women." (2 Sam 1/25–26) Later we shall see the mutual love of the *haberim* reflected in Jesus and his disciples.

Love of the neighbor is a fundamental law of the Torah. "You shall love your neighbor as yourself. I am the Lord." (Lv 19/18) Love for the neighbor's wife, his goods, lying, injuring him in any way, is against love. The neighbor for the Hebrews generally meant those who lived nearby.

The Israelite must love his neighbor. But what about foreigners? During the monarchy "foreigner" came to mean non-Israelite. The Israelites, as were many early peoples, were xenophobic, with the stranger looked upon as an enemy.

McKenzie (DOB, 847) notes that the Hebrew Bible is ambivalent toward the foreigner, sometimes commanding his extermination.

> And when the Lord your God gives them over to you [Hittites, Girgashites, Amorites, etc.] and you defeat them, then you must utterly destroy them. You shall make no covenant with them, and show no mercy to them. (Dt 7/1–2)

The fear of the foreigner seems to be that of syncresis, namely, the adoption of foreign beliefs, rites, and customs and the dilution of the race by intermarriage.

But though the foreigner is to be feared and even despised since he does not believe in Yahweh, yet when he comes into the land as a sojourner (*ger* or *tosab*) he is to be loved. "Love the sojourner, therefore, for you were sojourners in the land of Egypt." (Dt 10/19) In the East, with its fluid and mobile population, most are sojourners at one time or another due to wars, famine, drought, etc. Thus the ancient tradition of Eastern hospitality. Welcome the stranger. Give him everything that is yours, food, lodging, friendship, even female companionship. And you will be welcomed when you are a stranger.

The Rabbis

The rabbis taught and explained to the people of their time the Torah's teaching on love. Yahweh loves his bride Israel, chosen from among many. And he is compassionate with them, sending his Shekhinah among them.

The Torah is the law of love.

The Torah [that is practiced and studied] for its own sake [*lishmah*] is a law of love. The Law [that is practiced and studied] not for its own sake is a law without love. The Torah which is studied in order to teach, is a law of love. The Torah which is not studied in order to teach, is a law without love. (*Sukkah*, 49b)[5]

Love of God is shown in *kanwanah*, reverent and attentive prayer, and *lishmah*, observing the Law for its own sake. Man must love his neighbor as God loves him. "Yield your will to your friend; but let both his will and yours yield to the will of God." (*Derek Erez Zutta*, 1/8) And: "The rabbis have taught: it says, 'You shall not hate your brother in your heart.'" (*'Arakin*, 16b) The heart is the center of Hebrew love, as it is in most Eastern traditions.

Love that is based on passing beauty will soon fly away. "Whenever love depends upon some material cause, with the passing away of that cause, the love, too, passes away. But if it be not dependent on such a cause, it will not pass away forever." (*Aboth*, 5/19)

Man must love his fellow creatures and not hate them. The men of the generation which was dispersed over the earth (Gen. R. 1–9) loved one another. And so God did not destroy them, but only scattered them. But the men of Sodom hated one another. And so God destroyed them both from this world and from the world to come. (*Aboth R. Nathan*, vi, 12/26b)

And Rabbi Simeon B. Elazar said: "What a great oath was this word said, 'You shall love your neighbor as yourself.' 'I, the Lord have created him; if you love him, I am trustworthy to give you good reward. And if not, I am judge to punish you.'" (Aboth, 16/32b)

Yet the Israelite does not love all equally. The love-hate themes in the Bible usually spell degrees of love. Thus: "Love the wise and hate the disciple. . . . Love all and hate only the heretics, the apostates and informers." (Aboth, 16/32b) And:

"You shall not abhor an Edomite, for he is your brother"; good or bad, he is your brother. "You shall not abhor an Egyptian, for you were a sojourner in his land"; good or bad, among them you lived many years. But as to Amalek, "Remember what Amalek did to you." (Peshahim, R. 47b)

In both the written Torah of Moses and the oral Torah of the rabbis love of God and neighbor is a central theme. Since the Rabbi Jesus of Nazareth taught in this milieu, we should also expect him to teach the law of love. We shall see the love doctrine of the School of Jesus in the following chapter.

~§ VII ᙥ~

GOD IS LOVE

1 John, 4/8

The teachings of Jesus of Nazareth and his school are basically applications of the law of love from the Torah.

Agape

Much has been made of the use of the Greek word "agape" (love) in the New Testament vis-à-vis the eros of Greek philosophy. The New Testament writers may have avoided eros because of its sexual connotations, relying on agape and *philein* to express the uniqueness of Christian love when preaching to the Greeks. Also they may have felt that agape is much closer to the *hesed,* covenant love, of the Torah.

Nygren in his classical *Agape and Eros* distinguishes sharply between the two words. Thus agape is uncaused and spontaneous, not the product of man's work, but rather God's free gift. Agape is creative. "The man whom God loves has not any value in himself. His value consists simply in the fact that God loves him."[1] Whereas eros is man's way to God, agape is God's way to man. God loves man, not because man is lovable, but rather because God is love and so he cannot help but overflow in his largess. Nygren's view of agape reflects Luther, whom we will see in a later chapter.

Morgan feels that Nygren may have overdrawn the distinction between eros and agape. "Nygren fails to observe that one can argue at least equally well that the fact that Greek contains two distinct words for love does not prove that eros and agape are distinct and unrelated realities."[2]

All philological distinctions aside, love is the central theme of Christianity. The Rabbi Jesus is the key. He is the love of the Father overflowing in man. He is God's elect and beloved (*agapētos*). The New Testament election is Christological. Thus Christ is the only son and beloved of the Father. Williams writes: "There is one elect man and in some way all human history has to be interpreted from within his election and Jesus is the representative of God and everyman."[3]

Whereas the Hebrew Bible stresses God's love for his chosen people, the New Testament election is wider, reflecting the eschatological messianic kingdom which is to include both Jews and Gentiles. Thus the incarnate Messiah shows God's love for everyman. "The story of Jesus is the story of the only begotten son. The beloved, now fulfilling the divine purpose through enacting the life of love in the midst of the world's need."[4]

But is it not absurd for God to love man? The Greek gods did not love because they needed nothing. How can a god love man when he has everything? Here the distinction between agape and eros may be of help. God does not have acquisitive love, eros, but rather he has agape, *hesed*, a superabundance of love overflowing to the needy ones. Indeed, it appears absurd that God could love sinful man. But when we see God as self-giving love, the absurdity disappears.

This brings up once again the question of the changelessness of God. If God is almighty and unchangeable, the Unmoved Mover of the Greeks, how can he possibly love, which involves emotion, sympathy, and change? This is a dilemma which the Hebrew Bible answered with its colorful images of God as a spurned lover, as we have seen. The New Testament speaks of the Messiah as God's incarnate love and modern process thought has developed the theme further.

What about love and the Law? It would seem from some interpretations of Paul that love and the Torah are incompatible. Not so! The Torah's very heart is love. When the Torah no longer reflects and protects love, then it is not doing its job. Jesus came not to destroy the Law, but to fulfill it as a model of love. New Testament ethics, as those of the Torah, are rules of love. Besides the fundamental law of love there are special norms (*derek eretz*) to safeguard it.

The Synoptic Gospels

Jesus teaches the law of love. (Dt 6/5; Lv 19/18)

You shall love the Lord your God with all your heart, and with all your soul, and with all your mind. This is the greatest and first commandment, and a second is like it, you shall love your neighbor as yourself. On these two commandments depend all the law and the prophets. (Mt 22/37–40)

This is the overflowing agape of God which is fundamental to Christianity. It is not the acquisitive eros by which man loves God in order to get something out of him, or a love of friendship on an equal basis.

Our love is based on God's love, for it is the divine agape in us that overflows to the neighbor. This divine agape is spontaneous, uncaused by us and undeserved, a free gift of God to us and through us to our neighbor.

Who is the neighbor? Just as God loves all indiscriminately, saint and sinner, so also the Christian should love all. The neighbor in Jewish tradition tends to mean those who live nearby, as we have seen. When asked who the neighbor is, Jesus responds with the story of the good Samaritan, the traditional enemy who helps the fallen Jew. (Lk 10/29–37)

Love of enemies is an important teaching of Jesus and some feel that it is an overturning of the ancient custom of hating the enemy, although, as we have seen, the Torah is ambivalent. Jesus says:

Love your enemies, do good to those who hate you, bless those who curse you, pray for those who abuse you. . . . As you wish that men would do to you, do so to them. If you love those who love you, what credit is that to you? For even sinners love those who love them. (Lk 6/27–32)

Just as God loves all equally, good and bad, so the Christian should love all. And when he loves his enemies, they cease to be enemies and become friends.

Love of enemies ties in with forgiveness. And Jesus' parables such as that of the prodigal son illustrate this. Self-righteousness and love are incompatible. God's *hesed*, his covenant love, is a forgiving love. To love is to forgive. In the story of Mary Magdalene (Lk 7/36–50) it is the loving forgiveness of God which overflows as the oil which she pours out on the feet of Jesus. "Therefore, I tell you her sins, which are many, are forgiven, for she has loved much; but he who is forgiven little, loves little."

Agape flows through the parables of Jesus. Thus the vineyard

6. "She has loved much" (Luke 7/47)

workers with equal pay for all. And the prodigal son and lost sheep show the spontaneous love of the master. As Nygren comments: "All Christian ethics can be summed up in his words: freely you have received, freely give. Freely you have received the divine love, freely pass it on to men."[5]

The love-hate theme in the synoptics, as in Judaism, usually denotes grades of love. Thus when Jesus tells his disciples to love himself and to hate their parents, he may be pointing out the rabbinical tradition in which the disciple transfers his love and obedience from his parents to his teacher. (Lk 14/26)[6]

Also one should love God more than money. "No one can serve two masters, for either he will hate the one and love the other or he will be devoted to the one and despise the other. You cannot serve God and mammon." (Mt 6/24)

The Father's love appears foremost in the love of his beloved Son (*agapētos*). (Mt 3/17, 12/18) This is the very basis of the Christian trinity as interpreted by Augustine—lover, beloved, and love. The Father's love for his Son is the paradigm of his love for all men, for the Incarnation makes Christ one with mankind.

Paul

Paul takes up the agape love theme of his master Jesus and develops it in his famous letters to the Corinthians and Romans. Paul sees the Law for what it is, an outward expression of love. It is a love Torah. But sometimes the outer hedge of the oral Torah was overgrown in details so that it obscured what it was meant to protect, namely, the love core.

Paul writes to the Galatians (54) that love is the epitome of their ethical code.

For you were called to freedom, brethren; only do not use your freedom as an opportunity for the flesh, but through love be servants of one another. For the whole Law is fulfilled on one word. "You shall love your neighbor as yourself." But if you bite and devour one another, take heed that you are not consumed by one another. . . . The fruit of the spirit is love, joy, peace, patience, kindness, goodness, faithfulness, gentleness, self-control. Against such there is no law. (5/13–24)

The situation in Corinth needed correction and sexual abuses may well have been rampant. At any rate, Paul stresses agape in his letters to the Corinthians. McKenzie writes: "Agape thus becomes a kind of atmosphere in which God and the Christian live together. Communicated from God, agape permeates the Christian community and the individual Christian." (DOB, 522)

But how about those who are not Christians? McKenzie responds:

The Pauline concept of fraternal agape, it is true, seems to have no room for those who are not Christians, and in a sense, it has none. The union of hearts and the exchange of the duties of love which a community makes possible cannot be communicated to those who are not members of the community. (DOB, 522)

Thus agape would seem to be synonymous with the church and one would have to be a member of the Christian community in order to partake.

The Christian community of love is best experienced at the community meal, the agape, which was sometimes combined with the Eucharist. One who sins seriously against the community separates himself from the agape. How is excommunication compatible with the command to love one's enemies? Perhaps it is parallel to the mystery of God's love and his justice.

Paul tells the Corinthians (1 Cor 7) that since the time is short to the *eschaton,* the unmarried state is to be preferred to the married. Exclusive married love is a preparatory stage for the messianic kingdom in which there will be neither marriage nor the giving in marriage (Lk 20/34–36), but rather a universal agape for all. In other words, in the *eschaton* there is no reason for propagation since we shall have reached the goal.

It is argued whether Jesus and Paul preached the imminent coming of the kingdom. They both probably did. This would be a normal message in the expectant milieu of the Jewish community of the first century.

Paul says that agape builds up (*oikodomei*) the Christian community (1 Cor 8/1), whereas hate (*misis*) tears it down and knowledge (*gnōsis*) puffs up (*physioi*) and so is easily pricked. "If any one imagines that he knows something, he does not yet know as he ought to know. But if one loves God, he is known by him." (1 Cor 8/2–3) Paul may be opposing Christian agape to Greek *gnosis*. *Gnosis* puffs up while agape builds up.

Our *gnosis* is at best partial and will be done away with. Only agape will survive which gives a more penetrating knowledge in the Hebrew analogy of the knowledge shared by husband and wife.

It is true that there are many gifts that build up the Christian community, including prophecy (1 Cor 8/2–3) and authority (2 Cor 10/8). But love is the principal builder. "Therefore, encourage one another and build up one another, just as you are doing." (1 Thes 5/11)

Paul's love hymn in 1 Cor 13 is perhaps the best in any language.

If I speak in the tongues of men and angels, but have not love [agape], I am a noisy gong or a clanging cymbal. And if I have prophetic powers, and understand all mysteries and all knowledge, and if I have faith so as to move mountains, but have not love, I am nothing. If I give away all I have, and if I deliver my body to be burned, but have not love, I gain nothing.

Love is patient and kind. Love is not jealous or boastful;

it is not arrogant or rude. Love does not insist on its own way, it is not irritable or resentful; it does not rejoice at wrong, but rejoices in the right. Love bears all things, hopes all things, endures all things.

Love never ends; as for prophecies, they will pass away; as for tongues, they will cease; as for knowledge, it will pass away. For our knowledge is imperfect and our prophecy is imperfect; but when the perfect comes, the imperfect will pass away. When I was a child I spoke like a child, I thought like a child. When I became a man, I gave up childish ways. For now we see in a mirror dimly, but then face to face. Now I know in part; then I shall understand fully, even as I have been fully understood. So faith, hope, and love abide, these three; but the greatest of these is love.

Unlike human sexual love (eros), which seeks self-perfection in beauty and nobility, agape is a gift of God, disinterested, creative, and indiscriminately shared with all.

Paul uses the husband-wife analogy of Jewish tradition. (Rom 7/1–6; Eph 5/25) For Paul the church is the bride of Christ and as a messianic church (*ekklēsia*) it includes both Jews and Gentiles. As Yahweh is a jealous lover of Israel, so Paul writes:

I feel a divine jealousy for you, for I betrothed you to Christ to present you as a pure bride to her one husband. But I am afraid that as the serpent deceived Eve by his cunning, your thoughts will be led astray from a sincere and pure devotion to Christ. (2 Cor 11/2–3)

Paul fears the super-apostles teaching a different Jesus.

Paul also writes to the Romans on love. (57–58) The Christian lives in hope of sharing God's glory. Why? "Because God's love has been poured into our hearts through the Holy Spirit who has been given to us." (Rom 5/5)

God's Shekhinah, or his Holy Spirit, is a reflection and sometimes a personification of his love in rabbinical tradition.

She dwells in the temple and on those who pray and study Torah. She hovers over the sickbed and inhabits the home in which a loving wife and mother resides. She lies in the marriage bed between husband and wife. She is driven out by sin and hate. In later Judaism she is the spouse of Yahweh and identified with the Keneset Israel. The Christians, too, see the Spirit as the spirit of God's love.

At times Paul seems to have a low view of carnal love vis-à-vis heavenly agape. There have been many theories attempting to explain this, including the irrelevance of carnal love in the Messianic Age. Why marry if the end is near? Others see Paul living in licentious times, especially in certain port cities such as Corinth. In these circumstances one must bend over backwards in the opposite direction; thus celibacy would be preferred to marriage. Here we have some of the root reasons for the tradition of celibacy in the Christian church.

Paul is human and so feels the call to carnal love in himself, the *yezer hara* of Judaism (Rom 7/14–25), the law of the flesh fighting against the law of the spirit. But the law of the spirit of life in Jesus Christ sets Paul free from the law of sin and death. (Rom 8/2)

The Spirit helps us when we are weak. With the love of God we can do anything and nothing can separate us, death, life, angels, powers. "Nor anything else in all creation will be able to separate us from the love of God in Christ Jesus our Lord." (Rom 8/37–39)

Paul exhorts the Romans to show this divine agape to each other. "Let love be genuine. Hate what is evil, hold fast to what is good. Love one another with brotherly affection; outdo one another in showing honor." (Rom 12/9–10)

As we have mentioned, the Torah is a law of love and the only way it can be properly fulfilled is by love.

Owe no one anything except to love one another. For he who loves his neighbor has fulfilled the Law. The commandments: "You shall not commit adultery, you shall not steal, you shall not covet," and any other commandment, are summed up in this sentence. "You shall love your neighbor as yourself." Love does no wrong to a neighbor, therefore love is the fulfilling of the Law. (Rom 13/8–10)

Man's love of neighbor is based on God's love of man, his agape as shown through his divine Son. And this must be shared with one's neighbor. (Rom 15/7)

Faith in Christ and love are correlative, Paul writes to the Ephesians.

And that Christ may dwell in your hearts through faith; that you being rooted and grounded in love, may have power to comprehend with all the saints what is the breadth and length and height and depth, and to know the love of Christ which surpasses knowledge that you may be filled with all the fullness of God. (Eph 3/17–19)

Agape is the divine love which makes *gnosis* but a shadow. It is the fullness of God, whose love for his Son overflows into his Son's disciples.

Again to the Ephesians Paul teaches that love builds up not only the individual but the moral person of Christ.

Speaking the truth in love, we are to grow up in every way into him who is the head, into Christ, from whom the whole body, joined and knit together by every joint with which it is supplied, when each part is working properly, makes bodily growth and upbuilds itself in love. (Eph 4/15–16)

Love is the keynote of God, Christ, and the Christian. "Therefore, be imitators of God, as beloved children, and walk in love, as Christ loved us and gave himself up for us, a fragrant offering and sacrifice to God." (Eph 5/1–2)

As Christ loves his disciples, so husbands should love their wives.

Husbands, love your wives, as Christ loved the church and gave himself up for her, that he might sanctify her, having cleansed her by the washing of water with the word, that he might present the church to himself in splendor, without spot or wrinkle or any such thing, that she might be holy and without blemish.

Even so husbands should love their wives as their own bodies. He who loves his wife, loves himself. For no man ever hates his own flesh, but nourishes and cherishes it, as Christ does the church, because we are members of his body. "For this reason a man shall leave his father and mother and be joined to his wife and the two shall become one." This is a great mystery, and I mean in reference to Christ and the church. However, let each one of you love his wife as himself, and let the wife see that she respects her husband. (Eph 5/25–33)

Here again a comparison of human marital love with Christ's love for his church. Both loves are enduring. And indeed, human love cannot perdure alone without divine love.

How is Paul's beautiful sermon on married love to the Ephesians compatible with his earlier exhortation not to marry? (1 Cor 7) Conditions were undoubtedly different in Ephesus than they were in Corinth. Moreover, the old Jewish analogy of human and divine love would apply even more in the Messianic Kingdom.

Paul's *derek eretz*, his rules for Christian living, are specifications of love. Thus he exhorts his disciples to compassion, kindness, meekness, forbearance, forgiveness. "And above all put on love, which binds everything together in perfect harmony." (Col 3/12–14. Also Phil 1/9–11, 2/2–16; 1 Tim 1/5)

Love is as central to Paul as it is to the other rabbis. But with a difference. For Paul love is seen foremost in the Father's love of Jesus, his only Son, and the sacrifice of Jesus for the sins of all as the greatest love act. As the Father loves Jesus, so Jesus loves his disciples more than any other rabbi ever loved his followers. And the disciples are to love each other as Jesus loves them. Moreover, this Christian agape is to be seen in kindness, forgiveness, hospitality, etc.

John

The school of John also sings the hymn of love, and the Holy Spirit of divine love permeates it. The agape of John also has a threefold theme—namely, God, Jesus, and the disciples. The love instructions of John parallel those of the Jewish rabbis, but for John, as for Paul, Christ is love incarnate.

Proof of God's love for the world is that he gave up his only begotten Son, that we believing may enjoy eternal life. This is the father-son motif so popular in the Hebrew Bible. And there is no greater love than between a father and his first-born son. (Jn 3/16–21) And when one rejects this incarnate love, he may expect God's wrath. "The Father loves the Son and has given all things into his hand. He who believes in the Son has eternal life; he who does not obey the Son shall not see life, but the wrath of God rests upon him." (Jn 3/35–36)

Jesus' whole life shows himself as love incarnate, healing, forgiving, compassionate. He fights sin, which is a lack of love. (Jn 5/42–43) In laying down his life Jesus especially shows his great love. (Jn 10/17) And this is the paradox of love. "He who loves his life loses it, and he who hates his life in this world will keep it for eternal life." (Jn 12/25)

John brings out Jesus' special love for his disciples. "Having loved his own who were in the world, he loved them to the end." (Jn 13/1) Did Jesus love all his disciples equally? He seems to have a deeper love for Peter, James, and John. Thus John calls himself "one of the disciples whom Jesus loved." (13/23)

As Jesus loves his disciples, so they are to love each other. The Jewish rabbinical fellowship, the *haburah*, was not just a union of scholarship, but also one of love. "A new commandment I give you, that you love one another; even as I have loved you, that you also love one another. By this all men will know that you are my disciples—if you have love for one another." (13/34–35) Jesus addresses them as "little children" (*teknia*), a term of endearment used by the rabbis of their young students.

Again Jesus says: "This is my commandment that you love one another as I have loved you. Greater love has no man than this, that a man lay down his life for his friends." (15/12–17) This is what Jesus did and he asks his disciples to show the same love for each other.

As love is the shibboleth of the Christian, so hate seems to be the keynote of the world. "If the world hates you, know that it has hated me before it hated you." (15/18)

How do the disciples show their love? By observing what Jesus has taught them.

He who has my commandments and keeps them, he it is who loves me; and he who loves me will be loved by my Father and I will love him and manifest myself to him. . . . If a man loves me, he will keep my word, and my Father will love him and we will come to him and make our home with him. He who does not love me, does not keep my words; and the word which you hear is not mine but the Father's who sent me. (14/23–24; 15/9–11)

But in the end Jesus has to take leave of his beloved disciples in order to return to the Father. "I do as the Father has commanded me, so that the world may know that I love the Father." (14/31) But the Father loves the disciples because they have loved Jesus and believed that he came from the Father. (16/27)

Finally Jesus prays for unity in his school, the unity that is a sign of love.

The glory which you have given me, I have given to them, that they may be one even as we are one, I in them and you in me, that they may be perfectly one, . . . so that the world may know that you have sent me and have loved them even as you have loved me. Father, I desire that they also, whom you have given me, may be with me where I am, to behold my glory which you have given me in your love for me before the foundation of the world. O righteous Father, the world has not known you, but I have known you; and these know that you have sent me. I made known to them your name, and I will make it known that the love with which you have loved me may be in them and I in them. (17/22–26)

Perhaps the epitome of Christian love is found in the First Letter of John. The Christian is he who walks in the light of love. He who walks as Jesus walked, in him the love of God is perfected. (2/4–6)

Hate is incompatible with love. "He who says he is in the light and hates his brother is in the darkness still. He who loves his brother abides in the light, and in it there is no cause for stumbling." (2/9–10)

John speaks of two loves, namely, love of the world and love of God. What the "world" (*cosmos*) means here has been speculated on by many. It may mean the world of those outside the Christian community. *Cosmos* sometimes had this meaning for the Jews, that is, those outside the family of Judaism. At any rate, Jesus cautions his disciples against love of the world.

Do not love the world or the things of the world. If anyone loves the world, love for the Father is not in him. For all that is in the world, lust of the flesh, and lust of the eyes and the pride of life, is not of the Father, but is of the world, and the world passes away and the lust of it. But he who does the will of God abides forever. (1 Jn 2/15–17)

The two loves of John remind us of the two loves of Plato, one ending in beauties and the other in divine Beauty.

The Father-Son love union is strong in John, as we have

seen. As the Father loves Jesus, so he loves Jesus' disciples. "See what love the Father has given us that we should be called children of God; and so we are." (3/1) But the world does not recognize this nor does it know him.

In fact, the world hates the brethren.

Do not wonder, brethren, that the world hates you. We know that we have passed out of death into life because we love the brethren. He who does not love remains in death. Any one who hates his brother is a murderer. And you know that no murderer has eternal life abiding in him. By this we know love, that he laid down his life for us. And we ought to lay down our lives for the brethren. But if any one has the world's goods and sees his brother in need, yet closes his heart against him, how does God's love abide in him? Little children, let us not love in word or speech, but in deed and in truth. (3/13–18)

Love is creative, builds up, is life-giving. Hate destroys, tears down, murders. Love, as in Eastern traditions, resides in the heart. So the lover has the tender heart of God's *hesed*. John's final exhortation to love:

Beloved, let us love one another. For love is of God, and he who loves is born of God and knows God. He who does not love, does not know God, for God is love. In this the love of God was made manifest among us. That God sent his only Son into the world, so that he might live through him. In this is love, not that we loved God, but that he loved us and sent his Son to be the expiation for our sins. Beloved, if God so loved us, we also ought to love one another. No man has ever seen God. If we love one another, God abides in us and his love is perfected in us. (4/7–12)

God is love and his love is especially for his Son, whom he sent to save the world. Moreover, his divine love is seen in his Spirit, which he delegates to guide us. He who believes this will possess divine love, for God dwells in him and he in God.

> So we know and believe the love God has for us. God is love, and he who abides in love, abides in God and God abides in him. In this is love perfected in us, that we may have confidence for the day of judgment, because as he is, so are we in this world. There is no fear in love. But perfect love casts out fear. For fear has to do with punishment, and he who fears is not perfected in love. We love God because he loved us.
>
> If any one says, "I love God" and hates his brother, he is a liar. For he who does not love his brother whom he has seen, cannot love God whom he has not seen. And this commandment we have from him, that he who loves God should love his brother also. (4/16–21)

It is not enough just to say that one loves God. No, he must also show his love in action.

> Every one who believes that Jesus is the Christ is a child of God, and every one who loves the parent loves the child. By this we know that we love the children of God, when we love God and obey his commandments. For this is the love of God that we keep his commandments. (5/1–3)

The school of John's central theme is: God is love (*ho theos agapē estin*). (1 Jn 4/8) So that wherever true love is found, God is there. Since God is love, he is the originator of love. And he loves even the sinful and unlovable. This is the very essence of divine agape, self-giving and not acquisitive. God's love in us should spill over in our love for the brethren. We love because he loved us first.

Johannine love is fivefold. First of all, it is seen in God's love for his divine Son, whom he sends to save us and who is overshadowed by the Spirit of love. Secondly, we find God's love of men, his adopted children, brothers of Christ. Third, the brethren love Christ their adopted brother, teacher, and savior. And as brothers of Christ and children of the Father, they love each other. Finally, all love God their adopted father and the natural father of their adopted brother Jesus. God is present in all of these loves, for he is true love.

Christian, Jewish, and Platonic Love

What is the difference between Christian, Jewish, and Platonic views of love? Christian and Jewish love have a lot in common. And since Christianity grew up in the milieu of rabbinical Judaism, we should expect this. In both we find God's love for man and man's reciprocal duty to love God and his fellow men. But Christianity has a trinitarian view of God's love as the primordial love between Father and Son. This is the Spirit of divine love living among men.

The Holy Spirit of love is also strong in Jewish tradition. Later she will become the wife of Yahweh in the medieval Kabbalah, which we will see later.

There is little mention of a divine son in Hebrew literature, though Philo seems to call the pre-existing Logos the son of God. And the Messiah was to be divinely begotten, some believed. But Jewish monotheism was reluctant to accept anything like the Christian Trinity, though the Jewish mystics saw many divine manifestations.

Platonic love is more impersonal. For Plato the Good is not a person and is not incarnate. And though the Demiurge is an intermediary, he is not a loving savior by any means.

Nygren claims that Christianity's agape reversed the Greek eros.[7] Whereas the Greek gods cannot love, the God of Christianity and Judaism is love itself. Like the Greek gods, the God of Christianity and Judaism is self-sufficient, though his love is not acquisitive but self-giving, as we have seen.

Whereas the Greeks had no mutual relationship between the gods and men, in Christian agape God has begun a fellowship between himself and man. And although Aristotle admitted that God loves rational men, those closest to him (*Nic. Eth*, 10/9), the Christian God loves the weak, foolish, and sinful (1 Cor 1/27 f).

Christian love is paradoxical and even irrational, reversing the accepted Hellenistic values. Agape flies in the face of the *gnosis* of Greek philosophy. In fact, the only true *gnosis* of God can be obtained through agape.

Nygren seems to paint eros as basically egocentric. But in many ways it is theocentric, for man has a divine origin in the Good and he will not be happy till he returns whence he remembers. It is true that he hopes for happiness in the Good and Beauty.

In agape God comes to man and it is his love that enables man to love him in return and to love his fellow man. But the Greek eros also is of divine origin, a *daimōnion* between God and man. Both agape and eros seek to explain the relationship of human and divine love.

Although eros seeks enjoyment in love of man, it loves because man reflects divine Good and Beauty. Beautiful bodies and beautiful souls are just the first steps to Beauty itself. Agape, on the other hand, is divine love overflowing without regard to the beauty, intelligence, or youth of the beloved.

The eventual syncresis of these two views of love by Christian writers was inevitable. And it seems that the eros theme has not harmed Christianity as much as some would believe.

First, it is of no less divine origin than agape, and secondly, ascending eros is complementary to the descending agape. Eros could not ascend, unless somehow, somewhere it had descended. Thirdly, the ascending view of love has added much to the growth of mysticism in Christianity, Judaism, and Islam.

ᵰᵉ VIII ᵉ᷻

LOVE IS A KIND OF WARFARE

Ovid, The Art of Love, 2/511

While the Jewish and Christian rabbis were teaching divine love and universal agape in anticipation of the Messianic Age, we find the Romans more interested in the pleasures of human sexual love. One of their best-selling love poets is Ovid.

Ovid, Modern Lover

Ovid was born in 43 B.C. in a new era of Rome, the Augustan Peace. He is first of all a poet, like his colleagues Bassus, Macer, Ponticus, and Propertius. But he is also a lover who sees love as the central theme in man's life, especially in his youth. He was probably a teen-ager when he wrote his songs of Corrina.

Ovid is not the first Roman to write elegies of love. Gallus, Tibullus, Propertius, and Catullus preceded him. E. K. Rand comments: "If we would know the real history of Roman elegy and understand both Ovid and Catullus, 'Cherchez la femme.'"[1]

Ovid writes of Corrina: Is she his real beloved or a fictitious "every woman"? Like many youths, Ovid is lovestruck. He would marry three times and would sing love songs for almost twenty-five years. And some would say that he was eventually exiled for his risqué love talk.

Ovid is not only a poet, an elegist, but also a didactic, giving lessons in love as one would teach music, art, or writing. Yet he takes love in a light spirit, making fun of love's problems and heartbreaks as Horace had done.

As a poet in practical Rome, Ovid feels that his work is unappreciated. Money, power, and authority are the name of the game (*negotium*) in Ovid's Rome. All else is play or leisure (*otium*). H. F. Frankel writes:

Any poet whose work was unrelated to practical purposes because it was exclusively devoted to the concerns of the mind and heart, saw the fruits of his endeavors classified as playthings and relegated to some quaint limbo beyond the pale of consequential reality.[2]

Nevertheless, Ovid's love poems were popular.

Amores

This is Ovid's first published collection of 50–51 elegies. He wrote on love because that is what people were interested in. Are his love elegies his own personal experience? Undoubtedly his own love affairs are reflected in his poems. People write best about their own experiences. But he is trying not to limit his poems to his own adventures but to view the vagaries of love through the eyes of Every Lover. The classical author, be he Homer, Ovid, or Shakespeare, is only successful insofar as he can picture the sentiments and emotions of every man.

Ovid portrays love as a sickness, passion, sleepless nights. The only solution is to yield to the triumphal Cupid with his aides—Caresses, Confusion, Craze—while Conscience and Modesty are in chains.

Just is my prayer: let the maid who has lately made me her prey either give me love, or give me reason for ever to love!

Ah, I have asked too much—let her but suffer herself to be loved; may Cytherea hear my many prayers. (1/3/1–4)[3]

She is his one and only! "I am not smitten with a thousand! I am no flit-about in love! You, if there be any truth, shall be my everlasting care." (1/3/15–16) His lady love is married and he is jealous of her husband. He constantly eyes her at the banquet. "When you think of the wanton delights of our love, touch your cheeks with tender finger." (1/4/22) Love accelerates as difficulties mount. The nightly barred door between lover and beloved is a favorite theme. (1/6)

Ovid next tells of the contrite lover who has wounded his beloved in a lover's spat. (1/7) Though he is repentant, he asks if a lover who is never jealous or angry or who never strikes his beloved is still her lover. He had scratched her cheek, torn her dress, and now feels that he must have been mad. Ovid displays a certain kindness and thoughtfulness toward women and is able to see the world through the eyes of his beloved.

But love is basically war. "Every lover is a soldier and Cupid has a camp of his own." (1/9/1) An old man neither soldiers nor loves. Both lover and soldier are awake through the night. Both sleep on the ground. Both will take a long journey in pursuit, climbing mountains, bearing wind and storm. Each besieges the threshold and both attack while the enemy sleeps.

Love for a beautiful girl has started me from craven ways and bidden me take service in her camp. For this you see me full of action, and waging the wars of night. Whoso would not lose all his spirit, let him love. (1/9/44–45)

Love cannot be bought and sold. "Love is a child and naked. He has the years that know not greed and is unclad so that he may be open in his ways." (1/10/15) The harlot sells her body. But nature never requires gifts of the beloved. "The love that is to be of equal joy to both—why should the one make sale of it, and the other purchase?" (1/10/34) Perhaps there

is no harm in asking presents from the rich. But Ovid has only
his art to give.

Aurora (dawn) is the enemy of love. Love is a secret night-
time thing, destroyed by daylight. Ovid's Aurora elegy would
inspire medieval love songs, the French *aubade,* and the German *Tageliet,* celebrating the parting of lovers at daybreak.
The lovers lie happy in their sweet sleep at the hour of dawn.
"'Tis now I delight to lie in the tender arms of my love. If
ever, it is now I am happy to have her close by my side."
(1/13/5) Daybreak brings travel, soldiery, lust for wealth, the
antitheses of the lover's concerns—business, farming, school,
law.

Ovid chastises Aurora for breaking up love, accusing her of
hurrying to escape her aged husband. If she had a young and
handsome lover she would not be in such a rush.

Ovid writes that all lovers may see themselves in him. His
appeal is that he is Every Lover. "Let some youth who is
wounded by the same bow as I am now, know in my lines,
the record of his own heart's flame." (2/1/7–8)

He berates Bagoas, the stern guardian of his mistress. "Readily would you be compliant and yielding to lovers' prayers, if
you had ever grown warm with love for any woman."
(2/3/5–6)

No fixed beauty type attracts the poet, be she modest or
saucy, austere, intellectual, rustic, soft or hard, singer or
dancer, tall or short, light or dark, young or old. "In fine, whatever fair ones anyone could praise in all the city—my love is
a candidate for the favors of them all." (2/4/47)

Jealousy, the proof of love, rakes his soul. "Those kisses are
common to you with me, and common to me with you—Why
does any third attempt to share these goods?" (2/5/30–32) But
quickly he forgives.

He begs Cupid to leave him alone. "So many men there are
without love, without love so many maids!—There is your field
for great and glorious triumph." (2/9/15) He had served so

often in the wars of women's love that now he wants to live in peace.

But at last his beloved Corinna lies in his arms (2/12), in spite of her husband, keeper and locked doors. He is her slave. (2/17) But her beauty makes her hard and proud. First she repels him, then draws him on. "And kisses, O great gods, what kisses, and how many she would give." (2/19/17–18)

Since she partakes in divine beauty, she can swear falsely unharmed. (3/3/11) As a goddess she is above the law. Either God is naught, or "if there is a god, he is in love with the tender fair, and too quick to ordain that they alone may do all things." (3/3/25)

A watchful husband does not keep his wife from sin, for she can sin within. "She who sins not, because she may not, she sins!" (3/4/4) In fact, his guardianship escalates her desires. "Whatever is guarded, we desire the more and care itself invites the thief. Few love what another concedes." (25)

Love is ambivalent. To begin with, it is a hard but pleasing battle. "I have seen when the lover came forth from your doors fatigued, with frame exhausted and weak from love's campaign." (3/11/12–13) Love and hate are mixed. "I fly from your baseness—as I fly, your beauty draws me back. I shun the wickedness of your ways—your person I love. Thus I can live neither with you nor without, and seem not to know my own heart's prayer." (3/11/37–40)

He does not want to know her faults, for love is blind. He does not insist that she be chaste, only that she pretend to be chaste. "She does not sin who can deny her sin." (3/14/5) Be a double person—a wanton on the couch, but chaste outside. "Let a modest aspect deny the harlot's trade." (3/14/26)

Love is also the theme of Ovid's *Heroides*—fifteen letters written by wives of legendary fame displaying human qualities. Penelope faithful, Briseis forgiving, Dido desperate, Helen vain, Medea, Hypsipyle, Oenone, Ariande—passion, Laodamia solicitous, Phyllis trustful, Canace grief-stricken. Acontius and Cydippe, Hero and Leander, double letters of young love.

The Art of Love

Ovid wrote his *Ars Amatoria*[4] in his early mellow forties. A didactic poem in elegiac meter, it is a "how to" book. With skill and training in love one can be successful, like one who is learned in the art of writing, sculpture, sailing, or charioteering.

There are three steps: first finding your beloved, then winning her, and finally holding on to her.

First of all, where to find her? In Pompey's portico, Livian colonnade, feast of Adonis, Memphian shrine, law courts? The round theater is the best, or the circus. Show care and attention to your girl. Banquets give openings, too, but darkness and drink impair judgment of beauty.

First let assurance come to your minds that all women can be caught. Spread out your nets and you will catch them. Sooner would birds be silent in spring or grasshoppers in summer, or the hound of Maenalus flee before the hare than a woman persuasively wooed resist a love. (1/269–73)

Stolen love is pleasant to both man and woman, but a woman conceals her pleasure better. Sometimes the handmaid is the way to her mistress' heart, for she knows her mistress' moods. There are times proper for pressing a suit. Not on days when she expects presents—e.g., feasts or birthdays. Rather go to see her when the stores are closed. Ovid does not write for the well-to-do, but for men of modest means like himself who can ill afford to lavish presents on their beloveds. "A woman knows the way to fleece an eager lover of his wealth." (420)

Learn eloquence to be suasive, yet hide your powers. Be tricky, use cunning ambiguities, even pretending love. "Each woman thinks herself lovable. Hideous though she be, there is none her own looks do not please." (613–14) Yet sometimes simulated love comes true. Flattery is not out of place. "Even

honest maids love to hear their charms extolled." (623) Ovid
has no scruple about tricking women into love. "Deceive the
deceivers," he writes. (645) Tears are handy, and kisses, too.

Man must take the first step with entreating words, coaxing.
"Let love find entrance in friendship's name." (720–21) White
is the color of a lover and lean from nightly vigils. But suit
yourself to your beloved. The hearts of women are various and
there are a thousand roads to their hearts, and as many ways
to catch a fish.

In Book Two of his *Ars Amatoria,* Ovid tells how to hold
on to your beloved, once you have her. A girl may be won by
chance, but she can only be held by art and skill. Love can
be illusive. Magic and potions can never keep it alive.

First of all, if you want to be loved, be lovable (*ut ameris,
amabilis esto*). And add gifts of the mind to those of the body,
for beauty wanes. Learn the liberal arts and language. Be gentle and indulgent and not harsh. "Keep far away quarrels and
bitter-tongued affrays. With soft words must love be fostered."
(151–52) Quarreling is more proper for wives than for mistresses.

If she is not courteous, be persistent. Slowly she will comply.
Yield when she resists. Blame, approve, affirm, laugh, weep as
she does. Let her win at games, hold her parasol. Put on her
slipper, warm her hands. Drop everything at her command.
"Love is a kind of warfare. Avaunt ye laggards! These banners
are not for timid men to guard." (233–34) Endure night, storm,
marches in the camp of war.

Give small gifts such as fruits in season, and for a learned
lady—a poem of praise. Release a slave through her request.
"But whoever you are who are anxious to keep your mistress,
be sure she thinks you spellbound by her beauty." (295–96)
Praise her clothes, hair, body, voice, dance, but do not let your
flattery show. "Art, if hidden, avails; if detected, it brings
shame and deservedly discredits you forever." (313–14) Watch
over her health, especially in the uncertain air of autumn.
When she is sick, weep, make vows. Bring remedies.

While love wanders in youth, it gathers strength by experience. Let her see a lot of you, then not, for a rested field repays its trust. Do not be too submissive or overflattering to hide your past faults. These just stress your guilt. Rather: "By caresses must the former passion be disproved." (413–14)

But hearts grow listless when all is right. So sharp goads must be applied to call up love. Shock her with your guilt, make her fight, tear hair, weep, then "when she has raged her fill, when she seems your certain foe, then seek the treaty of a love embrace, that will make her gentle." (462–64)

By following Dr. Ovid's instructions one will surely win. "Whosoever loves wisely will be victorious, and by my art will gain his end." (511–12)

Do not let jealousy rule your lives. "Wherefore all the more, O lovers, detecting your mistresses, let them err, and erring think they have deceived. Detection fans the flame of passion." (557–59)

Do not call attention to a woman's faults. Time will heal all. Soften her shortcomings with pleasant names. Thus if she is too dark, call her a brunette. If she has yellow hair, she resembles Minerva; skinny—slender; heavy—mature. And especially do not harp on her age if she is old. (657 ff.)

Man and woman should enjoy each other equally. Pleasure given as a duty has no charm.

Love's bliss must not be hastened, but gradually lured on by slow delay. . . . But neither do you, spreading to full sail, leave your mistress behind, nor let her outstrip your speed. Hasten side by side to the goal. Then is pleasure full when man and woman lie vanquished both together." (717 ff.)

In Book Three, Ovid has some advice for the ladies in the ways of love.

It were not just that defenceless maids should fight with armed men. Such a victory, O men, would be shameful for you also. (5–6)

Here he praises women and criticizes men. "Often do men deceive, tender maids not often. Should you inquire, they are rarely charged with deceit." (31–32)

Be aware of onrushing old age! Have fun while it is still spring.

> That day will come when you, who now shut out your lovers, will lie, a cold and lonely old woman, through the night. Nor will your door be broken in a nightly brawl. Nor will you find your threshold strewn with roses in the morning. (71–75)

Time is the enemy of love.

Dr. Ovid recommends careful care of the body. Make your body attractive to men. Accentuate the positive. Earlier he had written a treatise on painting the face. As in agriculture, cultivation improves on nature. The root sense of cosmetics is an ordering of the disordered.

But he reminds his female disciples that facial beauty is fleeting.

> Love of character is lasting. Beauty will be ravaged by age, and the face that charmed will be ploughed by wrinkles. The time will come when it will vex you to look at a mirror, and grief will prove a second cause of wrinkles. Goodness endures and lasts for many a day. And throughout its years love securely rests thereon. (43–50)

Each girl should choose the adornments that enhance her natural qualities. Thus an oval face invites parted hair. Clothing should be chosen with care. Snow-white skin likes dark-gray color, while those of dark hue should dress in white. Shave your legs and underarms, use face powder, rouge and eye-shadow, eyebrow pencil, etc. But do not overdo it. And do not let your lover see you at your craft.

Beauty is proud and feels that it needs little instruction. But even the loveliest face has its inequalities. "Rare is the face that lacks a blemish. Hide your blemishes, and so far as you can, conceal any fault of body." (261–62) If you are short, sit or recline and hide your feet. If thin, wear loose clothing. And if pale, don purple stripes. Affect a lisp or a charming walk, bare shoulders and upper arms, learn to sing and dance and play games.

"Let the beautiful woman offer herself to the people to be seen. Out of many there will be one, perchance whom she may attract." (421–22) The fisherman always has his hook out. But avoid men who are elegant and pride themselves in their good looks. "What they have told you, they have told a thousand women. Their fancy wanders and has no fixed abode." (435–36)

When your lover writes, examine the letter to see if it is genuine. Then delay a bit. "Delay spurs lovers on, if but its term is brief." (475) Keep him in suspense, torn between hope and fear, let proper language be used in your reply. Since love letters can be used against you, learn to write in different hands, even using "she" for "he."

Beauty is seen best in peace, humility, and not melancholy but cheerful. Suit yourself to men of varied talents—rich, lawyer or poet. "Dissemble, and carry not greed on your open countenance. A new lover will take fright if he sees the net." (553–54)

The raw recruit, new to love and passionate, needs tender treatment, whereas the veteran comes gradually and prudently to love. His love is surer, but the other is richer, though brief. But keeping the lover in suspense is the secret. Tell of other rivals; close the door. His love will be inflamed by the competition.

Ovid is distinct on the proper positions of love which show off the body to best advantage. "Let the woman feel love's act, unstrung to the very depths of her frame, and let that act delight both alike." (793–94)

The Remedies of Love[5]

At age forty-three Ovid had been singing the songs of love for about twenty-five years. Why so long on this theme? Love has always been a favorite with poets. In fact, can love be expressed in any other manner? Also the popularity of his love hymns may well have filled his pocketbook. But in his forties a man sometimes begins to tire of love as his youthful passions wane.

Why did Ovid write *The Remedies of Love?* Was it a personal disillusionment? Love cannot solve all and sometimes it brings as much misery as happiness. Ovid wants to help those who are suffering from the miseries of love. About a third of his warnings against love seem to reverse earlier praises.

If any lover has delight in his love, blest is his passion. Let him rejoice and sail on with favoring wind. But if any endures the tyranny of the unworthy mistress, lest he perish, let him learn the help my art can give. (13–16)

Some lovers have been driven to suicide, others frustrated to tears. The same hand that heals can also wound, for the thorn is found near the rose.

Ovid's advice can also be used by spurned women. "A profitable aim it is to extinguish savage flames, and have a heart not enslaved to its own frailty." (54–55) Perhaps Phyllis, Dido, and many others could have been saved if they had listened to him.

Crush love while it is still young, advises Dr. Ovid, for delay allows it to mature and it is hard to stamp out. *"Principiis obsta."* Resist beginnings. But love seeks delay. "All love deceives and finds sustenance in delaying." (95) Advanced love is difficult to stem and deaf to counsel. But do not attack it at an inopportune time.

As he had noted well in his *Art of Love,* leisure is the garden of love. When dawn breaks and work comes, love flees. So now, using the same principle, Ovid advises his readers to use work as an antidote to love. "Take away leisure and Cupid's bow is broken, and his torch lies extinguished and despised." (139–40) And again: "Where sloth is, that boy is wont to follow. He hates the busy. Give the empty mind some business to occupy it." (149–50) Business, law, war, have little place for love. Aegis became an adulterer because he was a sluggard.

Animal husbandry and farming also are distracting. No thoughts of girls at night—too tired. "By these and other pursuits until you unlearn your love, you must craftily deceive yourself." (211–13) Take a trip. In order to recover his health one must undergo pain. And do not return too soon or love will renew its fight. Moreover, do not waste your time on magic or potions.

Underline your beloved's faults. She is greedy, selfish, false, lies with peddlers. Moreover, she has ugly legs and skinny arms and she is too short. Virtues and vices depend on one's point of view. Whereas before he glorified her faults in order to win her, calling her full-breasted when she was really fat, now when he wants to forget her she is beefy. Slender becomes bony, and honest, simple-minded.

Stress her faults by making her sing if she has a bad voice, dance if ungainly, laugh if she has bad teeth. Arrive early to see her half-painted face. Take an ungainly posture. Open all the windows so that her unsightly limbs come to light. Note well all of her faults and blemishes. These and other ugly sights have turned off lovers.

Have more than one mistress to divide the fires of love. Feign what you are not. Be cool to her, diminish your ardor. If she grants you a night, hesitate to come. "Since natures vary, I will vary my arts. The disease has a thousand forms, I have a thousand remedies." (525–26)

Be sated with her night and day. Plenty can destroy passion and her house can grow distasteful. Get rid of the fear that you may lose her! Near the Colline gate is a shrine where

Lethaean love dwells and where love is cured. Flee loneliness, for loneliness breeds love. Stay with a crowd. If you are alone, you will be sad and see your mistress before you, especially at night.

Love is contagious, so avoid young lovers. Shun your mistress or her friends and confidantes. Moreover, it is better to be silent than to tell her you do not love her. "He who says o'er much 'I love not' is in love." (648) Leave off your love slowly. Do not hate her, but just be indifferent to her. "He who ends love by hating, either loves still, or will find it hard to end his misery." (657–58) Those once united in love should not end up as enemies. "Where no quarrel comes, love unremembered slips away." Depart in peace. Do not take her through the courts and let her keep her presents. And if you happen to meet her, steel yourself against the foe. Try to remember your rival. Do not try to please her, but let her know that she is one of many.

We are slow to break off old loves because we hope that we are still loved. Do not let a woman's tears sway you and don't give reasons for the separation. "Silence is strength. To reproach a woman often is to ask to be satisfied." (697–99)

Compare your girl with real beauties and she will suffer by comparison, and contrast not only looks but also character and accomplishments.

Burn your old love letters and pictures and avoid the old trysting places. Love brought to life flames up like a cinder touched by sulphur. Avoid erotic plays and dances. May the gods give you strength to pass by the door of a deserted mistress. Your rival is no longer a foe but a friend. "As soon as you can embrace him, you are healed." (794)

Watch what you eat. No onions, but rue is all right. Watch out for Bacchus, for wine prepares the heart for love. Either do not imbibe at all, or else drown your sorrows in drunkenness. So ends Dr. Ovid's healing verses to make the lovesick whole again.

Other Works

Ovid turns more to mythology in his *Metamorphoses,* finished in a way in 7 A.D., starting with the dawn of creation and going down to his own time. Amatory stories of the gods, such as Jupiter and Phoebus and Mercury and Medea, are sprinkled throughout. The vengeful love of Medea, the unfilial love of Scylla, chivalrous love of Meleager, incestuous love of Byblis, and Narcissus' self-love.

He ends up with a vision of a greater Italy, a monument to the new Rome. His irreverent treatment of the gods signals the twilight of the gods in Roman culture. But irreverence and piety often go together.

Ovid's *Fasti* comments on the Roman feasts, showing an interest in Roman origins and the place of religion in Roman life.

In 8 A.D. Ovid was banished by Augustus to Tomis on the Black Sea. Some claim that he was exiled because of his too liberal writings on love, which inspired the emperor's daughter Julia to an affair with Silvanus. Others say that he may have been involved in a plot against Augustus.

Ovid is part of the new way with his liberal love poems and his irreverent *Metamorphoses* militating against Augustus' religious reforms. To the end he defended his love songs, which he felt were no worse than others had written nor as bad as the licentious vaudeville patronized by the emperor. Though his works were forbidden in the libraries, there were plenty of copies in private collections.

Ovid's Influence

The two greatest eras of Ovid's love influence are the Middle Ages and the Renaissance, when the reading of Ovid in the schools prompted elegiac comedies and tales.

Ovid is the high priest of the order of bards. Verses of the Goliards are found as early as the ninth century—gay and gracious, political and religious, sung by wandering minstrels in court and monastery.[6] We shall see Ovid's heritage more in detail in later chapters. In France and Germany troubadours and minnesingers continue the Goliard Ovidian love themes.

Ovid is the first of the medieval romancers, retelling the Greek myths in his own style. In turn, Ovid's stories are retold in long romances by men like Chrétien de Troyes. The twelfth century is the age of courtly love, and Ovid's *Art of Love* is the manual. Medieval love texts such as Andreas Capellanus' *The Art of Courtly Love* are modeled on it.

Besides inspiring romances, Ovid is quoted in classics, ethics, theology, and even medicine. In the later Middle Ages he would inspire Dante and Chaucer. Rand comments:

> The spirit of Ovid the lover, chastened and refined, comes to Dante through the troubadours and the singers of the *"dolce stil nuova."* It is exalted in the lyrics of the *Vita Nuova* and the *Convivio* and finally in the divine allegory of the *Commedia* to the heights of which Ovid never dreamed.[7]

Chaucer and Jean de Meun were other favorite pupils of Ovid's *Art of Love,* and in the Renaissance, Petrarch and Boccaccio. Rand writes:

> The idea of love that Ovid sets forth in his early poems was refined and etherealized as it passed into the medieval knightly code and the poetry of the troubadours whence it was exalted to the heights yet more sublime by Dante and Boccaccio.[8]

The Ovidian stream watered the ages of Louis XIV in France and of Elizabeth, the Restoration, and Queen Anne in England, to be succeeded by the more Platonic Romantic period.

Modern essays on human love have tended more toward the romantic and psychological, missing the elegiac flavor of Ovid.

But love is an art, a poem, a song, a dance, a painting or sculpture, and not a clinical science.

Let us now turn to another Roman school of love, with a more Platonic tinge, beginning with the Middle Platonists in Alexandria and perfected by such Neo-Platonic mystics as Plotinus and Augustine.

⊰ IX ⊱

LATE HAVE I LOVED YOU

Augustine, Confessions, *10/27/38*

We have seen the sexual *amores* of Ovid expressed in poetry and myth. They were popular in the everyday secular world of Rome, where love of boy and girl, wife and paramour, were celebrated. But there was another world of philosophers and mystics where Plato's love themes were going strong, first in Alexandria and then in Rome.

The Fathers and Plotinus

The Alexandrian Christian Fathers, as did their predecessor Philo, used the Greek "eros" in their writings on love. But others such as Marcion and Irenaeus resisted the trend. Still others—Methodius, Athanasius, and the Cappadocian Fathers—used "eros" and "agape" interchangeably.[1]

As was mentioned earlier, the two words may not be incompatible, for eros is of divine origin and in this sense is a divine gift. So divine eros can lead man back to God, whence he has come. Thus the popular themes of the heavenly ladder and the ascent of the holy mountain.

A famous Alexandrian philosopher who introduced eros to the West is Plotinus, melding Platonism with the mystery religions. The Alexandrian school of Platonism had sought to reconcile the dualism of God and matter with intermediaries.

Somehow, somewhere, the human soul had descended from God into matter and now seeks to ascend back to him.

As his mentor Plato, Plotinus teaches that the soul pursues Beauty, which is only reflected in earthly beauty.

So divine and precious is the soul, be confident that by its power you can attain divinity. Start your ascent. You will not need to search long. Few are the steps that separate you from your goal. Take as your guide the most divine part of the soul, that which borders on the superior realm from which it comes. (*Enneads,* 5/1/10)

It is eros which gives the soul its drive toward the heavenly. With the aid of eros the soul rises upward toward the Beautiful, reversing the order of descent. For Plotinus, God is eros. Not only is he worthy of love, but he is love itself and he is Beauty itself, the object of all love. (6/8/15)

Augustine, Philosopher of Love

It is Augustine, student of Plotinus, who is the great psychologist and theologian of love in the West and who has been credited with synthesizing Neo-Platonic eros with Christian agape, thus combining descent and ascent in *caritas.*

Let us see something of love in Augustine's early works (386–90), when his Neo-Platonism is still fresh. As time went on, he became less philosophical and more Scriptural, with added emphasis on God's grace.

One of the favorite topics of the philosophers is happiness. For all agree that man wants to be happy. The big question is: What is happiness? This was a natural for Augustine and his students in their discussions at Cassiciacum. These conversations in *The Happy Life* (386) are Augustine's first completed work at the age of thirty-two.

Like many young men, Augustine had sought happiness in various philosophers: the Manichees, Academics, Platonists. He explored for it in his sex life of fifteen years of common-law marriage and in his career as a rhetor. But none of these was satisfying. He concludes that God is the source of happiness. We are drawn to God, but held back.

As long as we are still seeking and not yet satiated by the fountain itself—to use our word—by fullness—we must confess that we have not yet reached our measure; therefore notwithstanding the help of God, we are not yet wise and happy. (4/35) (FOC)

7. "We are not yet wise and happy" (Augustine, *The Happy Life*, 4/35)

Also while at Cassiciacum he wrote his *Soliloquies*, a dialogue with himself on knowledge of God and the soul. We can know God through our study of the soul made in his image. This is Augustine's first mention of a psychological approach to God which would culminate in his *Trinity*. Since the soul must resemble its creator, why not study it as a way to God?

Augustine wants to know God and the soul which he loves. But his reason asks whether he does not know something like God. He answers: "If I knew anything like God, I would doubtless love it, but up to now I love nothing except God and the soul, neither of which I know." (*Sol.*, 1/2/7)(FOC)

But does not Augustine love his friends? Yes. "Because they have rational souls, which I love even in thieves. . . . And so I love my friends all the more the better use they make of the rational soul. Or at least according to the manner in which they desire to use it well." (*Sol.*, 1/2/7) Augustine's view of reason as the divine and lovable part of man reflects a major trend in Hellenistic philosophy.

Though Augustine loves his friends and knows them superficially—that is, by the senses—he does not yet know them interiorly.

The law of friendship is most just by which it is ordained that we should love a friend neither less nor more than one loves oneself. Accordingly, since I do not know myself, what shame can I possibly inflict on a friend when I say he is unknown to me, especially when I believe that he himself does not know himself? (*Sol.*, 1/3/8)

Augustine teaches the Platonic precedence of love in cognition, a keen insight which would be rediscovered by modern educators and psychologists.

Are there lesser loves than the love of God? Yes, the love of friends, health, wealth, honors, wife, etc. But all of these loves are undermined by the fear of loss, for friends depart, health weakens, money is lost, dishonor comes, a wife dies.

Augustine pursues divine love. "And this boon grows on me day by day, for the more my hope increases of seeing that Beauty which I so long for, the more is all my love and delight turned toward him." (*Sol.*, 1/10/17)

Augustine is accused of having a negative view of sex. But he speaks as a man of experience, for he had had sexual intercourse for about fifteen years. But it was a joy that he found ephemeral. Moreover, he disdains sexual delights purely for the pleasure of it, though he knows it is necessary for the propagation of the race.

Probably many factors besides his disillusionment with sex turned Augustine from marriage. Perhaps the cataclysmic approach of the fall of Rome turned him toward monasticism, as it had many in this period. Why bring children into a collapsing world? Also rampant promiscuity in the falling empire may have turned him to celibacy, as it had others.

But Augustine is not recommending that all give up married love, only he himself who had experienced its dissatisfaction. "I know of nothing which brings the manly mind down from the heights more than a woman's caresses and that joining of bodies without which one cannot have a wife." However, one who takes a wife to devote himself to children is worthy of admiration, but not of imitation. (*Sol.*, 1/10/17) The child-orientation of Roman marriage is reflected in the marriage laws of the time. Augustine concludes: "On this account, for the sake of freedom of my soul, I have enjoined myself—with due justice and good reason, I think—not to covet, not to seek, not to marry a wife." (*Sol.*, 1/10/17)[2]

Augustine is often the *bête noire* for the proponents of free love. However, his main point is often missed, namely, that this is not the highest form of love. First of all, human love is necessarily ephemeral, for time is its enemy. Augustine seeks a more durable love than the unsatisfying sexual love which he had so long experienced.

The next year (388) in Rome, Augustine begins his role as the defender of his new faith against the Manichees, portraying divine love as the foundation of Christian morals, which are superior to those of the Manichees.

Taking up the theme of *The Happy Life* and the *Soliloquies*, he claims that happiness is the enjoyment of man's chief good, which cannot be lost unless by man's own free will. One cannot be happy who does not possess what he loves or who loves and has something hurtful or if he has something that he does not love.

What is happiness, then? Having one's chief loved good at hand. Man's chief good cannot be inferior to him or he himself will become inferior.[3] And human love always carries with it the risk of loss. So what remains? God. "God then remains, in following after whom we live both well and happily." (*Morals of the Catholic Church*, 7)

Both the Old and the New Testament teach love. "If then to those who love God all things issue in good, and if, as no one doubts, the chief and perfect good is not only to be loved, but to be loved so that nothing shall be loved better"—our chief good must be God and no one but our own selves can separate us from him. (MCC, 11)

It is Christ, love incarnate, and his Spirit who unite us to God. Why? Because through love we become conformed to Christ by the Holy Spirit.

Augustine is writing on the morals of the Catholic Church. But morality is virtue and virtue is love.

As to virtue leading us to a happy life, I hold virtue to be nothing else than perfect love of God. . . . Temperance is love giving itself entirely to that which is loved; fortitude is love readily bearing all things for the sake of the loved object; justice is love serving only the loved object, and therefore ruling rightly; prudence is love distinguishing with sagacity between what hinders it and what helps it.

The object of love is God, so that temperance keeps whole and entire for God, fortitude bears up under everything for God, etc. (MCC, 15)

We have been talking about love of God, around which the whole of Christian morality revolves. But what of love of self and neighbor? First Augustine explains self-love. "It is impossible for one who loves God not to love himself. For he alone has a proper love for himself who aims diligently at the attainment of the chief and true good"—God.

And we should show our love for our neighbor by trying to draw him to the same highest good which we are pursuing. Both divine love and neighborly love are first in their own way. Thus the love of God is first in beginning, while love of neighbor is first in coming to perfection. (MCC, 26) Augustine then concludes with examples of Christian anchorites and cenobites and others living lives of perfect charity.

Augustine's dialogue "On Music" was started in 387, before

his conversion, and was finished in 391. It is one of his treatises on the liberal arts. In the Sixth Book on the hierarchy of numbers he speaks of delight (*delectatio*) in parallel terms with love. "For delight is a kind of weight [*pondus*] in the soul. Therefore delight orders the soul." Thus we should order ourselves between the higher and the lower, avoiding the troubles of the lower, and taking delight in the higher. (6/11/29) Delight, like love, is a weight bearing man toward the object of his love, as the weight of a stone carries it to the earth or the weight of a flame rises up to the heights.[4]

Everyone loves beautiful things. But improper love turns us away from God.

Then the love of acting on the stream of its bodily passions turns the soul away from the contemplation of eternal things, diverting its attention with the care of sensible pleasure. It does this with reacting numbers. But the love of operating on bodies also turns it away, and makes it restless. This it does with advancing numbers. . . . But the general love of action turning away from the true arises from pride by which vice the soul has preferred imitating God to serving him. (6/13/39–40) (FOC)

The soul is nothing of itself, but is from God. By staying in order, it is quickened in mind and conscience by the presence of God. But puffed with pride, it is out of order, disordered, goes out empty, and becomes less and less, putting itself away from God.

It is the love of lower beauty that soils the soul, causing disorder. "That soul keeps order, that, with its whole self, loves him above itself, that is, God, and fellow souls as itself. In virtue of this love, it orders lower things and suffers no disorder from them." (6/14/46) "And so let us put our joy neither in carnal pleasure, nor in the honors and praises of man, nor in the exploring of things touching the body from without, having God within where all we love is sure and unchangeable." (6/14/48)

Delight in music and in love are proper orderings. When things are out of order in the musical world—cacophony. Dissonance and lack of harmony can be in both music and love.

Pastor of Love

In his priestly years—from 391 onward—Augustine is less philosophical and more pastoral in tone, beginning with his *Confessions* (397), written to help others along his path of love, others trapped in the same culs-de-sac of earthly delights which he had experienced.

Augustine's *Confessions* are a song of love. "For love of your love I perform this task." (11/1/1)[5] Man is made for God and his love will never rest till he possesses his beloved. "Our heart is restless until it rests in you." (1/1/1)

In reviewing his early life, Augustine regrets some loves which went against the will of his parents. (1/10/16) "I was disobedient, not out of desire for better things, but out of love for play." In Book Two he further recalls his youthful lusts.

What was there to bring me delight except to love and be loved? But that due measure between soul and soul, wherein lie the bright boundaries of friendship, was not kept. Clouds arose from the slimy desires of the flesh and from youth's seething spring. They clouded over and darkened my soul, so that I could not distinguish the calm light of chaste love from the fog of lust. (2/2/2)

Sin for Augustine, reflecting Plato, is a settling for a love of creatures which mirror divine beauty in lieu of Beauty itself.

There is a splendor in human bodies, both in gold and silver, and in all things. For the sense of touch, what is suitable to it affords great pleasure and for each of the other senses there is a just adaptation of bodily things. Worldly honor, too, and the power to command and to rule over others have their own appeal, and from them issues greed for revenge. But even to gain all these objects we must not depart from you, O Lord, or fall away from your law. This life which we live here has its own allurements which come from its particular mode of beauty and its agreement with all these lower beauties.

The friendship of men bound together by a loving tie, is sweet because of the unity that it fashions among many souls. With regard to these things, and others of like nature, sins are committed when, out of an immoderate liking for them, since they are the least goods, we desert the best and highest goods, which are you, O Lord, our God, and your truth and your law. These lower goods have their delights, but none such as my God, who has made all things, for in him the just man finds delight, and he is the joy of the upright of heart. (2/5/10)

Earthly beauty can require only partial love and give partial joy. When total love is given to the exclusion of divine love, when human beauty does not lead to divine beauty, sin arises.

A catalyst in Augustine's conversion is Cicero's *Hortensius*.

How I burned with a desire to fly away from earthly things and upwards to you, and yet I did not know what you would do with me! For with you there is wisdom. Love of wisdom has the name philosophy in Greek, and that book set me on fire for it. (3/4/8)

By profession Augustine is a rhetor, but by interest a philosopher. In the finest tradition of the Greek wisdom lovers, Augustine seeks wisdom which can be found only in God.

Augustine is a man of many loves. Besides his youthful lusts, his filial love of Monica, his paternal affection for Adeodatus, and his sexual love of his anonymous consort, he also deeply experienced the love of friendship. But he saw all these loves end in death. Friendship unites two souls into one, but destined to be split. At the sudden death of a close friend, Augustine cried out: "I marveled that other men should live, because he whom I had loved as if he should never die was dead." (4/6/11) With half of his soul gone, Augustine fears that his half may go, too.

Human friendship and love, though great, are ephemeral.

But blessed is the man who loves you and his friend in you, and his enemy for your sake. For he alone loses no dear one to whom all are dear in him who is not lost. But who is this unless our God, the God who made heaven and earth and fills all things because by filling them he made them. (4/9/14)

The divine light illumines his friendship. "You beat back my feeble sight, sending down your beams most powerfully upon me, and I trembled with love and awe." (7/10/16)

Augustine is not a pessimist or an exaggerated dualist who sees material things as evil, as the Manichees did. No, all created things are good, but they are corruptible and so tend to lose their goodness. And they must be good, for if they were not good to begin with, they would not be corruptible. But all of these things reflect and praise their creator, the highest and incorruptible good. (7/12/18–19)

What is evil? It is a disordered love centering on lower loves in lieu of the higher. "It is a perversity of will, twisted away from the supreme substance, yourself, O God, and towards lower things." (7/10/22) Though he is borne down by the weight of carnal lust, there still remains in Augustine a remembrance of God.

The books of the Platonists attracted Augustine, but they also puffed him up with their wisdom. What he needed was the humble charity of Christ in the Gospels.

Augustine had many loves. But how does the love of God compare with these? "Not with doubtful, but with sure knowledge do I love you, O Lord. By your word you have transfixed my heart, and I have loved you. Heaven and earth and all things in them, behold! Everywhere they say to me that I should love you."

It is not beautiful bodies, or temporal fame, or shining lights, or sweet songs, delightful flowers or shapely legs!

Yet I do love a certain light, a certain voice, a certain odor, a certain food, a certain embrace, when I love my God. A light, a voice, an odor, a food, an embrace for the man within me, where his light, which no place can contain, floods my soul; where he utters words that time does not speed away; where he sends forth an aroma that no mind can scatter; where he provides food that no eating can lessen; where he so clings that satiety does not sunder us. This is what I love when I love my God. (10/6/8)

For thirty-two years Augustine had pursued mortal beauties until at last he had found Beauty itself.

Too late have I loved you, O Beauty, so ancient and so new. Too late have I loved you! Behold you were within me while I was outside. It was there that I sought you, and, a deformed creature, rushed headlong upon these things of beauty which you have made. You were with me, but I was not with you. They kept me far from you, those fair things which, if they were not in you, would not exist at all.

You have called to me, and have cried out, and have shattered my deafness. You have blazed forth with light, and have shone upon me, and you have put my blindness to flight! You have sent forth fragrance, and I have drawn in my breath, and I pant after you. I have tasted you and I hunger and thirst after you. You have touched me, and I have burned for your peace. (10/27/38)

It is the weight (*pondus*) of his love that moves Augustine toward God, where he will find rest. As fire rises and stones fall, as oil rises and water sinks until they find their place of natural rest, so: "My love is my weight. I am borne about by it, wheresoever I am borne. By your gift I am enkindled, and we are borne upwards. We glow with inward fire and we go on. We ascend steps within the heart and we sing a gradual psalm." (13/9/10) But this weighty love is not something that man has acquired. No, it is God's gratuitous gift to him.

When he was consecrated bishop of Hippo (395), Augustine's philosophy of love took on more of a pastoral hue. Thus in 399 he writes a work, *On Catechizing*, to encourage the catechists in their difficult work.

The first aim of the catechist should be to teach his disciples that Christ came to instruct in love. Why else did Christ come than to manifest God's love for us sinners and to give us an example to love each other?

Even if at first we found it irksome to love him, now at least, it should not prove irksome to return that love. For there is nothing that invites love more than to be beforehand in loving. And that heart is overhard which even though it were unwilling to bestow love, would be unwilling to return it.

There is no greater reason either for the birth or growth of love than when one who as yet does not love, perceives that he is loved. Or when he who loves already hopes either that he may yet be loved in return, or actually has proof that he is loved. (4/7) (ACW)

If this is true in natural passion, how much more so in friendship.

For what else do we have to be on our guard against in an offense against friendship than that our friend should think either that we do not love him, or that we love him less than he loves us? (4/7)

If a friend believes that we love him less than he loves us, will not his love cool, especially if it is of a utilitarian type?

Though love of friendship is great when traded on an equal basis, the love of a superior for an inferior is even greater. "For love is more welcome when it is not burnt up by the drought of want, but issues forth from the overflowing stream of beneficence. For the former springs from misery, the latter from commiseration." (4/7)

This is the love of God which Christ came to teach us.

> Christ came chiefly that man might learn how much God loves him, and might learn this to the end that he might begin to glow with love of him by whom he was first loved, and so might love his neighbor at the bidding and after the example of him who made himself man's neighbor by loving him, when instead of being his neighbor, he was wandering far from him. (4/8)

This is the epitome of the Scriptures and of all catechizing, too, namely, that God has loved us first and that we should love him and our neighbor in Christ's example.

Love, not utility or gain, should prompt one to become a Christian. The catechumen, finding himself loved by God, wishes to love him in return. (5/9)

Bishop Augustine also teaches love in a second work, *On Christian Teaching* (394–426). Here he distinguishes the two loves, *frui* and *uti* (enjoyment and use). The things of the world are used to bring man to his final end. "But because of their eagerness to enjoy the creature in place of the creator, men have been conformed to this world and have been fittingly called the 'world.'" (1/12/12) (FOC) The enjoyment of temporal things does not lead to happiness since there is a constant risk of loss. The enjoyment of eternal things alone can bring happiness. (1/22/20)

But how about human love, *frui* or *uti?*

> We have been commanded to love one another. But the question is: whether man is to be loved by man for his own sake or for another reason. If he is loved for his own sake, we are enjoying him [*frui*]; if he is loved for another reason, we are using him [*uti*]. (1/22/20)

Augustine prefers *uti* to *frui* in the case of man as with other creatures. Thus he should use his love of his fellow man to reach God.

The same holds true of man's self-love.

No one ought to enjoy himself, if you observe clearly, because he should not love himself for his own sake, but because of him whom he ought to enjoy. . . . If he loves himself for his own sake, he does not refer himself to God. But, since he has turned to himself, he is not turned toward something unchangeable. (1/22/21)

A man cannot enjoy himself perfectly, for God is the only one in whom he can find total delight. "Therefore, if you ought to love yourself, not for your own sake, but on account of him who is the most fitting object of your love, no other man should be angered if you love him also for the sake of God." (1/22/21)

So one should love his neighbor with reference to God. "Thus loving him as himself, he refers all the love of himself and the other to that love of God which suffers no trickle to be led off from itself by those whose diversion its own volume might lessen." (1/22/21)

There are four things to be loved: things above, ourselves, things equal to ourselves, and things below. "Concerning the second and the fourth no rules have been given. For, however far a man errs from the truth, there remains in him a love of himself and of his own body." (1/23/22) Man is between God and creatures and it is unjust of him to expect lower creatures to serve him, if he in turn refuses to serve God.

Though no man needs be told to love himself or his own body, he needs a reminder to love God and his neighbor.

Now the purpose of this charge is charity, a two-fold love of God and neighbor. . . . Since the love of God has precedence, and since the measure of that love has been so defined that all other loves are to fuse in him, it seems that no mention has been made about our love of ourselves. (1/26/27)

But we should love our neighbor as ourselves.

The just and holy person "has a well-regulated love and neither loves what he ought not, nor fails to love what he should." (1/27/28) Sinners as sinners should not be loved. Man is loved for God and God for his own sake.

> And if God is to be loved more than any man, each one ought to love God more than himself. Thus another man should be loved more than our own bodies, because all those things are to be loved for the sake of God. (1/27/28)

Another man can enjoy God with us, whereas our body cannot. All men should be loved equally. But is there not a hierarchy of love among men? One must decide who is more in need. (1/28/29)

How should we act who are united by the love of God, the enjoyment of whom constitutes our happy life and from whom all who love him receive their existence and their love of him? He wants us to love in order to share his love with us, rewarding us with himself, the object of our love. So one even loves his enemies in compassion since they have removed themselves from the reward of divine love. (1/29/30)

But the big question remains. How can God love us? The Greek gods had no need of man and so did not love him.

> How does God love us? If he enjoys us, he needs a benefit that is ours—something no sane man would say, because he himself is our every good or else it comes from him.

If God, then, does not love us for enjoyment (*frui*), does he do so with the love of use (*uti*)? Augustine replies: "If he neither enjoys nor uses us, I cannot discover how he loves us." (1/31/34) But the use God makes of us is not the way man uses creation to help his ultimate enjoyment of God. "God refers that use which he is said to make of us to our benefit, not to his own benefit, but only to his goodness." For we exist only because of a superabundance of his goodness. (1/32/35)

For Augustine *caritas* (love or charity) and *cupiditas* (lust) are exact opposites. Thus "charity is a motion of the soul whose purpose is to enjoy God for his own sake and one's self and one's neighbor for the sake of God," whereas *cupiditas* is enjoying oneself, neighbor, or any creature without any reference to God.

Unbridled lust in ourselves is vice, while aimed at others it is crime. Charity, on the other hand, used for oneself is utility, whereas for another it is kindness. "The more the power of lust is destroyed, the more the power of charity is strengthened." (3/10/16)

In conclusion, love is the central message of the Scriptures. So when one becomes a Christian, he should do so out of love for God, who has loved him first through his Son, Jesus Christ.

Augustine's many pastoral sermons also reflect his concern for love. We will glance at two of these, namely, 21 and 34. In Sermon 21 Augustine speaks on Psalm 63 (11): "The just man will rejoice in the Lord."

Love is based on hope.

You love money, but you would not love it if you did not hope. You love your wife not already wed, but about to be wed. Perhaps your beloved fiancée will be hated as a wife. Why? Because as a wife she does not appear the same as she was imagined as a fiancée.

However, God, who is loved when absent, does not diminish when he is present. No matter how much the human mind exaggerates God's goodness, it is still less than he is. Thus it is necessary that the possession of God find more than the mind could have imagined. So we will love him more when we see him, if we could have loved him even before we saw. (1) (PL, 38/142)

Love seeks the good in the loved object. Thus even the misguided love of sin seeks a good. "You do not love sin. But merely love evilly that which you love, becoming ensnared in sin." (3) All creatures of God are good. It is only when we replace God with creatures that we sin.

Augustine contrasts delight in the world with delight in
the Lord. "For he delights in the Lord when he destroys all
delights in the world, and remains in the Lord in whom he rejoices and there remains in him a simple, perfect and immuta-
ble delight of heart." (9) After all, creatures are gifts of
God, who can give or take as he pleases. Thus when all of
Job's possessions are taken away he can still rejoice in the
Lord.

Augustine's Sermon 34 is on Psalm 149 (1, 2): "Sing
the Lord a new song." (PL 38/209 ff.) "A new man knows a
new song. A song is a thing of joy, or better a thing of love.
So whoever knows how to love a new life, knows how to love
a new song." (1/1)

> Charity is from God! There is no one who does not love.
> But it is asked what he loves. So we do not admonish not
> to love, but that we choose what we love. But what do we
> choose unless first we are chosen? Because we do not love
> unless first loved. Hear John the Apostle [Jn 13/23; 1 Jn
> 4/10]: . . . We love. How can we? Because he loved us
> first. . . . He whom we love gave himself and he also gave
> that by which we love. What did he give by which we love?
> Clearly hear Paul: "The charity of God is diffused in our
> hearts." Whence does this love come? From us? No! Then
> whence? "Through the Holy Spirit who is given to us" [Rom
> 5/5]. (1/1)

Loving (*diligere*) is really choosing (*eligere*), both deriva-
tives of *legere* (to choose or select). Augustine says that wrong
loves are really wrong choices, whereas right loves are right
choices. When we choose God it is because he has chosen us
first and given us the grace to choose him in return. When
someone makes himself God, giving divine love to self or to a
creature, trouble ensues.

A lascivious and impure person loves a beautiful woman.
Bodily beauty moves him, but inside he seeks a return of

love. For if he hears that she hates him, does not all his heat and desire of her lovely body cool? And he recoils and turns offended from his desire and begins to hate what he loved.

Has her shapely body changed? Is not everything still there that he has chosen? Everything is there all right! He loved in her what he saw and in his heart he wanted what he did not see. If he knows that he is loved in return, how his love would grow stronger. She sees him, he sees her. No one sees love. Thus love is loved which is not seen. (2/4)

Augustine's graphic description of unrequited love seems to be experiential. Love is an invisible, intangible thing. Indeed it is divine, even as its divine author and object is invisible. When we love God, we possess him. "God you do not see. Love him and you possess him. . . . God, in short, offers himself to us. He cries to us. 'Love me and you will have me, because you are not able to love me unless you have had me.'" (3/5)

What is the price of charity (*caritas*)? It is dear (*cara*) indeed! Though we can buy wheat with money, a farm with silver, pearls with gold, one must pay his very self in order to buy charity.

If you want to have charity, seek yourself and find yourself. Why do you fear to give yourself, lest you be used up? Indeed, if you have not given yourself, you destroy yourself. Charity speaks through Wisdom and says something to you. Are you not frightened at what it says: "Give yourself." . . . "Son, give me your heart" [Prov 23/26]? (4/7)

The price of charity is self-gift. God gave himself to man so that man could give himself to God.

We should love God with our whole self and our neighbor as ourself.

Do you want to hear why you love yourself? You love yourself because you love God with your whole self. Do you think that God profits anything when you love him? Or because you love God he gains anything? And if you do not love him, does he lose anything?

When you love, you are the one who profits, for you will be there where you will not perish. But you will answer: When did I not love myself? You did not love yourself when you did not love God who made you. But when you hated yourself, you thought that you were loving yourself. "Who loves iniquity, hates his own soul" [Ps 10/6]. (5/8)

The City of Love

Augustine's later works (411–430) are even more Scriptural and less philosophical. Whether attacking the Donatists or commenting on the Psalms or on John or explaining the mysteries of the Trinity, Scripture is the mainstay of his argument.

As we have seen, the Psalms, songs of love, are important in Jewish and Christian liturgy. And Augustine uses them as springboards for his sermons on love.

In his Commentary on Psalm 9 (15), Augustine calls love the foot of the soul. When depraved it is called lust, and when upright, love or charity. The foot of sinners is caught in a snare and most difficult to pull out.

In his second sermon on Psalm 31, Augustine speaks of active love.

Love itself cannot be idle. What but love is the active force, even for evil in man? Find me a love idle and unproductive! Crime, adultery, villainy, murder, excesses of all kinds, are they not the work of love? . . . Am I telling you "Love nothing"? Nonsense!

Lazy, dead, detestable, wretched will you be if you love nothing. Love, but take care what it is you love. The love of God, the love of one's neighbor, are termed charity. The love of earthly things, the love of this world, are termed

passion. Bridle your passion, stir up your charity. (2/5)
(ACW)

Those in Christ's body are united in their love of him. So
our love of Christ is not a jealous love. Not as a man craving
to see a certain woman in the nude, but who does not want
others to see her bare.

No, the love of a Christian is not at all like this. He wants
others to love Christ as well. "Shame on those who love God
in such a way as to begrudge him to others." People of the
world are attached to an athlete or an actor and try to persuade others to support him.

Yet a Christian never raises his voice in church to invite
others to join him in loving God's truth! Stir up this love in
yourselves, then, brethren, and cry out to one another, saying "O magnify the Lord with me." Let there be this glowing desire in you.

Why am I quoting and explaining these words to you? If
you love God, carry along all those who are connected with
you, and everybody in your house, and make them love God.
If Christ's body, that is to say, the unity of the church, is
the object of your love, urge them on to delight in it. Cry
"O magnify the Lord with me" [Ps 33/2/6]. (ACW)

The lover finds his strength in the Holy Spirit.

For whatever thing is difficult in a commandment, is a light
thing to a lover. Nor on any other account is rightly understood the saying "My burden is light" [Mt 11/30]. But because he gives the Holy Spirit whereby love is shed abroad in
our hearts [Rom 5/5] in order that in love we may do freely
that which he that does in fear does slavishly. Nor is he a
lover of what is right, when he would prefer, if it were possible, that what is right should not be commanded [Ps 68/16].
(NPNF)

All of man's good works are really one work of love, for

love is the fulfilling of the law. "There is, therefore, one work, in which are all 'Faith which works by love.'" (Gal 5/6; Ps 90/17)

Love is the law of the city of God.

What is the city of God but the holy church? For men who love one another and who love their God who swells in them constitute a city unto God. Because a city is held together by some law, their very law is love. And that very love is God. For openly it is written "God is love" [1 Jn 4/8]. He, therefore, who is full of love is full of God. And many, full of love, constitute a city full of God [Ps 99/4]. (NPNF)

This theme is taken up again in Augustine's *City of God*.

In his sermons on the Trinity, Augustine reaches a new psychological level of love talk. First of all, God is love. Secondly, man is made to the image of God's self-love, so that man's self-love must somehow reflect God's love.

Justice is the basis of love, writes Augustine.

He, therefore, who loves men ought to love them either because they are just or that they may be just. So ought he to love himself also, either because he is just or that he may be just, for in this way he loves his neighbor as himself without any danger. (8/6/9) (FOC)

As in some of his other works, Augustine makes the sharp distinction between true love (*caritas*) and desire (*cupiditas*). "But this is true love, that while holding fast to the truth, we may live justly. And, therefore, we may despise everything mortal for the sake of the love of men whereby we wish them to love justly." (8/7/10)

Scripture commands love of God and neighbor.

But he who loves God must logically do what God commanded, and loves him just as much as he does so. Therefore he must also love his neighbor since God has commanded this. . . . But this also follows logically, for he who loves his neighbor must also love love itself above everything else. But "God is love and he who abides in love abides in God." Therefore, he must needs love God above everything else. (8/7/10)

Let no one say: "I do not know what I should love." Let him love his brother and he will love the same love, for he knows the love by which he loves more than the brother whom he loves. And so God can now become more known to him than his brother, actually more known because more present, more known because more within him, more known because more certain. Embrace love, God, and embrace God by love. (8/8/12)

God is love, Scripture says. But where is the triune nature of God in this? Augustine shows the threefold nature of love. We love love (God) and our brother: lover, love, and beloved. "If he loved him whom he sees by human sight with a spiritual love, he would see God, who is love itself, with that inner sight by which he can be seen." (8/8/12)

Now love is of someone who loves, and something is loved with love, so then there are three: the lover, the beloved and love. What else is love, therefore, except a kind of life which binds or seeks to bind some two together, namely, the lover and the beloved? (8/10/14)

When the mind loves itself, it makes known two things, the mind and the love.

Yet mind and love are not two spirits, but one spirit; not two essences, but one essence; and still the two are one, the lover and the love, or, so to say, the beloved and the love. And these two are truly said to be related. The lover is referred to the love and the love to the lover, and love is of someone who loves. (9/2/2)

But how is the trinity reflected here?

Just as there are two things, the mind and its love, when it loves itself, so there are two things, the mind and its knowledge, when it knows itself. Therefore, the mind itself, its love and knowledge are a kind of trinity. These three things are one and when they are perfect, they are equal. (9/4/4)

If one loves himself either more or less than he should, for example, if he deifies himself—sin.

Augustine continues:

In these three, when the mind knows itself and loves itself, a trinity remains: the mind, love and knowledge; and there is no confusion through any commingling, although each is a substance in itself, and all are found mutually in all, whether each one is in each two, or each two in each one, consequently all are in all. (9/5/8; 9/12/12)

This, then, is the trinity of the human soul: mind, love, and knowledge, reflecting in highest manner the triune image of its creator.

Another human triad which reflects the divine trinity is the mind remembering, understanding, and loving itself. (14/8/11)

Hence this trinity of the mind is not on that account the image of God because the mind remembers itself, understands itself and loves itself, but because it can also remember, understand and love him by whom it was made. And when it does so, it becomes wise. But if it does not, even though it remembers itself, knows itself and loves itself, it is foolish. Let it, then, remember its God, to whose image it has been made, and understand him and love him. (14/12/15)

Forgetting God is sin. And what is more wretched than for one to be without him whom he cannot be without? (14/12/15)

Though God is love, love is the special appropriation of the Holy Spirit.

When God, the Holy Spirit, therefore, who proceeds from God, has been given to man, he inflames him with the love for God and his neighbor, and he himself is love. For man does not have the means to love God, except from God himself [Rom 5/5]. (15/17/31)

The Spirit is especially called the Gift for no other reason except love. And he who does not have it even with all other gifts is nothing. (1 Cor 13/1–3)

Furthermore, if among the gifts of God, none is greater than love, and there is no greater gift of God than the Holy Spirit, what is more logical than that he himself should be love, who is called both God and of God? And if the love whereby the Father loves the Son and the Son the Father, reveals in an ineffable manner the union between both, what more fitting than that he who is the Spirit, common to both, should be properly called love? (15/19/37)

So for Augustine, God is a trinity of love which is especially appropriated to the Holy Spirit. And man reflects the triune God especially when he remembers, understands, and loves God.

The later Augustine is a Scripture fan, as we have seen. And what better place to find love than in the School of John? (414–16)

A man's love is determined by the object of his love.

Those who for their love of the world are called the world. By loving we dwell with the heart. But because of their loving the world, they deserved to be called after the name of that in which they dwelt. . . . For those who do not love the world in the flesh, indeed, sojourn in the world, but in their hearts they dwell in heaven. (2/11)(NPNF)

Love of God and neighbor are interrelated.

He who commanded you this love in two precepts did not charge you to love your neighbor first, and then God, but first God and afterwards your neighbor. You, however, as you do not yet see God, earn to see him by loving your neighbor. By loving your neighbor, you purge your eye for seeing God [1 Jn 4/20]. . . .

Therefore, love your neighbor, look at the source of the love of your neighbor. There you will see God. . . . Where does your way go, but to the Lord God whom we ought to love with the whole heart and with the whole soul and with the whole mind? For we are not yet come to the Lord. But we have our neighbor with us. (17/8–9)

The mind is drawn to God by love.

I say it is not enough to be drawn by will; you are drawn even by delight. What is it to be drawn by delight? "Delight yourself in the Lord and he shall give you the desires of your heart" [Ps 37/4]. There is a pleasure of the heart to which that bread of heaven is sweet.

Thus a man is drawn to Christ when he delights in truth, blessedness, righteousness, and life everlasting. "Give me a man that loves, and he feels what I say. Give me one that longs, one that hungers, one that is traveling in this wilderness, and thirsting and panting after the fountain of his eternal home. Give such and he knows what to say." (26/4) This is the weight of love, drawing man to God.

The Holy Spirit is the personification of divine love. Why was the Spirit sent after the Resurrection?

In order that our resurrection of love may be inflamed, and may part from the love of the world to run wholly towards God. For here we are born and die. Let us not love this world. Let us migrate hence by love, by love let us dwell above, by that love by which we love God. . . .

If we live, if we believe in him who is risen again, he will give us, not that which men love here who love not God,

or love the more the less they love him, but love this the
less, the more they love him. . . . Because such is what he
promised to us that love him and grow with the charity of
the Holy Spirit. (32/9)

When the Holy Spirit came upon the early Christians, they
became a community of love.

A considerable community was created, in which all receiving the Holy Spirit, by whom spiritual love was kindled, were
by their very love and fervor of spirit welded into one. . . .

If by approaching God many souls by love become one
soul, and many hearts one heart, what of the very fountain
of love in the Father and Son? Is it not still more so here
that the trinity is one God? For thence of that Holy Spirit,
does love come to us, as the Apostle says: "The love of God
is shed abroad in our hearts by the Holy Spirit which is given
to us" [Rom 5/5].

If, then, the love of God, shed abroad in our hearts by
the Holy Spirit which is given to us, makes many souls one
soul and many hearts one heart, how much rather are the
Father and Son and Holy Spirit one God, one light and one
beginning? (39/5)

Christ has given us a new commandment to love each other
as he has loved us! "This is the love that renews us, makes us
new men, heirs of the New Testament, singers of the new
song." The twofold commandment of love of God and neighbor does not contradict.

For on the one hand, he that loves God, cannot despise his
commandment to love his neighbor. And, on the other hand,
he who in a holy and spiritual way loves his neighbor, what
does he love in him but God? That is the love distinguished
from all mundane love, which the Lord specially character-
ized, when he added "As I have loved you." For what was
it but God that he loved in us? Not because we had him,
but in order that we might have him, and that he may lead

us on, as I said a little while ago, where God is all in all.
(65/1)

Likewise, when a physician loves the sick, he loves in them the
health that he desires to recall. So we should love one another,
hoping to have God in us. He loved us that we might love each
other united in a body of which he is the head.

Charity or love is the greatest and it fulfills the law.

And although in charity, that is in love, are comprehended
the two commandments, yet it is here declared to be the
greatest only, and not the sole one. . . . Love is the fulness
of the law [Rom 13/10] and so where there is love what
can be wanting? And where it is not, what is there that can
possibly be profitable? The devil believes but does not love.
No one loves who does not believe.

One may indeed hope for pardon who does not love, but
he hopes in vain. But no one can despair who loves. Therefore where there is love, there of necessity will be faith and
hope. And where there is the love of our neighbor, there
also of necessity will be the love of God. For he that loves
not God, how loves he his neighbor as himself, seeing that
he loves not even himself? (84/3)

Few men have this motive for loving each other—that God may
be all in all!

Peter made a threefold love commitment to Jesus. Jesus
asked: "'Do you love me?' 'Feed my sheep.' That is, 'If you
love me, think not of feeding yourself, but feed my sheep as
mine.'" Since the Gospel uses *diligere* and *amare*, it would
seem that liking and loving are similar. Elsewhere (in Jn 8/5)
Augustine identifies *amare* with carnal love and *diligere* with
a higher love.

Let us, then, love not ourselves, but him. And in feeding his
sheep, let us be seeking the things which are his, not the
things which are our own. For in some inexplicable way, I
know not what, everyone that loves himself and not God,

loves not himself, and whoever loves God and not himself, he it is that loves himself. (123/5)

Augustine also remarks on the First Epistle of John, the love testament of the School of John.

The deeds of men are only discerned by the root of charity. For many things may be done that have a good appearance, and yet proceed not from the root of charity, for thorns also have flowers. Some actions truly seem rough and savage, though they are done for discipline at the bidding of charity.

Once for all, then, a short precept is given you. Love, and do what you will, whether you hold your peace, through love hold your peace. Whether you cry out, through love cry out; whether you correct, through love correct; whether you spare, through love spare. Let the root of love be within, of this root can nothing spring but what is good. (7/8)

If any of you perhaps wish to keep charity, brethren, above all things do not imagine it to be an abject and sluggish thing; nor that charity is to be preserved by a sort of gentleness, nay not gentleness, but tameness and listlessness. . . .

Let charity be fervent to correct, to amend. But if there be good manners, let them delight you. If bad, let them be amended, let them be corrected. Love not in the man his error, but the man, for the man God made, the error the man himself made. Love that which God made, love not that which man himself made. (7/11)

A father sometimes corrects his son fiercely. But:

It is the fierceness of love, the fierceness of charity, a sort of fierceness without gall after the manner of the dove, not of the raven. Whence it came into my mind, my brothers, to tell you, that those violaters of charity are they that have made the schism. As they hate charity itself, so they hate also the dove. (7/11)

Brotherly love is the theme of the Epistle of John, with less stress on the love of God and nothing at all on the love of enemies.

Extend your love to them that are nearest. Yet do not call this an extending. For it is almost loving yourself, to love them that are close to you. Extend it to the unknown, who have done you no ill. Pass even them; reach on to love your enemies. This at least the Lord commands. Why has the apostle here said nothing about loving an enemy? (8/4)

How should we love men, *amare* (carnal love) or *diligere* (a higher love)? Not as a glutton loves food!

Whenever we love [*amamus*] in the way of food, to this end we love it that it may be consumed and we may be restored. Are men to be so loved as to be consumed? But there is a certain friendliness of well-wishing by which we desire at some time or other to do good to those whom we love. What if there be no good that we can do? The benevolence, the wishing well is of itself sufficient for him that loves.

But what of those not in need? Can we still love them? "With a truer touch of love you love the happy man to whom there is no good office you can do. Purer will that love be and far more unalloyed." Love for the lowly tends to be patronizing and can lead to pride. "Wish him to be your equal, that you both may be under the one Lord, on whom nothing can be bestowed." (8/5)[6]

John's school of love plays a strong part in the later Augustine, as the school of Plato did in his younger days.

A pastoral handbook of Augustine's later episcopal days is his *Enchiridion* of the Christian way of life as seen in the theological virtues, particularly charity. (421–422) Charity is the crown of the virtues. Why is charity so important? "A man with right love, also has right faith and hope. But one who has no love, believes in vain even though what he believes may be the truth." (31/117)(ACW)

Man has four states: first, before the Law, second under the Law, third under grace, and fourth full and perfect peace. In the third stage: "If God looks upon him, and he then believes that God helps him to carry out his commands and begins to be moved by the Spirit of God, then, with charity the dominant force in him, his desires run counter to his flesh." Though tempted, he does not yield to lust. (31/118)

The whole Law depends on charity, for God is charity.

Every commandment, therefore, has for its end charity, that is, it is charity that determines every commandment. But whatever is done either through fear of punishment or from some carnal motive so as not to be determined by that charity which the Holy Spirit diffuses in our hearts, is not done as it ought to be done, all appearances notwithstanding. (32/121)

So all the commandments—whether they be: Thou shalt not commit adultery, kill, etc.—"All these things are carried out in the right manner when they are motivated by love for God, and because of God, for our neighbor." (32/121)

Love holds sway here and in the world to come. Thus we love God now through faith, then by sight. Here we love our neighbor through faith also, for we do not know what lies in his heart. But in the next world all will be revealed. "Who then can fathom how great love will be in the world to come, where there will be no passion for it to overcome or even to restrain?" (32/121)

Finally, a brief look at Augustine's *City of God* (413–423). Here he repeats some of his earlier love themes, namely, that man's highest good is God and his love is a weight drawing him to God. The eternal law of love expresses this. Man's egocentricity is the enemy of love.

Augustine's central thesis describes two cities, of God and of man, based on two loves.

What we see, then, is that two societies have issued from

two kinds of love. Worldly society has flowered from a selfish love which dared to despise even God, whereas the communion of saints is rooted in a love of God that is ready to trample on self. In a word, this latter relies on the Lord, whereas the other boasts that it can get along by itself.

The city of man seeks the praise of men, whereas the height of glory for the other is to hear God in the witness of conscience. The one lifts up its head in its own boasting. The other says to God: "You are my glory, you lift up my head!" [Ps 3/4]. (14/28)[7]

In the city of the world the rulers and people are dominated by the lust for domination, whereas in the city of God all serve each other in charity. The one city loves its leaders as symbols of strength, the other loves God as its strength.

Love is the foundation of a city writes E. Gilson. "If we give the name 'city' to any group of men united by a common love for some object, we say that there are as many cities as there are loves."[8] Those with earthly love (*cupiditas*) form an earthly city, and those of heavenly love (*caritas*) form a heavenly city. The two cities have coexisted since the beginning of the world. And in fact in each man's heart there are two loves, though he often tends more to one city than to another.

The people in a city are united by their common love, and most societies pursue peace. To have peace, order must be maintained, the harmony of a number of wills working for a common end. Peace of the individual home or city depends on harmony. Augustine comments: "The peace of the heavenly city lies in a perfectly ordered and harmonious communion of those who find their joy in God and in one another in God." (19/13)

The only city worthy of the name is the heavenly one, but in the earthly life the two cities are intermingled.

The church is the kingdom of God. (20/9) But is it also the city of God? There are two kingdoms of God: one temporary and earthly and including sinners and one final, which includes only the elect. This is the city of God.[9]

The two cities here below are contemporaneous and interwoven in each one of us, in the family and in the city and state. Can there ever be a perfect city of divine love on this earth? The history of monasticism has been a long-enduring attempt to reach this ideal, with cities in the desert or on islands, etc. Augustine himself was drawn to this type of life. But even here the city of man tended to creep in.[10]

In concluding our discussion of Augustine's theology and psychology of love, let us remark once again that he started out Platonic and ended up Pauline and Johannine. His theology of love was to influence generations of theologians and mystics, including Bernard, Aquinas, and Luther, whom we will see in later chapters.

A couple of centuries after Augustine, Plato and the Bible would once again inspire mysticism, this time among the Islamic Sufi, whom we will see in the following chapter.

⇜ X ⇝

IT IS THE FLAME OF LOVE
THAT FIRED ME

Rumi, Mathnawi

In the last chapter we saw Augustine's loving ascent to God with its Neo-Platonic nuances. A century or two later the prophet Mohammed would preach a self-giving love of Allah which was destined to sweep the Arab world. Aided also by Platonism, it would influence other traditions as well.

Mohammed and the Love of Allah

Mohammed (570–632) was born in Mecca in the Arabian Peninsula as Ubu'l Kassim. As a merchant and camel driver he came into contact with many peoples and many religious traditions, including Christians and Jews.

The people of Mecca claimed to be descendants of Abraham through Ishmael and believed that their temple, Ka'bah, was built by Abraham himself for the worship of the one true God, the house of Allah. When idolatry crept in, a few zealous souls called Hunafa resisted to honor their one God, Allah. Among these was Mohammed.

Mohammed taught that there is only one God, Allah, and one can be saved only by submission to him (Islam). And he dedicated himself to Allah as his prophet. His visions and revelations, written down in the Koran and Hadith, would be the seed of Islamic mysticism. He chose faithful saints and disciples (*auliya*), and his personal experiences of God (*karamat*) led him to a closer union with Allah.

About age forty Mohammed experienced a conversion in the cave of Hira, where he was called to prophecy by the angel Gabriel. He and his family meditated in the desert for one month out of the year. Periodic revelations to him confirmed earlier prophets as Abraham, Moses, and Jesus.

Though his mystical experiences belong to his early Meccan period, as with so many other religious leaders, they inspired his prophecies, teaching, correcting, reforming, and governing throughout his whole life.

The Koran abounds in mystical reflections. For example: "Allah is the light of the heavens and of the earth. His light is as if there were a lustrous niche, wherein is a lamp contained in a crystal globe, the globe as bright as a glittering star." (24/36)[1]

Allah is described as merciful and loving. (11/91; 85/15) But love of God and man is mutual and man must show his love of God. "Allah loves the righteous." (3/77) "Surely Allah loves those who put their trust in him." (3/160) "Indeed, Allah loves those who turn to him often and Allah loves those who are clean and pure." (2/223)

A. J. Arberry comments:

> The conception of a remote indifferent potentate of the universe is wholly overthrown by this doctrine of the merciful Allah ever taking the first step towards man, the election of his creation to draw him by the powerful cords of love.[2]

The mutual love of God and man provides the great Sufi doctrine of love (*mahabba*) and the trinity of lover, beloved, and love.

The passing away of earthly attributes (*fana*) to free oneself for union with God is also strong in Moslem tradition. Poverty helps toward this end, for the poor man is stimulated to trust in God and trust leads to a higher state of love.

> And my servant continues to draw near to me through the works of supererogation until I love him and when I love him, I am his ear, so he hears by me; and his eye so that he sees by me, and his tongue so that he speaks by me, and his hand so that he takes by me.[3]

Love leads from ascetical works to contemplation and union with God—the basis of Sufi theosophy. Parallels may be seen in Hindu and Christian mysticism. God loves man, for he sees himself in him. Thus it behooves man to look inside himself to see God.

Mohammed reached the height of mystical experience when he was borne up to the seventh heaven by a winged horse to the near presence of God. The prophet said: "I am not as one of you. Verily I pass the night with my Lord, and he gives me food and drink." And: "I am with God in a state in which none of the cherubim nor any prophet is capable of being contained with me."[4] This night journey of Mohammed is the supreme mystical experience.

Early Islamic Mystics

The first century of Islam brought rich conquests and wealth and power with its ensuing problems. Though some leaders kept to the simple life, the transferal of the capital from Mecca to Damascus registered a decline in the spiritual life.

But some pious Moslems were inspired to withdraw from this luxurious life in the monastic tradition. And their poverty and asceticism was to be the foundation of Sufism, named after their woolen cloak.

Though they felt that Christian monasticism had failed and, indeed, at this time (8th cent.) it was in decline in the East,[5] some such as Ibrahim ben Adham learned asceticism from the

Christian monks, putting a premium on meditation and silence.

The self-discipline and trust in God of these early Moslem ascetics would develop into full-blown Sufism. Moreover, their indifference to the world has a strong Koranic basis. As with Hinduism, the Jewish rabbis, and the Christian monks before them, this often led to abstention even from the legitimate pleasures of marriage and family.

For example, Rabi'a, a female mystic of Basra in Iraq (8th cent.). When many men seek the hand of this gorgeous woman, she replies:

> The contract of marriage is for those who have phenomenal existence. But in my case there is no such existence, for I have ceased to exist and have passed out of self. I exist in God and am altogether his. I live in the shadow of his command. The marriage contract must be asked for from him and not from me.[6]

Rabi'a approaches Paradise. But when she yearns for it, God rebukes her. She wants no reward for worshipping God out of selfish fear of Hell or hope of Paradise.

> Two ways I love you: selfishly
> And next, as worthy of you.
> It is selfish love that I do naught
> Save think on you with every thought.
> 'Tis purest love when you raise
> The veil of my adoring gaze,
> Not mine the praise in that or this,
> Yours is the praise in that or this,
> Yours is the praise in both I wish.[7]

And again:

The groaning and the yearning of the lover of God
    will not be satisfied until it is satisfied in the Beloved.
I have made you the companion of my heart.
But my body is available to those who desire its company.

And my body is friendly towards its guests.
But the Beloved of my heart is the guest of my soul.

My peace is in solitude, but my Beloved is always with me.
Nothing can take the place of his love and it is the test
for me among mortal beings. Whenever I contemplate his
beauty, he is my *mihras* [mosque niche facing Mecca], towards him is my *qibla* [part of mosque towards which prayer
is directed].

O healer of souls, the heart feeds upon its desire and it
is striving towards union with you that has healed my soul.
You are my joy and my life to eternity. You were the source
of my life. From you came my ecstasy. I have separated myself from all created beings. My hope is for union with you,
for that is the goal of my quest.[8]

Self-denial, which slowly developed into complete disregard
for the world, led to an overwhelming passion for God. It is
fitting that this should occur in desert areas, where man is naturally removed from distractions and close to God. Some would
say that desert people are natural monotheists, while farmers
are polytheists.

The Christian monks found God in their isolation in the des-
erts of Egypt, Syria, and Palestine and on remote islands of
the Mediterranean and Irish seas.[9] And, as we have seen, some
early Islamic ascetics learned from the monks.

Asceticism, as many religious traditions teach, is a necessary
prelude to the love of God. Arberry writes:

When warmed by spiritual emotion, it [asceticism] converts
into ardent fervor, rejoicing in hardship and delighting in ecstatic experience. Subjected to the searching light of speculative reason, it is transformed into the hard discipline that is
the necessary prelude to a proved theosophy.[10]

The lover of God is not concerned with externals or the
world, but with reflection, solitude, and silence.

When others look at the lover, he does not see them. When

he is called, he does not hear. When misfortune comes upon him, he is not grieved, and when success looks him in the face, he does not rejoice. He fears no man and makes no request of anyone [save God].

God enlightens the heart of his lover and all veils are removed so that she may contemplate the invisible. (Al-Antaki) (9th cent.) (RMI, 10)

The translation of the works of Plato and Aristotle into Arabic gave a new slant to Islamic mysticism. We have seen earlier that some of the Greek philosophers were contemplatives, exalting the speculative *theoria* and the ascending eros. Moslem mystics, as the Christians before them, would make use of Greek nuances.

An outstanding Sufi author of the ninth century is al-Muhasibi. Born in Basra and educated in Baghdad, he knew philosophy and theology as well as Jewish and Christian traditions. He taught self-discipline and self-examination and, above all, love.

When love is established in the heart of a servant, there is no place there for the remembrance of men or demons or of paradise or hell nor anything else except the remembrance of the beloved and his grace. The love of God in its essence is really the illumination of the heart by joy because of its nearness to the beloved, for love in solitude rises up triumphant and the heart of the lover is possessed by the sense of its fellowship with him, and when solitude is combined with secret intercourse with the beloved, the joy of that intercourse overwhelms the mind, so that it is no longer concerned with this world and what is therein.

To that one whom God has placed in the rank of his lovers, he gives the vision of himself, for he has sworn saying, "By my glory I will show him my face and I will heal his soul by the vision of myself." The hearts of such lovers are held captive in the hidden shrine of the divine loving kindness. They are marked out by their knowledge of the revelation of the divine majesty. Being transformed by the joy of vision, in contemplation of the invisible, and of the enveloping glory of God. And from them all hindrances are removed for they tread the path of friendship with God and are transported into the garden of vision, and their hearts dwell in that region where they see without eyes, and are in the company of the beloved, without looking upon him, and converse with an unseen friend. (RMI, 16)

Dhul'l-Nun, an Egyptian contemporary of al-Muhasibi, is half mystic and half alchemist. Poetry attributed to him is quite passionate, a Sufi trait that would influence later European courtly love songs and Christian mystic writings.

> I die, and yet not dies in me
> The ardor of my love for you,
> Nor has your love, my only goal,
> Assuaged the fever of my soul.
> To you alone my spirit cries;
> In you my whole ambition lies,
> And still your wealth is far above
> The poverty of my small love.[11]

Abul Yazid, a Persian (9th cent.), feels the intoxication of divine love in *fana*, a passing out of self and into God. His soul flies like a bird in quest of God and God speaks to him.

O my chosen one, approach unto me and ascend to the heights of my glory and the plains of my splendor and sit upon the carpet of my holiness, so that you may see the working of my grace in my appointed time. You are my chosen and my beloved and my elect among creatures.

Drinking of the fountains of grace, he is brought nearer to God than the soul is to the body. (RMI, 25)[12]

Fana was to become a pillar of Sufism. Thus, when one disdains the world as nothing, he easily passes away into God. Man must die to self and the world in order to live in God.

Al-Junaid of Baghdad (9th–10th cent.) says that man searches

to be as he was, as a lover yearning for his beloved, enjoying
the suffering of separation. "He makes them absent [from this
world] when they are in union with him, and makes them
present [in this world] when he has separated them from himself." When they are separated, they seek God in his creation.
By combining union and separation al-Junaid avoids the apotheosis of man which some say his contemporary al-Hallaj
preached.

> I am he whom I love and he whom I love is I.
> We are two spirits dwelling in one body.
> When you see me, you see him.
> And when you see him, then you see us both. (RMI, 34)

Al-Hallaj was crucified for his heresy.
The love allegory is popular with the Sufis. Thus al-Huri:

> So passionate my love is, I do yearn
> To keep his memory constantly in mind.
> But O, the ecstasy with which I burn
> Sears out my thoughts and strikes my memory blind.
> And, marvel upon marvel, ecstasy
> Itself is swept away, now far now near.
> My lover stands, and all the faculty
> Of memory is swept up in hope and fear.
>
> Lo! I have severed every thought from me
> And died to selfhood, that I might be yours.
> How long, my heart's beloved? I am spent!
> I can no longer endure this banishment.[13]

Medieval Theosophy

Sufi sects grew up based on the teachings of their founders.
But when orthodox Moslems called the Sufi heretics, they re-
sponded that the basic Sufi teachings go back to the Prophet.
Al-Makki (10th cent.) abhors the abstract scholasticism of

his time. "Gone now was the instruction [*ilm*] of the Pious, vanished the intuitive knowledge [*ma'rifa*] of the firm of faith —the teachings of piety, the inspiration of rectitude and belief."[14]

It was the old battle between the learned scholastics (*ulama*) and the romancers called gnostics (*'arifin*). It seems that some of the former had little grounding in religion or faith. In the tenth and eleventh centuries attempts were made to correct Sufi aberrations and to systematize Sufi thought. Also some tried to reconcile the Sufi way with orthodoxy.

Al-Qushairi (11th cent.) wrote his *Risala*,[15] a classical description of the Sufi mystical way in which he draws the important distinction between *maqam* (station), progress by the mystic's own effort, and *hal* (state), a free spiritual gift of God. The *maqam* is earned, while the *hal* is a grace. Sufi synergism with man and God working together toward salvation and union, with man taking the first steps, reminds one of other ascetical traditions.[16]

The first *maqam* is *tauba* (conversion), the determination to abandon the world and devote oneself to the service of God. Perhaps a parallel here might be the Christian call to the monastery or religious life. Other stations are: *mujahada*, a striving for the mystic way; *khalwa wa'uzla*, seclusion or withdrawal; *taqwa*, awe of God; and *wara*, abstaining.

The last three steps in the Sufi way to God are *hal*, where God takes over. First, *ma'rifa* (gnosis), a special secret knowledge which comes into the mystic's heart only when he has stilled all its motions. Then *mahabba* (love), which is the result of God's love for man. And finally *shauq*, a yearning to be constantly with God.

One of the greatest reconcilers of Sufism with orthodoxy is the Persian al-Ghazali (11th–12th cent.), who converted to the Sufi way at the age of thirty-six.

> Once I had been a slave: lust was my master,
> Lust then became my servant, I was free:

Leaving the haunts of men, I sought your presence,
Lonely, I found in you my company.
Not in the market place is found the treasure,
Nor by the ignorant, who know not you
Who taunt me, thinking that my search is folly.
But at the end, you will be found with me. (RMI, 67)

The mystical way drew al-Ghazali—stressing experience over words.

I apprehended that the mystics were men who had real experiences, not men of words, and that I had already progressed as far as was possible by way of intellectual apprehension. What remained for me was not to be attained by oral instruction and study but only by immediate experience and by walking in the mystical way.[17]

Neo-Platonism was strong at the time, with men like al-Farabi and Ibn Sina (Avicenna), though many objected to their positions which seemed to contradict Islamic tradition. Al-Ghazali incorporated some of their theories, while rejecting others.

It cannot be denied that where beauty is perceived, it is natural to love it, and if it is certain that God is beauty, he must be loved by that one to whom his beauty and his majesty are revealed in God and in him alone are all these causes of love combined and all things loveable found in their highest perfection. . . .
Finally man loves God, because of the affinity between the human soul and its source, for it shares in the divine nature and attributes, because through knowledge and love it can attain to eternal life and itself become godlike. Such love when it has grown strong and overwhelming is called passion ['ishq] which has no meaning but that of love firmly established and limitless. It is reasonable to give this passionate love to that one from whom all good things are seen to come. (RMI, 71)

Especially with his Ihya 'Ulum al-Din (*Revival of the Religious Sciences*), in which he discusses epistemology, theology, law, mysticism, etc., al-Ghazali made the Sufi mystical way acceptable to Islam alongside law and the speculation of the theologians.

One of the greatest of the medieval Arab mystic theologians is Ibn al-Arabi (12th–13th cent.). Born in Murcia, Spain, he studied Sufism at Seville, traveled in the East, finally settling in Damascus. He has been called the greatest mystical genius of the Arabs and seems to make use of many systems, including both Sunni and Sufi.

Al-Arabi teaches a sainthood (*wilaya*) in which all the prophets and saints are manifestations of the spirit or reality of Mohammed. As Mohammed is the Seal of the prophets, so al-Arabi is the Seal of the saints. He would influence both Moslem and Christian mystics.

Al-Arabi is ecumenical, reflecting, perhaps, his Spanish origins encompassing the three great religions. Ecumenism is natural to the mystics, who cherish direct union with God rather than the mediation of priests and churches. Thus M. Smith writes: "Because to the Sufis love was the real essence of all religion, most of them, but especially the later Sufis, were universalists, admitting all faiths to contain something of the truth and all worshippers, who were lovers of God, to be striving towards the same goal."[18]

Al-Arabi comments:

My heart can take on any appearance. The heart varies in accordance with variations of the innermost consciousness. It may appear in form as a gazelle meadow, a monkish cloister, an idol temple, a pilgrim Ka'bah, the tablets of the Torah for certain sciences, the bequest of the leaves of the Koran.

My duty is the depth of love. I accept freely and willingly whatever burden is placed on me. Love is as the love of lovers, except that instead of loving the phenomenon, I love the essential. That religion, that duty, is mine, and is my faith. A purpose of human love is to demonstrate ultimate, real love. This is the love which is conscious, the other is that which makes man unconscious of himself.[19]

Human love reflects the divine. "The ordinary lover adores a secondary phenomenon. I love the real." The ravishing beauty of a lovely young girl should turn one higher. "If someone seeking her, lowers his aspirations [to feel in terms of ordinary love] —there are always others who will not do so."[20]

Let us turn for a moment to the Persian Sufi poets of the Middle Ages, didactic, romantic, and lyrical. Ansari (11th cent.) speaks of divine love as an intoxication greater than the bliss of wine.

> I am intoxicated with love of You
> And need no fermented wine.
> I am your bird
> Free from need of seed
> And safe from the snare of the fowler.
> In the Ka'bah and in the temple
> You are the object of my search.
> Else I am freed
> From both these places of worship . . .
>
> O Lord, intoxicate me with the wine
> Of your love.
> Place the chains of slavery on
> My feet;
> Make me empty of all but your love,
> And in it destroy me and bring me
> Back to life.
> The hunger you have awakened culminates
> In fulfillment.

Ansari laments the pleasures of the world that had taken him away from true love.[21]

One of the most famous Persian poets is Jalal-ud-din Rumi

(13th cent.), founder of the Mevlevi order of dervishes. Rumi summed up Persian Sufi traditions of love, especially in his *Mathnawi*.

Early the language of human romance had been used in Sufi literature to explain the experience of the love of God as it had been applied in many other religious traditions. Love allegories abound in the Persian authors. For example, the story of Joseph and Potiphar's wife. The "Ghazal," a short Arabic love poem, the sweet talk of youths and maidens, was borrowed by the Persians.

The imagery of the allegories is ambivalent, showing the human side with its divine application.[22] Thus *rukh* (face) becomes the revelation of divine beauty in attributes of grace. *Zulf* (tress) is the divine majesty seen in attributes of omnipotence. *Lab* (lip) is the life-giving property of God and his keeping man in existence, while *sharab* (wine) is the ecstatic experience of the beloved destroying the foundations of reason.

The allegories of love, worship, faithlessness, and shame prompt the lyrics of Sana'i, Rumi, and other Persian poets. But there is an ambivalence in these love poems as there is in the Hebrew Greatest Song. In other words, where does the human love end and the divine begin?

Arberry notes that several of the Sufi bards also honored kings and princes as court poets. So their poems are double allegories. "The reference is made simultaneously to the Divine Beloved, and to the very earthly patron whose favor is no less difficult to win."[23] So God shares with a human beloved the poet's passion.

The same could also be said of the wine allegory. Does it mean spiritual intoxication or bodily or both?

Let us see some of Rumi's imagery first in his lyrical poems *Diwan-i Sahms-i Tabriz*.

That spirit which wears not true love as a garment is better not to have been. Its being is nothing but a disgrace.

Be drunk in love, for love is all that exists. Without the commerce of love there is no admittance to the beloved.

They say "What is love?" Say "the abandonment of free will." He who has not escaped out of free will, no free will has he.

The lover is an emperor. The two worlds are scattered over him, and the king pays no heed to the scattering.

Love it is and the lover that remain till all eternity. Set not your heart on aught but this, for it is merely borrowed.

How long will you embrace a dead beloved? Embrace the soul which naught embraces.

What was born of spring dies in the season of autumn: Love's rose bower receives no replenishment from spring.

The rose that comes of spring, the thorn is its companion. The wine that comes of pressed grapes is not exempt from crop-sickness.

Be not an expectant spectator on this path; for by Allah there is no death worse than expectancy.[24]

Perhaps Rumi's greatest mystical verse is his *Mathnawi*, a poem in rhyming couplets. Here he recounts the story of a lover who had given up all for his beloved.

For your sake I did such and such, in this war I suffered [wounds from] arrows and spears. Wealth is gone and strength is gone and fame is gone. On account of my love for you many a misfortune has befallen me. No dawn found me asleep or laughing. No eve found me with capital and means. . . .

His beloved responds:

You have done all this. Yet open your ear wide and apprehend well. For you have not done what is the root of love and fealty. This what you have done is only the branches.

What is the root?

The root thereof is to die and be naught. You have done all [else but] you have not died. You are still living. Hark, die if you are a self-sacrificing friend.[25]

Sufi love is irrational.

When you gamble away [sacrifice] your intelligence in love of the Lord, he gives you ten like it or seven hundred. Those women [of Egypt] when they gambled away [sacrificed] their intelligences, sped onward to the pavillion of Joseph's love.

[Love which is] the cupbearer of life took away their intelligence in one moment. They drank their fill of wisdom all the rest of their lives.

The beauty of the almighty is the source of a hundred Josephs.

O you who are less than a woman, devote yourself to that beauty.

O [dear] soul, love alone cuts disputation short, for it [alone] comes to the rescue when you cry for help against arguments.

Eloquence is dumfounded by love. It dare not engage in altercation.

For he [the lover] fears that, if he answer back, a pearl [his inner experience] may fall out of his mouth. (5/3236-42)

Moorish Love Songs

Let us now see some Spanish Sufi love poems which inspired the medieval troubadours of courtly love and the mystics, while the Arab philosophers made their impact on the universities.

In the eighth century Moslems under Tariq and Musa b.

Nusayr invaded Spain. But there was anarchy and confusion until the Berber tribes came in from North Africa. The Berber chief Abdul-Rahman kept the Arabs and Christians in check, with his dynasty lasting 250 years. By the ninth century the Malikite tradition of the East became the law of Spain. And in the tenth century Abdul-Rahman III consolidated Spain, uniting Arabs and Spaniards into a high culture.

Romantic poetry became popular, anticipating medieval chivalry: songs of beauty, the rejected lover and the cruel lady. For example, al-Mutamid, eleventh-century king of Seville, in "The Letter":

> I wrote, and in my heart was burning
> The grief of parting and that yearning
> They only realize.
> Who lose eternal paradise.
> My pen no single letter traced.
> But that my tears as swiftly raced
> To write upon my cheek
> The words anguished heart would speak.
> But for the quest of glory high
> My lovesick heart were lief to fly
> To thee this hour, as flows
> The dew upon the waking rose.[26]

The *zajal* and *muwashshah* are favorite poem types with rhyming stanzas and subordinate rhymes punctuating the verses. A golden age of literature flourished under Abdul-Rahman III and his successor, Hakam II. A large library was founded as well as schools and a university at Cordova (10th cent.).

The eleventh century saw the fall of the Spanish Umayyads, and though Cordova was still the literary center, independent dynasties flourished at Seville, Almería, Badajoz, Granada, etc.

When al-Mutamid of Seville feared the Franks, he asked help from the Berbers of North Africa, defeating Alfonso IV in 1086. The age of tyrants began and a literary age dawned with poets in every Andalusian court.

For example, Ibn Zaydun (11th cent.) writes to his beloved Wallada:

> All stirs in me the memory of that fire
> Which in my tortured breast will ne'er expire.
> Had death come ere we parted, it had been
> The best of all days in the world I ween.
> And this poor heart, where you are everything,
> Would not be fluttering now on passion's wing.
> Ah, might the zephyr waft me tenderly,
> Worn out with anguish as I am, to you.[27]

The greatest poet of the age is Ibn Hazm of Cordova (11th cent.), who came from a family of Christian converts to Islam. He wrote many works, including *The Ring of the Dove* (*Tauck al-Numara*).

Of its three sections, the first describes the root principles of love—the signs of love, those who fall in love while asleep, by description, at first sight, etc. The second explains the accidents of love and good and bad attributes, such as a helping friend, union, and secrets. And the third talks of the misfortunes of love: the reproacher, spy, slanderer, the last two chapters treating of the vileness of sin and the virtue of continence.

What is love? There are many varieties.

> The noblest sort of love is that which exists between persons who love each other in God: either because of an identical zeal for the righteous work upon which they are engaged, or as the result of a harmony in sectarian belief and principles or by virtue of a common possession of some noble knowledge.[28]

Other loves are based on kinship, familiarity, comradeship, elevation, on a shared secret, and passionate love of union of souls. But all of these loves increase or decrease with their causes. "The only exception is the love of true passion which has the mastery of the soul. This is the love which passes not away save with death." True love is a fusion of souls!

Love—May God exalt you!—is in truth a baffling ailment and its remedy is in strict accord with the degree to which it is treated. It is a delightful malady, a most desirable sickness. Whoever is free of it likes not to be immune, and whoever is struck down by it yearns not to recover. (31)

The signs of love are well known. The brooding gaze at the beloved. The lover centers his talk on his desire. He is confused and excited when he unexpectedly meets her. He will give to the limit of his capacity and delights at finding himself in a narrow space with her. He is depressed at separation and heals quickly any contentions. He desires to hear his beloved's name and has a fondness for solitude. Sleepless, he wastes away.

Trepidation anticipates meeting the beloved, or when an obstacle prevents it, weeping is another sign of love, as is close attention to everything the beloved does.

What about love at first sight? Ibn Hazm replies:

I indeed marvel profoundly at all those who pretend to fall in love at first sight. I cannot easily prevail upon myself to believe their claim and prefer to consider such love as merely a kind of lust. As for thinking that that sort of attachment can really possess the inmost heart, and penetrate the veil of the soul's recess, that I cannot under any circumstances credit. Love has never truly gripped my bowels, save after a long lapse of time and constant companionship with the person concerned, sharing with him all that while my every occupation, be it earnest or frivolous. (56)

There is an agony in separation from the beloved.

Life holds no joy for me, and I do nothing but hang my head and feel utterly cast down. Ever since I first tasted the bitterness of being separated from those I love. It is an anguish that constantly revisits me, an agony of grief that ceases not for a moment to assail me. My remembrance of past happiness has abated for me every joy that I may look for in the future. I am a dead man, though counted among the living. Slain by sorrow and buried by sadness, entombed while yet a dweller in the face of this mortal earth. Allah be praised, whatever be the circumstances that befall us. There is indeed no other God but he. (56)

In love the lover submits totally to the beloved.

One of the wonderful things that occur in love is the way the lover submits to the beloved and adjusts his own character by main force to that of his loved one. Often and often you will see a man stubborn by disposition, intractable, jibbing at all control, determined, arrogant, always ready to take umbrage. Yet no sooner let him sniff the soft air of love, plunge into its waves and swim in its sea, than his stubbornness will have suddenly changed to docility, his intractability to gentleness, his determination to easy-going, his arrogance to submission. (87)

Nothing surpasses union with the beloved.

> One day, I answer, she I love
> All other earthly things above
> Lay in my arms, and like a thought
> Her lips with mine I sinfully sought.
> And though the years before I die
> Stretch out interminably, I
> Shall only count my life in truth
> As that brief hour of happy youth. (119)

When the lover at last sees his long separated beloved, she is withered and bewildered.

Women are as aromatic herbs which if not well tended soon lose their fragrance. They are as edifices which if not constantly cared for, quickly fall into ruin. Therefore, it has been said that manly beauty is the truer, the more solidly

established, and of higher excellence, since it can endure—
and that without shelter—onslaughts the merest fraction of
which would transform the loveliness of a woman's face
beyond recognition. Such enemies as the burning heat of the
noon day, the scorching wind of the desert, every air of
heaven, and the changing moods of the seasons. (214)

Ibn Hazm cherishes chastity and union of spirit as more
beautiful than union of body.

The finest quality that a man can display in love is continence; to abstain from sin and all indecency. For so he will
prove himself to be not indifferent to the heavenly reward,
that eternal bliss reserved by God for those who dwell in his
everlasting kingdom. Neither will he disobey his master who
has been so gracious to him . . . (262)

Sometimes the greatest act of love can be abstention.
The ideal of passion is frequently sung in Moorish love poems. Thus Ibn al-Farid (12th–13th cent.) chants:

> Inflict upon me what trials and travails
> Soever you will, save only that of banishment
> From your presence. I shall ever remain
> Your faithful and submissive lover; I shall
> Ever employ industry to forestall your wishes.[29]

Moorish poetry was meant to be sung. So Arab verses had to
be adapted with shorter lines, each line divided by a middle
pause. There were two main types of poetry, one learned and
literary and the other popular. Though the popular was looked
down upon, some men of letters tried their hand at it.
For example, Ibn Quzman of Cordova (12th cent.), who
raised the popular *zajal* to literary rank, writes of love as a
passion.

Love is a burden. What heart were stout enough to bear
its load, did not beauty quicken the spirit and multiply its
power. . . . The very victims of love are grateful for their

sufferings and sing the praises of the power that anguishes them. (*zajal* 117)

Augustine, centuries before, had described love as a weight, as we have seen.

Quzman continues: "O joy of love! In you is life, in you is death! Since my eyes met yours, I am like to die, and no pang equals what I endure." (*zajal* 115)[30]

Moorish poetry probably influenced the troubadours of Provence. The first troubadour, William of Poitiers, had connections with Spain by marriage and expeditions. In fact, in the twelfth century the land of the troubadours was a part of Spain, with Alfonso II of Aragon holding rights over the county of Toulouse.

Domains of Provence were part of the kingdom of Aragon till the annexation of Languedoc to France in the thirteenth century. The troubadours went back and forth. And the Moslems and Christians seemed to peacefully coexist until the Berber invasion of the twelfth century.

The Spanish contact with the Moslems turned the courts of Castile and Aragon into splendid affairs with poets, troubadours, jongleurs, music, and dancing. Moorish jongleurs and jongleresses were popular in Europe and the toing and froing of the troubadours helped the Moorish love songs to inspire Provençal bards. And Spanish Sufi illuminists may have swayed the great Dante (13th cent.).

Another Christian mystic, Ramón Lull (13th cent.), also shows Sufi strains in his book of the Lover and Beloved, which would later inspire Teresa of Avila.

Let us now turn for a moment to the Sufi orders which did so much to spread the Islamic doctrine of divine love.

Sufi Orders of Love

Islamic asceticism started with individuals much as its counterpart in other traditions.[31] Gradually disciples gathered around the heroes and began the teacher-disciple relationship so central to Sufism (*shaikh-murid*). Convents were founded in which the saint taught and where his followers resided and learned and prayed with him. Initiation came with the donning of the *khirqa* frock.

By the twelfth century these isolated convents had banded together into Sufi ways (*tariqa*) or brotherhoods following the way of a certain master with their own rituals and disciplines.

The number of professional Sufis residing in convents and performing the rituals is small, while the number of laity who follow the services is large. Sufi ways are not monastic orders as in other cultures, though there are some semblances.

Sufi orders had rules for common life concerning cleanliness, gossip, prayer, reading of the Koran, reciting *dhikri*, kindness to the poor and needy, etc.[32]

> Furthermore, let them spend their hours of leisure in one of three things: either in the study of theology or in some devotional exercise (*wirdi*) or in bringing comfort to some one. Whosoever loves this community and helps them as much as he can is a sharer in their merit and future recompense.[33]

Parallels are found in other monastic traditions.

Interestingly, the *shaikh* is not mentioned in the Sufi rules. He is a guide in spiritual matters, a teacher but not an abbot or superior. Rather obedience is to the community.

Certain classes of people, occupational guilds, districts and towns, were linked with the orders. Also some had circles of women.

Some Sufis seem to have been celibate. Separate *khanaqah* (cloisters) were instituted for the married whose wives and children lived in separate compounds. In general, Sufi, like other monks, felt that family life did not ease the path to divine union.

Each order has its own ritual (*tariqa*) based on *dikr*, or recollection, leading to union with God, especially reciting the names of God. Breath control, music, dancing, teaching, and singing helped.

When one joins a Sufi way, he removes himself from the world and directs himself to God along the approved path, transcending self but not necessarily a mystical experience, though this often follows.

From the twelfth century there was an ordering of the mystical experience. "The realization that this experience can be induced for the ordinary man in a relatively short space of time by rhythmical exercises: posture, breath control, coordinated movements, and oral repetitions." Analogous approaches can be found in yoga.

Dervishes used every technique to open up to the supernatural, including sacred numbers and symbols, colors, perfumes, incense, rituals, invocations, and even drugs. Their goal seemed to be more ecstasy (*wajd*) than God encounter. The Sufi way is for the elite who have a certain mystical sensitivity. But the orders tried by their devotional techniques to give this illusion to the ordinary man, though some felt this to be a degeneration.

> For the ordinary lay member, participation in the ritual of the *dikr*, which for him only occasionally leads to the trance-ecstasy, provides at lowest a release from the hardships of everyday existence, and, at a higher level, some measure of freedom from the limitations of human life and a glimpse at the transcendental experience (*hal*).[34]

Sufism declined (15th–16th cent.) when cultivation of saints, superstition, and magic overshadowed the speculation and orthodox piety of the great mystics. Contempt for rituals, omission of prayers, and scorn for learning grew.

The orders ruled the masses and politics led to further abuses with each village dominated by a local saint. Yet even in its darkest hour Sufism boasted some men of genuine piety, such as al-Sha' Rani (15th–16th cent.), and new orders continued to develop into modern times, such as the Tijaniya and

Sanusiyya, the former more peaceful, while the latter had military and political ambitions.

In later chapters we will see the Christian troubadours and mystics inspired by the Sufi love poets. But first a look at the Jewish Kabbalah, another medieval love sect which grew up alongside Islamic and Christian love.

❦ XI ❧

THROUGH HIS UNION WITH THE SHEKHINAH HE HAS BECOME MALE AND FEMALE

Zohar, 1/49b

We have seen the love of God and man in the Hebrew Bible. God loves Israel as a man should love his wife. Though the Prophets experienced mystical love, it was not as popular among the scholarly rabbis.

H. Gersh clarifies the purpose of Jewish mysticism. "God cannot be perceived by the senses, and only dimly, if at all, by the intellect. He can be experienced only through a mystic union between man and the heavens."[1] Thus man can bring himself closer to the End of Days, the World to Come, and the Time of the Messiah. The mystical experience is a prolepsis of that of the Messianic Age or Heaven.

Intermediaries play a strong part in Jewish mysticism, for they are the links between God and man. The mystic secrets are not received through contemplation or by philosophical speculation but by psychic experience. In a sense this is a type of direct experience rather than through rabbis and torahs, though Scripture, prayer, and ritual also are used by the Jewish mystics.

Gersh comments: "Jewish mysticism is essentially an attempt to harmonize universal reason with the Scriptures. And the allegorical interpretations by the (philosophical) Aristotelians as well as the (symbolic) Palestinians may justly be regarded as its starting point."[2]

Jewish mystic trends began early. We find them in the Prophets. In the first century Philo writes about the Platonic emanations. The rabbis speculated on the mysteries of Genesis and the visions of Ezekiel, using foreign themes with upper and lower worlds, angels and demons. But they looked with suspicion on those who tried to pierce the divine mysteries.

During the Ghonic period after the close of the Talmud, books on mysticism appeared, such as *Hekalot* (*Halls*) and *Sefer Yetzirah* (*Book of Formation or Creation*) (8th cent.), combining Jewish mysticism, Platonic emanations, and the magical use of letters and numbers. In the early medieval period Jewish mysticism moved from Babylonia and Palestine to Europe.

A spur to the growth of Judaism especially in Spain was Jewish liberation from the Visigoths by the conquering Arabs (8th cent.). I. Zinberg remarks: "In a few generations these Spanish Jews, no longer spiritually impoverished, became the most important bearers of culture, both general and Jewish. And for this they were indebted mainly to their liberators and teachers, the Arabs."[3]

Arabs and Jews speaking a common language interacted and developed a marvelous culture. Zinberg adds:

> Under the influence of the rich and beautiful Arabic, refined taste developed among the Spanish Jews, and the feeling for beauty produced an interest in the poetic treasures of the bible and the language in which it was written. As Arabic poetry flowered in Spain [10th cent.], the Jews became envious, and among them the desire arose to create not only religious but secular poetry in Hebrew, employing Arabic form and principles of meter.[4]

The Sufi, too, inspired Jewish mystic trends in Spain. For example, Bayha ben Joseph Ibn Pakuda's *Hovot ha Levavot*

(11th cent.) is divided into ten gates parallel to the ten levels
that the Sufi must traverse to reach the true love of God.

The Greatest Song, celebrating the marriage of Yahweh and
Israel, was a favorite of Jewish poets. For example, Ibn Gabirol
(11th cent.):

> Arise, open the locked gate
> And send back to me the hart that has fled.
> On the day you return to me
> You will rest between my breasts,
> There you will place upon me your sweet odor.
> —Tell me, O lovely bride,
> How does your beloved look,
> The beloved whom you bid me send back to you?
> Is he beautiful-eyed, ruddy and lovely to look at?
> —My friend and my beloved is this,
> Arise now, anoint him.[5]

By the thirteenth century there were two schools of Jewish
thought in Spain, the abstract speculative philosophers of the
Maimonides school and the mystical strain of the Kabbalah,
teaching the "torah of the heart."

Kabbalah romanticism seemed to appeal more to lower
classes who could not comprehend the noetic games of the
philosophers. Perhaps a parallel might be drawn between the
early Jewish scholarly halakists and the popular haggadists
who preached to the common people. Islam, too, had its philosophers and Sufi poets, head and heart, as we have seen.

Persecution, too, stimulated mysticism. Disillusioned with
the world, the mystics long for the divine.

Primordial Hierogamy

Before looking more closely at the Kabbalah teaching on love,
we should see something of the masculine and feminine in
God. Why? Human love imitates and reiterates the divine.

Man can best picture God in a human manner, for he is made in God's image.

Primitive man saw life beginning with the primordial hierogamy, the divine marriage of the sky god and the earth goddess. Many early creation accounts describe this mating.

The Hebrew creation story, however, has God creating by himself without the aid of a female partner, though eventually the Hebrews did develop masculine and feminine aspects in God which culminated in the mating of the divine King with his Shekhinah in the Kabbalist tradition.

We have seen in an earlier chapter the Torah theme of Israel as the wife of Yahweh, with the Torah as the marriage contract and the exile a punishment for the adulterous wife. Later the Kabbalists would celebrate, in a special manner, Pentecost, the Feast of Weeks, commemorating the marriage of Yahweh and Israel.

The masculine and feminine in the godhead may be reflected in the temple cherubim locked in marital embrace. In the second temple pilgrims were allowed to see the male and female cherubim intertwined. The custom may have been introduced in the third century B.C. under Greek or Egyptian influence. The priests cried out: "Behold your love before God is like the male and female." (B. Yoma, 54a) On the seventh day of Succoth (Booths) there was a great rejoicing in male and female.

R. Patai feels that the view of the cherubim in sexual embrace may have fired orgiastic unions.[6] This had happened before at the sight of the golden calf in the desert. (Ex 32/6)

Orgy has traditionally been associated with fertility rites of cosmogonic and hierogamic myths and cycles. Sometimes it played out the chaos which preceded the order of creation at the New Year. In the last century of the second temple the sages put a stop to the orgies by placing the women in the balcony.

Philo of Alexandria (1st cent. A.D.) sees a masculine and feminine aspect of God. Taking the middle ground between

the Biblical literalists and the radical allegorists, he tries to
show the compatibility of the Greek Prime Mover with the
Jewish personal God.

In describing creation, Philo speaks more of procreation.
God the Father, Reason, unites with the Mother, who is God's
Knowledge and Wisdom. The Mother, receiving the seed of
God's Reason, begets her only son, the visible world.[7] God is
the husband, Reason, dropping his seed of happiness for the
race of mortals into the virgin soil.

Patai outlines Philo's parallels in the godhead.[8] Thus Elohim
and Yahweh parallel father and mother, husband and wife,
creator and nurturer, reason and wisdom, gentle and chastis-
ing, masculine and feminine cherubs. In Philo's scheme the
mother is educator and chastiser, while the father is compassionate. This bifold view of God is seen also in the Talmud and
flourishes later in the Kabbalah.

But there was a fear among the rabbis of separating the
divine hypostases and so lead to polytheism. At this period
the Christian Trinity was being formulated and some would
say that this belief was one cause in the final split between
Christianity and Judaism. Rabbi Eliezer cries out: "If he trans-
lates [and they saw the God of Israel] 'And they saw the glory
of the Shekhinah of the God of Israel,' he blasphemes because
he makes three [deities], namely, glory, Shekhinah and God."
(Mid. Hag. Ex 555)

Patai sees no great problem in different aspects or manifestations of the godhead since divine indeterminacy may be
seen even in the Bible.[9] For example, when God appears to
Abraham as three men. (Gen 18) So there is no impending
catastrophe in divine pluralism, as we shall see in the Kabbalah.

The Kabbalah

Judaism had traditionally resisted the pantheistic and cosmological myths of the East which unified God, man, and the world of nature. There had long been a rift in Judaism between the scholarly halakic rabbis poring over the books of the Law and the popular maggids with their haggadic stories so appealing to the laity.

The medieval Jewish philosophers more in the halakic style wanted a pure God unencumbered by myth and anthropomorphism.[10]

The Kabbalah is the medieval counterpart of the Haggadah, filled with myths, stories, wonders, appealing more to the common people.

Kabbalah means tradition. "The very doctrine of which centres about the immediate personal contact with the divine, that is to say, a highly personal and intimate form of knowledge is conceived as traditional wisdom."[11] This is the secret tradition of deep mysteries for the chosen few who pass it on to their disciples. At certain periods the Kabbalist influence widened to include many, showing them God's secret revelations to Adam.

To the Kabbalists the unity of God is not a philosophical proof but a living dynamic unity.

What to the Jewish theologians were the attributes of God, are to the Kabbalists potencies, hypostases, stages in an intradivine process. And it is not for nothing that the images with which he describes God are first and foremost images pertaining to the organism.[12]

The Kabbalah tended to restore the mythical character of the Torah which had been lost by the rabbis in their divorce of law from history. Kabbalah restores the Torah as a *corpus mysticum* rather than a desiccated body of law, symbols replacing concepts. Foreign myths inspired Kabbalah as well as a natural psychological development, and the problem of evil asserted itself in a complex demonology that appealed to the masses.

The ten Sephirot are central to Kabbalah. Mediating between Heaven and earth, they are the channels through which God's purely spiritual power becomes physically creative. They are divine manifestations, emanations through which God is known. The Sephirot had names, qualities, gender, and color. They are: Kether (crown), old one; Hochmah (wisdom) (m.); Binah (understanding) (f.); Hesed (kindness) (m.); Geborah (power) (f.); Tipheret (glory or beauty) (m. and f.); Hod (splendor) (f.); Yesod (foundation); Malkut (kingdom), called Shekhinah (f.).

Man has a threefold soul: *neshamah* (intellect), *ruah* (emotion), and *nefesh* (animal nature), represented by groups of three Sephirot starting from the top.

How did the Sephirot develop and why? They restored myth once again to the creation account over against the philosophical *creatio ex nihilo*, with the world of divine being overflowing into the worlds of creation. God overcomes nothingness, the first and highest Sephirah, and the second is the World Seed.

It is the World Seed, the supreme formative and male-paternal potency, which is sown in the primordial womb of the Supernal Mother; who is the product but also the counterpart of the original point. Fertilized in this womb, the World Seed—through her—emanates the other seven potencies, which the Kabbalists interpret as the archetypes of all creation, but also as the seven "first days" of the first chapters of Genesis or, in other words, as the original stages of interdivine development.[13]

The primordial man, Adam Kadmon, is another central theme in the Kabbalah. Similar to Philo's existential man, he reflected in himself all of creation—e.g., the ten Sephirot. After creation the Holy One is experienced as the Heavenly Man. Thus the first Sephirah, Kether, is his head, Hochmah brain, Binah heart, Yesod genitals, etc.

For the Kabbalists, the Torah was created before the world. So the letters of the Torah are primordial and have mystical powers. Each letter has a numerical value leading to magical sequences and magic words. Thus the numerical value of God (Yahweh) equals the numerical value of Adam.

Gersh sums up the Kabbalist contribution to Judaism:

> In the end Kabbalah served two major purposes. It elevated prayer, the mystic union of man with God, to a central position in Judaism, whereas formal Talmudic study tended to deemphasize it; and it moved the Jews away from the dead end of Aristotelianism. But in so doing, Kabbalah also gave to Judaism—particularly to the Chasidim—a burden of magic and superstition that was foreign to its ethical rationalistic basis.[14]

The Shekhinah

The Shekhinah becomes God's feminine presence and consort in Kabbalist literature. She was seen in a shadowy way in the visible divine presence as a cloud in the temple.

God's Wisdom (Hochmah) is hypostatized in the late Biblical period, and in the Wisdom of Solomon (8/3) is seen as God's wife.

In the Talmud the Shekhinah dwells in the temple until sin drives her out. (*Rab*, 12/6) She accompanies Israel in exile and consorts with Moses when he separates from his wife. (*B. Shab.*, 87a) She helps the sick and repentent sinners. She rests between husband and wife in the marriage bed, rests on the wise, rich, heroes, etc.

Is the Shekhinah an angel? No, she is above the angels, for they must cover their faces before her splendor. By the third century we find the Shekhinah confronting God as Israel's Paraclete.

The Christians, too, had a great devotion to the Paraclete, who was a member of the divine family along with the Father and the Son. Does the Christian Holy Spirit have any of the feminine nuances of the Jewish? She, too, is the soul of the body of the church, which is the spouse of Christ. Moreover, in the early church hierarchy the deaconesses were seen as the images of the Holy Spirit.[15]

There was a gradual evolution of the Shekhinah from the early presence of God to a personification closely associated with Israel. And the distance grew between the Shekhinah and God. Thus she acts in an anthropomorphic manner with a voice of her own that sounds like the tinkling of a bell or the chirping of a bird.

In the *Bahir* (12th-cent. Provence work) the Shekhinah becomes a quasi-independent feminine aspect of God. In the Sephirot there are upper and lower Shekhinot. Thus the third Sephirah, Binah, is the upper mother or upper Shekhinah from whom the other seven potencies emanate. Of these the first six are parts of the primordial man's body and epitomized in the phallic "foundation" (Yesod), which is also symbolic of the righteous one (Zaddik), who keeps the genitals under control.

The tenth Sephirah, the lower Shekhinah, is not strictly a part of man but rather his female complement, as mother, sister, wife, and daughter. According to the Kabbalists, following many primordial cosmogonic myths, the pre-existing soul of man is androgynous. The two halves split, with one half going to the male child and the other half to the female. Thus man must search out his "better half."

In the *Bahir* the Shekhinah is the personification of the feminine aspect. She is identified both with the mystical body of Israel and with man's soul (*neshamah*). Moreover, she is ambivalent—both merciful mother of Israel and stern judge.

The Shekhinah's exile is a forceful theme in the Kabbalah. In the Talmud the Shekhinah accompanied Israel in her exile, whereas in the Kabbalah a part of God is exiled from himself. The queen or daughter of the king is banished and sometimes is even overpowered by the other side. Sin separates the masculine and feminine in God.

Adam's sin is repeated in our own. Adam's mistake was that instead of contemplating all the Sephirot, he concentrated on the last one, the Shekhinah, mistaking it for the whole godhead. Since then there has been a cleavage between the upper and lower, masculine and feminine, the tree of life and the tree of knowledge.

"For the religious feeling of the early Kabbalists the exile of the Shekhinah was a symbol of our own guilt, and the aim of religious action must be to end this exile or at least to work in this direction."[16] All is done "for the sake of the Shekhinah." Only when God is once again united to his Shekhinah can the powers of generation flow once again.

For his sin, Adam was banished and sparks of the Shekhinah were scattered everywhere. And sparks of Adam's own soul were scattered into exile, where they are dominated by the shells (*kelippoth*).

Each soul's sin relives Adam's sin and when he obeys the Law he helps bring home the fallen sparks of the Shekhinah and of his own soul as well. In her exile Israel must go throughout the world to gather the sparks of the Shekhinah by her good deeds.

The *Zohar*, a thirteenth-century work of the Spanish Kabbalist Moses de León, has much to say about the Shekhinah's antipathy to sin.[17]

The created Torah is a vestment of the Shekhinah. And if man had not been created, the Shekhinah would have been without a vestment like a beggar. Hence when a man sins, it is as though he strips the Shekhinah of her vestments. And when he carries out the precepts of the Law, it is as though he clothes the Shekhinah in her vestments. (*Zohar*, 1/23b)

It is by the sin of unchastity that the Shekhinah is banished. When man unites with the evil temptress Lilith, the Shekhinah flees, as we shall see later. As we have seen in an earlier chapter, the punishment of an adulteress in ancient Judaism was often a shameful public stripping and being sent naked into a desert exile. (Hos 2/3)

The *Zohar* teaches the necessity of the male and female in man, paralleling divine and cosmic unity.

> Adam and Eve, as we have said, were created side by side. Why not face to face? For the reason that heaven and earth were not yet in complete harmony. "The Lord God had not caused it to rain upon the earth" [Gen 2/5]. When the lower union was rendered perfect, Adam and Eve turned face to face. Then was the upper union perfected. (1/34a)

When the lower world was made perfect, the upper also was made perfect. The lower world is made to support the upper, turning face to face with it.

The mist rising up from the earth (Gen 2/6) is like the yearning of the female for the male. Without the mist from below, God will not send his rain from above. The ancient theme of the hierogamy of the sky god and the earth goddess. Applied to Israel—"If the community of Israel failed to initiate the impulse, the one above would not move to go to her, and it is thus the yearning from below which brings about the completion above."

God made man male and female. Modern anthropologists defend the early androgeneity of man. "'Let us make man!' The word Adam [man] implies male and female, created wholly through the supernal and holy wisdom. 'In our image, after our likeness,' the two being combined so that man should be unique in the world and ruler over all." (1/47a)

God gave man two inclinations (*yezerim*). "With the good

inclination for himself and the evil inclination to turn towards the female."

The good inclination and the evil inclination are in harmony only because they share the female who is attached to both. In this way first the evil inclination goes for her and they unite with one another, and when they are united, the good inclination which is joy, rouses itself and draws her to herself, and so she is shared by both and reconciles them. (1/47a)

The Lord gave man this double inclination. He made man male and female together, and not separated, so as to turn face to face. Since man was created by God male and female, he must be always male and female.

But how can a man be male and female when he is on a journey alone? When the poor man travels, the Shekhinah accompanies him. Before he sets out he should pray to the Shekhinah. "When he has offered his prayer and thanksgiving and the Shekhinah rests on him, then he can depart, for through his union with the Shekhinah he has become 'male and female' in the country as he was 'male and female' in the town." (1/49b) Furthermore, he must take care lest by sinful conduct he lose the Shekhinah.

When he returns home, he must give his wife pleasure, for she procured the Shekhinah for him. Why must he give her pleasure? "One reason is that this is a religious pleasure, and one which gives joy to the Shekhinah also. And what is more by its means he spreads peace in the world." (1/50a) And if he refuses his wife, he sins, for he takes away from his heavenly partner.

The other reason is "that if his wife becomes pregnant, the celestial partner imparts to the child a holy soul, for this covenant is called the covenant of the Holy One, Blessed be He." (1/50a) Peace is brought to the house in which the religious duty of conjugal intercourse is enjoyed with gladness in the presence of the Shekhinah. Students of the Torah set the ex-

ample by their intercourse with their wives on the Sabbath
eve.

Kabbalists kept a parallel between the primordial hierogamy
and earthly marriage. Thus the Jewish man has two females,
mother and wife, as the male God has two women. "He is
beatified by two females, one of the upper and one of the
lower world—the upper one to pour blessings upon him and
the lower one to be supported by him and to be conjoined
with him." (1/50a) On a journey he has only his celestial
mother, but while united to his wife, the upper and lower
Shekhinah are joined.

The Kabbalists, as did many other cultures, saw a divine
family: father, mother, son, and daughter. It is normal for man
to see a divine family on which his own is modeled. Even the
Christians had a divine "household" of Father, Son, and Holy
Spirit, but with little stress on the feminine aspect of the Holy
Spirit. Some see the Virgin Mary, the mother of Jesus, as a
goddess in the medieval period. Certainly she is linked with
the Shekhinah in the conception of God's Son.

The two pairs of the Kabbalist tetrad are an upper and
lower male-female, the father begetting the mother and both
together generating the son and daughter.

Father and mother are always together in androgynous
union.

> The female spread out from her place and adhered to the
> male side and she came to unite with him face to face, and
> when they were united they appeared as veritably one body,
> and from this we learn that the male alone appears as half
> a body. . . . And female likewise. But when they join in
> union, they seem as veritably one body. (3/29a)

This is especially true on the Sabbath when the Shekhinah-
Matronit clings to her King.

The androgyny of God and man are persistent themes in
the Kabbalah. Things are best when male and female are
united and things are worst when they are separated.

In most divine families mother and father slip into the background and pre-eminence is given to the son and daughter, as the younger generation takes over.

In the *Zohar* there are many names given to the son and daughter as they are seen under different aspects. Thus the son is called: King, Holy One Blessed be He, Zoharariel, Aktariel, Four God, Heaven; while the daughter is: Malkhuth, Shekhinah, Matronit, Pearl, Community of Israel, Female, Earth, Night, etc.

The son and daughter marry as the King and his Matronit or Shekhinah, and the Jerusalem temple is built for their wedding chamber. Incest among the gods should not be shocking, for it was popular in royal families. Whereas the marriage of the older couple is steady and mature, that of the young lovers is stormy. One reason for this is the close association of the Shekhinah with the people of Israel.

When Israel disappointed the King, she was sent into exile and the Shekhinah accompanied her. The final alienation came when the temple bedchamber was destroyed. But the King is weak without his Shekhinah. The separation of masculine and feminine is bad for God and man.

A man's union with his wife imitates and depends upon the divine union. In fact, they partake in each other. In a sense, when a man departs from his wife in an adulterous union, God is also separated from his Shekhinah.

Is this celestial tetrad of father, mother, son, and daughter polytheistic? Patai remarks:

> The lone, aloof God, adored by the Jews up to the time of the Kabbalist upsurge, could not satisfy the emotional craving which sought a reflection of earthly life in the heavenly realm . . . and vice versa. Human existence always appealing to Jewish consciousness in the multiple form of man, wife and children, could not be recognized as the true reflection of God, in whose image man was said to have been created, as long as that God was alone.[18]

This is why we find a divine family in most other cultures as well. The Jewish Kabbalah succeeded in removing the noncorrespondence between the divine and the human. Human marriage not only imitates the divine family but also recapitulates and even promotes it.

The Shekhinah, daughter of the celestial mother and father and wife of the King, is often called Matronit or matron in the Kabbalah. Matronit imitates many popular goddesses with seemingly contradictory qualities: chaste and promiscuous, motherly yet warlike and bloodthirsty. By Kabbalist times Matronit seems to be a full-fledged goddess distinct from her divine husband. Paradoxically she remains a virgin while at the same time a lover of gods and men. For example, Moses left his wife Zipporah in order to marry the Shekhinah-Matronit. (1/21b–22a)

As we have seen, the King and Matronit, brother and sister, are produced simultaneously, androgynously, back to back, then separated. Their wedding is described in the *Zohar-Hadash*. At midnight in the temple Matronit and the King meet, accompanied by maids and youths. When alone, they embrace and kiss and the King leads her to the couch. There, with his left hand under her head, his right arm embraces her and she presses her image on his body while he plays between her breasts. Reminiscences of the Greatest Song.

Though some say that the King comes down to his temple bed every night, others claim that he comes only on the midnight of the Sabbath. (3/296a) At this hour scholars and their wives couple in celebration of the primordial hierogamy. In one sense the human love commemorates the divine and in another sense it brings about the divine union.

Similar rites celebrating the heavenly hierogamy are seen in other cultures. For example, the human representatives of Shiva and Shakti in Hinduism. We will see more of the Jewish Sabbath rites later. Also in the human conception that corresponds to the divine, the child generated receives a soul procreated in the celestial union.

There is an annual Kabbalist cycle parallel to the yearly courses found in other religions. Thus when the people of Israel sin, their divine counterpart, Matronit, couples with Samael (Satan). (2/219b) Meanwhile the King withdraws to Heaven till the Day of Atonement, when Satan is defeated and Matronit can ascend to Heaven and her King.

When the temple bedchamber is destroyed, the King is separated from his denuded Matronit. Lonely, he takes up with a slave girl of Matronit named Lilith, while Matronit consorts with foreign gods. Yet she is still attracted to pious men who study law and do good deeds.

Matronit is the mother of Israel and her protector against sinners and pagans. She is even at times pictured as a cosmic female monster, with her son Metatron and daughters Lilith and Naamah.

Patai sees Matronit as mother, nurse, lover-bride, wife, seductress, warrior-protectress. "The goddess thus speaks to man with four tongues: keep away from me because I am a virgin; enjoy me because I am available to all; come shelter in my motherly bosom; and die in me because I thirst for your blood."[19]

Lilith Succuba

We have seen the Shekhinah-Matronit of the Kabbalists. She is the spouse of the King and blessed the union of the Jewish couples. We have also seen how the lonely King consorted with her errant handmaid Lilith.

Lilith has a long history as a she-devil going back to ancient Sumeria, 2500 B.C. There she visited men at night and bore them ghostly children. She also had a male counterpart, incubus.

One tradition has Lilith as Adam's first wife who left him and promiscuously propagated demons. She had control over small babies, but made a pact with the angels that she would not harm them if they were protected by an amulet. When Adam and Eve separated for 130 years as penance for their sins, Lilith tempted Adam, begetting demons.

Lilith is best known as the temptress of men who sleep alone, for from their seed she makes demons.

> She roams at night and goes all about the world and makes sport with men and causes them to emit seed. In every place where a man sleeps alone in a house, she visits him and grabs him and attaches herself to him and has her desire from him, and bears from him. And she also afflicts him with sickness, and he knows it not. And all this takes place when the moon is on the wane. (1/19b)

Lilith turns from her consort Samael in order to enjoy men and use their semen to produce devils. Even in lawful marital intercourse Lilith is there seeking seeds, for her consort Samael was castrated by God to keep down the demon supply. She has power over children conceived in candlelight, or with a naked wife, or at forbidden times. And she can kill these children at will. Lilith sometimes has a companion seductress, her sister Naamah, also a child killer and mother of demons.

Lilith had her hour of triumph at the destruction of the temple in Jerusalem, when the King sent away his Matronit and took Lilith as his consort. Due to the sins of Israel, Israel and the Shekhinah had to leave the King. Only when the Messiah comes—and tradition has him coming at the hour of midnight—will the King and his Matronit come together again.

As Patai remarks,[20] there are interesting parallels between Matronit and Lilith—virgin and promiscuous queen, consort of gods and men, mother and killer of children. They seem to personify the dualism of sexual love—namely, divine and diabolic. Sex can be divine, uniting the Shekhinah with her King. Or it can be illicit, joining the King with Lilith. This is the ambivalence of man himself with his twofold *yezerim*.

The Sabbath Bride

We have been primarily interested in the correlation of human and divine love in the Jewish Kabbalah. It reaches its height in the celebration of the Matronit as the Sabbath bride.

But first a few words on the Kabbalist liturgy. As we have seen, the Kabbalists fled the desiccated god of the philosophers for the more attractive ancient mythological gods with all of their richness. Scholem observes:

> Kabbalist conceptions which exerted an influence on ritual were exclusively those in which contact was renewed with a mythical stratum whether disguised in allegory or directly communicated in symbols.[21]

The sacred action, the enactment of the Law, and even pious practices (sex) are related to the mythical world. Liturgy is basically the re-enactment of myths.

But it is not just enough to perform the ritual. No. One must have a mystical intention which accompanies the act. This is *kavannah*. For example, any potent person can perform the sex act. But does this automatically unite him with the divine hierogamy? No! The rite itself is only the body of which the *kavannah* is the soul, uniting upper and lower worlds in one mystical act. Both *tikkun*, the positive restoration of right order, and *berur*, the containing of the other side, help in uniting the upper and lower worlds.

Four major themes in Kabbalist rituals are: harmony of powers of judgment and those of mercy; the sacred marriage or conjunction of masculine and feminine; redemption of the Shekhinah from her entanglement with the other side; and finally a mastery over the powers of the other side.[22]

Now let us look at some of the Kabbalist rituals that commemorate the divine hierogamy, the union of the two Sephirot, Tipheret and Malkut, the male and female aspects of God, the

King and his consort—Shekhinah and Israel. For the Kabbalists the marriage of God and Israel is the outward sign of
the interior divine marriage.

The Feast of Weeks or Pentecost commemorates the marriage of Yahweh and Israel on Mount Sinai. And there was a
special significance in the night before.

> For in this night the bride makes ready for marriage with
> the bridegroom. And it was thought fitting that all those
> "belonging to the palace of the bride" (mystics and students
> of the Torah) should keep her company and partake through
> a festive ritual in the preparation for her marriage.[23]

The mystics clothe the bride in her proper ornaments, the
twenty-four books of the Bible. He who reads selections from
the twenty-four books with mystical interpretations is called
the "Best man of the Shekhinah." And next morning when the
King comes, the bride calls her best man to her side.

From the beginning of the sixteenth century the whole night
before the Pentecostal mystic marriage was spent in songs and
in readings from the Bible, *Mishnah*, and *Zohar*. On the next
day the Torah is lifted up in the synagogue while some read
the marriage contract between the bridegroom God and the
virgin Israel.

The Sabbath is the weekly celebration of this marriage and
a special feast of the Kabbalah. The Sabbath goddess becomes
identified with the Shekhinah.[24]

Philo, looking through the eyes of others, sees the Sabbath,
seven, as a mystical number, unbegotten and unbegetting. But
for himself she is the daughter of God, begotten, motherless,
beauty, virgin, incorruptible, sovereign leader.[25]

In the Talmud, Rabbi Yannai cries out on Friday evening:
"Come, O Bride, come, O Bride." (*B. Shab*, 119a) The six
days of the week have their own pairs, but the seventh day
is the mate of the community of Israel. (Ex 20/8; *Gen. Rab.*,
11/8)

The black Jews of Ethiopia deified the Sabbath.

Those who observe the Sabbath rest and love her, are her people whom she claims for God and whom she rescues from the last judgment even if they sinned. To love and honor the Sabbath is the same as loving and honoring God.[26]

Ethiopian Christians saw a parallel between the Virgin Mary and the Sabbath and to this day the Sabbath is the special day of Mary in the Christian church.

In the Kabbalah:

The feminine Sabbath (night) is mystically identified with the Shekhinah or the Sephirah of Kingship, while the male Sabbath (day) is the Yesod (Foundation) or the Tipheret (Beauty), that is, the male aspect of the Deity. Since the Shekhinah is also identified with the Community of Israel, in this manner she becomes the bride or mate of the Sabbath-Yesod.[27]

An elaborate cushioned seat is prepared for the bride. And as the rabbis used to go out on the road singing, "Come, O Bride," so we must sing and rejoice at table. The Lady Sabbath must be received with lighted candles, beautiful clothes, and finely appointed house. This causes the evil Lilith to sulk in the dark as a widow in mourning.

The good inclination is the holy Matronit, the holy kingdom which descends on the Sabbath. . . . And the king proceeds to receive her with many hosts. And the evil inclination, the evil handmaid, remains in darkness like a widow without her husband, without a chariot. (*Zohar*, 3/272b)

In a sense, on the Sabbath eve a man must make his choice between his Sabbath bride and the evil seductress Lilith.

The Safed community in Palestine (16th cent.) had an elaborate Sabbath ritual beginning with a procession to the surrounding hills Friday evening to welcome the Sabbath, intoning the Sabbath Song (Lekha Dodi):

> Come, my friend, to meet the bride,
> Let us receive the face of the Sabbath.
> Come in peace, O crown of her husband,
> In joy and jubilation,
> Amid the faithful of the chosen people,
> Come, O Bride, come, O Bride.

The fields of Safed with the arrival of the Sabbath-Shekhinah become "the Sacred Apple Orchard" sanctified by the union of God and his bride, producing the souls of the just. (*B. Taanith,* 29b) The whole procession resembles a Jewish wedding rite in which the bride is led from her home to the wedding canopy.

When the men returned from the Sabbath ritual, they were received by their wives, the earthly representatives of the Shekhinah. "With whom he was about to perform that night the sacred act of cohabitation in imitation of and in mystical sympathy with, the supernal union between God, the King and his wife Matronit-Shekhinah-Sabbath."[28]

There in the home a liturgy similar to the wedding rites is performed with myrtle twigs, walking around the table singing songs and reciting proverbs (31/10–31) in praise of the woman of strength who as her husband's partner fulfills the Kabbalah ideal of male and female togetherness. Here the Shekhinah is identified with the wife.

During the Sabbath meal an Aramaic hymn of Isaac Luria is sung, proclaiming the union of the King with his Sabbath bride.

> Let me sing the praises of him who enters the gates
> Of the orchard of apple trees, holy are they.
> Let us invite her now, with a freshly set table,
> With a goodly lamp which sheds light on the heads
> Right and left and the bride in between

Comes forth in her jewels and sumptuous raiments.
Her husband embraces her, and with her Yesod,
Which gives her pleasure, he presses her mightily.
Cries and sighs have stopped and ceased,
New faces come, spirits and souls.
He brings her great joy, in a double measure
Light pours upon her, and blessings on end.[29]

The Sabbath evening meal lasted till midnight, when, according to Kabbalist tradition, husband and wife had intercourse, the key event of the Sabbath ritual, uniting man and wife, God and his Shekhinah.

This is especially true of the Torah students. Married to the Torah or the Shekhinah during the week, they returned to their wives Friday nights. (*Zohar*, 1/50a)

They castrate themselves for the duration of the six days of the week, tiring themselves out with the study of the Law, and on Friday night they spur themselves to copulation because they know the supernal mystery of the hour in which the Matronit couples with the King. (*Zohar*, 2/89a)

Patai comments:

In the Kabbalistic view when the learned men, familiar with the heavenly mysteries, couple with their wives on Friday nights, they do this in full cognizance of performing a most significant act in direct imitation of the union which takes place at that very time between the supernal couple. If the wife conceives at that hour, the earthly father and mother of the child can be sure that it will receive a soul from the Above, one of those pure souls which are procreated in the divine copulation of the King and Matronit. . . .

But even more than that, when a pious earthly couple performs the act, by doing so they set in motion all generative forces of the mythico-mystical universe. The human sexual act causes the king to emit his seminal fluid from his divine male genital and thus to fertilize the Matronit who gives birth to human souls and angels.[30]

If the human couple love properly, they aid the celestial hierogamy and receive as a reward a divinely procreated soul for their child. But if they couple in a sinful manner, Lilith takes over the child. Also Lilith covets wasted seed to use as bodies for her demonic sons and daughters, as we have seen.

This mutual coupling of man and wife, God and his Shekhinah, on the Sabbath midnight is a true joining of human and divine love, a uniting of Heaven and earth which is only vestigially celebrated in temple prostitution and orgy.

But are not the scholars always united to the Shekhinah, in effect married to her in their Torah studies as Moses was before them? Yes, they are united with Heaven because the Shekhinah who is united to God is also joined with them.

Nevertheless, the Torah scholars still have an obligation to their wives. And in some places in the *Zohar* it is the debt to one's wife which is principally in mind in the Sabbath rituals. On the other hand, there is evidence that some scholars, especially those with raised families, left home for considerable periods of Torah study in union with the Shekhinah. Christian monastic and priestly celibacy may be related to this tradition. In effect, the Christian monk is married to the Shekhinah, the soul of the church, as the Jewish scholar is married to the Shekhinah, the soul of Israel. Both are dedicated to the study and recitation of the Torah.[31]

The mystical marriage with the divinity would play an important part especially in Christian mysticism in medieval and Renaissance times, as we shall see later.

The Hasidim

Having seen the medieval and Renaissance Kabbalists of Spain and Palestine, with their myths and celebrations of human and divine love, let us turn to another group of medieval Jewish mystics, namely, the German Hasidim, who remained aloof from the philosophical and theological discussions of the Jewish communities of Spain and Italy.[32]

The Crusades and persecutions helped give rise to the Hasidim. Whereas the Kabbalists were more of an elite sect, the Hasidim seem to have made an impact on many of the ordinary German burghers, especially in the twelfth and thirteenth centuries.

It seems that German Jewish mysticism even preceded the Middle Ages. The Mercabah variety came from Italy perhaps in the ninth century. German mysticism was especially strong at the approach of the Messianic year 5000 (1240) as predicted by Eleazar of Worms. The philosophical thought of Saadia and the Neo-Platonism of Abraham ibn Ezra and others mixed with magic, occult, and demonology.

Despite Crusades and persecutions, no apocalypses or specific prophecies of the coming of the Messiah. Yet Hasidism is basically eschatological in hue: paradise, redemption, resurrection, beatific vision, reward and punishment, especially in Judah the Hasid.

Three main things constitute a Hasid: the ascetical renunciation of the things of the world; serenity of mind; and an altruism that is sometimes extreme.

Hasidic asceticism rejects in a monastic way the ordinary pleasures of life for the pleasures of the next world. "By renouncing the temptations of this world, by averting his eyes from women, he becomes worthy of an after life in which he will see the glory of the Shekhinah with his own eyes and rank above the angels."[33] Besides the regular *halakah*, there is a higher heavenly law binding only the Hasidim.

Hasiduth leads to a state of pure love of God. "When the soul thinks deeply about the fear of God, then the flame of heart-felt love bursts in it and the exultation of innermost joy fills the heart . . ." The pleasures of family, wife, and children mean little now. "All the contemplation of his thoughts burns in the fire of love for him."[34]

The choosing of heavenly or divine love over human is a contrast with the Kabbalah, where union of husband and wife cooperated with and in a sense brought about union of God and his Shekhinah. We find a similar thought in *Sefer Hasidim*. (14)

The joy of this love is of such intensity and so overpowers the heart of those who love God, that even after many days of not being with his wife and having a great desire for her, in the hour that a man ejaculates, he does not find it as satisfying as the intensity and power of loving God and finding joy in his creator.[35]

Innocent family pleasures, such as walks, meeting with women, songs, etc., take second place. "In order that his heart may be whole in the joy of God, toiling and laboring in that which is the will of the Creator."

This love of God is overpowering.

He must love the Creator with a great and strong love until he becomes sick because of his love, as the man who is love-sick for the affections of a woman and reels constantly because of his love, when he sits, rises, goes and comes. Also when he eats and drinks. He neither sleeps nor slumbers because of this love. Greater than this should love of the Creator be in the hearts of those who love him and they should be absorbed in it constantly, as we were commanded. "With all your heart and with all your soul . . ." [Dt 6/4]. And this is what Solomon in his wisdom said by the way of simile. "For I am love-sick" [Cant 2/5].[36]

As in medieval Christian love poetry and Islamic as well, terms of erotic passion are used to describe the mystic union with God. But such usage goes back to the Talmud and Torah. In a later time Israel Baal Shem would say: "If the force of sensual love is so great, how great must be the passion with which man loves God."[37]

Monastic apathy and ataraxy, going back to the Stoics and found in many other traditions, is also strong in the Hasidim. Indifference to praise or blame, equanimity, ataraxy. Thus Isaac of Acre, a Spanish Kabbalist (13th–14th cent.): "He who is vouchsafed the entry into the mystery of adhesion to God, *devekuth*, attains to the mystery of equanimity, and he who possesses equanimity attains to loneliness, and from there he comes to the Holy Spirit and prophecy."[38] Meister Eckhart, a German Christian mystic of the same period, echoes similar thoughts. Hasidic ataraxy may well have come from the Christian monks, but it is found in many other cultures as well.

As Scholem writes, Hasidic saints combined two major facets of religious life: radical, antisocial introspective devotion to the ideal and loving care for the community.[39]

Magic, word studies, and penance were popular. But is not the Messiah to suffer for our sins? (Is 53/5) A Hasid responds: "I do not want anyone but myself to suffer for my sins." (*Sefer Hasidim*, 1556)

Divine immanence and omnipresence is a popular theme in Hasidism. No longer a transcendent king on a throne, God is now a friend, I and Thou, closer to man than his own soul is to his body. The "Song of Unity" of the Hasidim:

Everything is in you, and you are in everything; you fill everything and encompass it. When everything was created, you were in everything; before everything was created, you were in everything. Before everything was created, you were everything.[40]

As with the Sufi, there is a danger here of immanentism and identification of God and the world, God and man.

Other popular Hasidic themes: Kavod or divine Glory or the Shekhinah as revealed to prophets and mystics—both inner and outer Spirit. The vision of the visible Kavod is the aim of Hasidic askesis. Sometimes the visible Glory is seen as the holy cherub on the throne of Merkabah. Moreover, God's Holiness and Greatness are seen as created hypostases of his Glory.

The eighteenth-century Hasidim are not related directly to their medieval predecessors, except in their mutual interest in mysticism, yet a mystic life which inspires social action.

Like the earlier Hasidim, the later stressed divine immanence, union with God in thought and prayer. Faith in the Zaddikim and rapturous delight in worship helped lift the hearts of a depressed people. Yet Hasidism was feared by the old-line rabbis as an innovation. It would influence Jewish culture. For example, musician Ernst Bloch, poet Judah Leib Peretz, and scholar Martin Buber.

Having seen the Moslem and Jewish love themes in the Middle Ages, let us turn to Christian love, first as sung by the troubadours and then in monastery and university.

❧ XII ❧

LOVE IS A CERTAIN
INBORN SUFFERING

Andreas Capellanus, The Art of Courtly Love, *1/1*

In this and the following chapter we will see Christian medieval love themes which grew parallel with Islamic and Jewish traditions.

The Rise of Courtly Love

Courtly love appeared in Languedoc in southern France at the end of the eleventh century. We have seen earlier the influence of Sufi love songs in this area.

In the South of France courtly love appeared to flourish amidst a certain softness of life, typified by the landless and footloose knight. As C. S. Lewis writes:

> The unattached knight as we meet him in the romances, respectable only by his valor, amiable only by his courtesy, predestined lover of other men's wives, was therefore a reality. But this does not explain why he loved in a new way.[1]

The Provençal court of the twelfth century was an island of leisure in an often barbarous countryside. Since there were few women—the lady of the court plus her daughters and handmaids—and many men, including knights, lesser lords, pages, etc., in the service of the lady and her lord, some of the latter had little hope of marriage. This setting naturally lent itself to polyandry, the medieval version of which was called courtly love.

The very artificial nature of feudal marriage also fostered courtly love. Rather than based on love, the average feudal marriage was founded on political or economic expediency. And often when a particular alliance folded, the marriage was dissolved. Lewis comments: "Any idealizing of sexual love in a society where marriage is purely utilitarian, must begin by being an idealization of adultery."[2]

The Cathars grew up in the same period and are said by some to have been influential in the development of courtly love. They were a Christian sect known as the Church of Love, or the Albigenses, from the town of Albi in southern France. Dualists who proclaimed God as love and the world as evil, they had two degrees: beginners living in the world and the perfect, who were celibate.

Some feel that the wandering troubadours of southern France may have been Cathars.[3] Both Cathars and troubadours extolled chastity; both received the single kiss of initiation from their lady; both scoffed at marriage; both reviled the clergy and feudal lords. The troubadours led a life of the wandering poor and used Catharist liturgical expressions in their songs. Whether the Cathari influenced the troubadours of southern France cannot be said with certitude. But both grew up in the same area and their concern with love may have had similar roots.

The troubadours are priests of the religion of love. Ovid had celebrated *amor*, as Plato had eros. There seems little doubt that Ovid inspired the courtly tradition perhaps more in the North than in the South. The new religion of love is a rival of the established church and even a parody of it. Ovid is its doctor and his *Art of Love* its gospel.

But there is a certain ambivalence in it all. Lewis warns: "We must be prepared for a certain ambiguity in all those poems where the attitude of the lover to his lady or to Love looks at first sight like the attitude of a worshiper to the Blessed Virgin or to God."[4] We have seen this ambivalence of love before and we will see it again.

By the end of the twelfth century the love religion had spread in two directions. One went from Provence down to Italy through the poets of the *dolce stil nuovo* to the *Divine Comedy* of Dante. Another wave blew North to meld with Ovidian and Celtic traditions already popular there.

We have seen some of the factors behind the rise of courtly love in twelfth-century France. Its characteristics include: humility, courtesy, adultery, and a religious devotion to love. Its attributes may be seen in the lays of the troubadours and medieval love manuals such as Andreas Capellanus' *Art of Courtly Love*. It thrived in the courts of Eleanor of Aquitaine and her daughter Marie of Champagne. Both the poets and the scientists of love wanted to show the proper psychology and methodology of courtly love constantly beset by its enemies.

The Troubadours

These are the love poets and singers of southern France in the twelfth and thirteenth centuries. And their hymns to their castle ladies paved the way for love literature of future generations.

"Troubadour" comes from the vulgar Latin word *tropar* or the Provençal *trobar*—to find. And it is related to the "tropes" of Latin rhetoric and Christian liturgy. But the stress, as in French *trover* and Italian *trovare*, is on discovery, invention, and creativity.[5]

Their love poems are often ambiguous, reflecting the church-court, religious-secular situation of the times. For example, praise of courtly ladies and the Virgin. Some music was used both for church liturgy and for love poems.

Duke William of Aquitaine was not a Bernard of Clairvaux, although the two men shared the Platonic-Christian ethos of the day, a world spirit that stressed the correspondence of things. While Bernard wrote traditional praises of Our Lady, William wrote to his own, voicing in an original fashion the ego of lyric expression for the first time in the post-classical world.[6]

There was a tradition in the Latin literature of eighth-to-tenth-century Europe in which the women of the courts were praised, mirroring the *Ave Maria* tradition of the period. But there was more deference to the lady than in later Provençal poems. There also may have been inspiration from the popular love hymns sung at the spring festivals. But this is more true in the North.

Provençal love poems reflect the resurrection of Europe from the Dark Ages. "Just as the Provençal poem often bursts forth with a shaft of spring sunlight, singing birds, budding flowers, and green-growing trees, so the external world was flowering in church and court alike."[7] The Provençal poems are creative, with stanzaic patterns and rhyme schemes with Ambrosian, Ovidian, and perhaps Sufi antecedents.

It is a lively and fun-filled song. Thus the frolic of clowns and jugglers often accompanies the poems of the troubadours. These are lively times with millennial expectations, heresies, Crusades, schools, cathedrals, monasteries, and poets. And the troubadours sing in the *langue d'oc* of Provence, where *oc* means "yes." They sing of moderation, service, prowess, long expectation, secrecy, pity, all leading to the joys of true love.

William of Poitou, the ninth Duke of Aquitaine, is the first of the troubadours. Vigorous, brash, amorous, and proud, experienced in women, a good composer and singer, wealthy landowner, Crusader. His songs have youth, wit, and joy. He allegedly founded an abbey of whores. When his legal wife was driven away, he carried off the wife of a certain viscount,

engraving her figure on his shield. His liberal loves clashed
with the church.

> I'll write a poem, then take a nap,
> And things stand in the sun.
> Some ladies are really misguided.
> I know which ones:
> Those who turn the love of a knight
> Into grief. (1)

> Then Lady Agnes to Lady Emma:
> He's just what we're looking for.
> For the love of God, let's put him up.
> He's a mute.
> He'll never be able to tattle about
> What we do. (6)[8]

> I've got two pretty good fillies in my corral:
> They're ready for any combat—
> They're tough.
> But I can't keep them together:
> Don't get along. (3)

> If I could tame 'em the way I want,
> I wouldn't have to change
> This set-up,
> For I'd be the best-mounted man
> In all the world. (4)[9]

Marcabrun, a twelfth-century troubadour, cried out against
the free love of William.

> Gallantry's been banished
> While whoredom's honor still grows,
> For the married men have grabbed it,
> Turning themselves into swains.
> Hearing one brag is as wonderful
> As watching a dog knead dough. (5)

As long as Marcabrun has life,
One of that barbaric tribe will get
No affection from him.
For they're all just evil givers,
Forgers of a wicked creed,
Through France and through Guyenne. (6)

Marcabrun compares low love with good love:

Low loving spreads, confounding
Control with gluttonous appetite.
Searching for that sweet dish of meat,
Ever warmed by those nasty fires—
Ay!
Once a man slips in there—
For real or just for a try—
Yeah!
But to leave his skin behind in the pot. (3)

Good love packs a panacea
To heal his loyal followers;
But low loving spanks his disciples
And sends 'em straight to Hell—
Ay!
As long as the geld lasts here,
The poor fool thinks he's loved.
Yeah!
But once the geld's gone, botch up. (4)

Low living lays a marvelous trap
Luring the duke into his lime
From top down to his toes;
All messed up! Shall I? No?
Ay!
Want a blond, brunette, or black?
And will I do it? Or won't I?
Yeah!

This way a fool gets a skinny rump. (5)
Who has good love as a neighbor
And lives within his bondage,
Sees honor and worth inclining
And Value—not any danger—
Ay!
Does so much with honest words
He need never fear the wrath—
Yeah!
Of that lecher-loving Sir Aigline. (8)[10]

Low love seems to be an unbridled lust leading to Hell, while good love is the brotherly love of Christian charity leading to Heaven. Can this also be the refined love (*amor fina*) between lady and knight, or lady and husband? In contrast with William of Aquitaine, Marcabrun's poems mirror the church's mind.

Andreas Capellanus

Besides the lays of the troubadours, courtly love is seen in the love manuals, such as Andreas Capellanus' *Art of Courtly Love*. This is a handbook of love-making by a court chaplain of the late twelfth century at the direction of the Countess Marie of Champagne, and it reflects a strong Ovidian hue. It was inspired by the ambiance of Queen Eleanor's court at Poitiers, 1170–74, though written later when Countess Marie was at Troyes as regent for her son.

What is love? Andreas responds:

Love is a certain inborn suffering derived from the sight of and excessive meditation upon the beauty of the opposite sex, which causes each one to wish above all things the embraces of the other and by common desire to carry all of love's precepts in the other's embrace. (1/1)[11]

How can love be suffering? First of all, the lover fears that he may lose his desire, since so many things can come between him and his beloved. This inborn suffering comes from seeing and meditating.

> For when a man sees some woman fit for love and shaped according to his taste, he begins at once to lust after her in his heart. Then the more he thinks about her the more he burns with love, until he comes to a fuller meditation.

Meditation on her body leads to action looking for time and place and intermediaries. (1/1)

Love must be between the opposite sexes (1/2) and the enjoyment of her embraces.

> In the sight of a lover, nothing can be compared to the act of love, and a true lover would rather be deprived of all his money and of everything that the human mind can imagine as indispensable to life rather than be without love, either hoped for or attained.

> Love (*amor*) gets its name from hook (*amus*), to capture or be captured. "For he who is in love is captured in the chains of desire and wishes to capture some one else with his hook." (1/3)

Love changes a man. It causes the ugly to become beautiful, the humble noble, and the proud humble. It even makes the lover chaste.

> Because he who shines with the light of one love can hardly think of embracing another woman, even a beautiful one. For when he thinks deeply of his beloved, the sight of another woman seems to his mind rough and rude. (1/4)

Among the many barriers to love, including youth and blindness, is also an excess of passion.

> Because there are men who are slaves to such passionate desire that they cannot be held in the bonds of love—men who, after they have thought long about some woman or even enjoyed her, when they see another woman straightway desire her embraces. . . . (1/5)

They lust after every woman they see like a shameless dog.

How is love acquired? By a shapely figure, excellent character, readiness in speech, great wealth, and readiness to grant that which is sought. The first three are important, and excellence of character takes precedence over beauty. Beauty never pleases if it lacks goodness. "It is excellence of character alone which blesses a man with true nobility and makes him flourish in ruddy beauty." (1/6)

Andreas then recounts some ideal dialogues between lovers of the same or of different classes. The lover praises his beloved, she demurs, etc. How one should court a woman of the upper class and her gentle response. In his dialogue (5) between the noble man and noble woman, Andreas presents the twelve rules of love.

1. You shall avoid avarice like a deadly pestilence and shall embrace its opposite.
2. You shall keep yourself chaste for the sake of her whom you love.
3. You shall not knowingly strive to break up a correct love affair that someone else is engaged in.
4. You shall not choose for your love anyone whom a natural sense of shame forbids you to marry.
5. Be mindful completely to avoid falsehood.
6. You shall not have many who know of your love affair.
7. Being obedient in all things to the commands of the ladies, you shall ever strive to ally yourself to the service of love.
8. In giving and receiving love's solaces let modesty be ever present.
9. You shall speak no evil.
10. You shall not be a revealer of love affairs.
11. You shall be in all things polite and courteous.
12. In practicing the solaces of love you shall not exceed the desires of your lover. (1/6)

Courts of love decided violations of the rules of love. For example, when a knight spread abroad the details of an affair, violating the rules of secrecy: "A court of ladies having been summoned in Gascony, it was established by everlasting decree, with the wholehearted consent of the court, that the knight be deprived of every hope of love, and that in every court of ladies or chevaliers, he be always considered approbrious and contemptible to all." (2/7/18) Sometimes the Countess Marie or Queen Eleanor would decide a love dispute.

In his dialogue (7) between a man of higher nobility and a woman of simple nobility, Andreas asserts the courtly thesis that love cannot exist in marriage. Why not?

I am greatly surprised that you wish to misapply the term "love" to that marital affection which husband and wife are expected to feel for each other after marriage. Since everyone knows that love can have no place between husband and wife.

They may have affection, but this is not love. "For what is love but an inordinate desire to receive passionately a furtive and hidden embrace?" The marital embrace cannot be furtive since husband and wife belong to each other, and have no fear of others objecting to their intercourse. How can someone make furtive use of what already belongs to him? Similarly, between father and son there is affection but not love.

Also that essential ingredient of love, jealousy, is missing in marriage. Lovers welcome jealousy as the mother and nurse of love, jealousy which is the fear of the loss of the beloved and anxiety lest love not be reciprocated.

Andreas writes of courtly love. Marriages of the time were often forced arrangements of political or economic advantage, so lovers sought furtive and jealous rendezvous outside the marriage. Also the *debitum* of marriage can hardly be conducive to spontaneous love.

In his dialogue between two of high nobility, Andreas speaks of pure and mixed love.

It is the pure love which binds together the hearts of two lovers with every feeling of delight. This kind consists in the contemplation of the mind and affection of the heart. It goes so far as the kiss and the embrace and the modest contact with the nude lover, omitting the final solace, for that is not permitted to those who wish to love purely. (8)

This pure love perhaps resembles the Tantric *shakti* yoga, which also stops short of intercourse, and the Moslem *al-hawa-al-ludri*, and possibly the *subintroducta* of early Christianity. Andreas says that this pure love is really virtuous and does not hurt anyone and God sees little wrong with it. Sometimes moderns call this love "the third way"!

On the other hand, mixed love goes all the way, culminating in the final act of lust. This is a short-lived love and it leads only to injury to the other and to God and can only bring remorse. Andreas does not condemn mixed love outright, but prefers pure love.

How about the love of the clergy? The law of clerical celibacy was enforced by the monk-pope Gregory VII in the eleventh century. But celibacy means that the clerk cannot marry; it does not mean that he cannot love. And one would judge from the literature of the time that not only was clerical love not unknown, but clerics make the best lovers. The clerk, like his lay brother, is weak and prone to sins of the flesh. Clerical love is preferred because of the clerk's vast experience and caution, restraint, and prudence.

Ideally a clerk as a clerk should not love.

But since hardly anyone ever lives without carnal sin, and since the life of the clergy is, because of the continual idleness and the great abundance of food, naturally liable to temptations of the body than that of other men, if any clerk should wish to enter into the lists of love, let him speak and apply himself to love's service in accordance with the rank or standing of his parents, as we have already fully explained in regards to the different ranks of men. (1/8)

It seems that the high rank of the clerichood would render love most difficult if not impossible. So the clerk should pursue love on the level of his former rank. Interestingly enough, clerical marriage in the Western church always followed this pattern, namely, laicization back to one's former rank. Also later in Reformation times many of the clerics, forsaking their priesthood, picked up with the lowliest of servant wenches, perhaps indicating that they themselves may have derived from the lower classes.

Nuns are definitely off limits for lovers and liable to punishment by God and man. Nuns are married to God, who is a jealous lover, as the hymns of Bernard of Clairvaux and William of St. Thierry attest.

Love is not something that can be bought or sold, for this would be next to harlotry. (1/9) Nor can love be had with an easy woman who gives herself to whomever asks. (1/10)

In Book Two, Andreas writes in Ovidian fashion how love may be kept once it has been won. First of all, keep it a secret. Be restrained with your beloved, come to her aid in time of need, and apologize if you have done her wrong. Dress well, be generous, courageous, selfless. Solaces of the flesh may be taken, but not in a wearisome manner. (2/1)

How can love be increased? (2/2) By separation, by jealousy. Love generally does not last once it has been made public. Parental objections, certain ways of walking and dressing, increase love. Love can be decreased by the opposite. (2/3) Too much contact, foolishness, cowardice, blasphemy, uncharitableness, etc.

What terminates love? (2/4) Infidelity, when love is made public, a new love, inequality of love, marriage, impotence, insanity. If terminated through ignorance, love may be revived, otherwise usually not.

Andreas then gives a number of love norms:

1. Marriage is no real excuse for not loving.
2. He who is not jealous cannot love.

3. No one can be bound by a double love.

4. It is well known that love is always increasing or decreasing. . . .

7. When one lover dies, a widowhood of two years is required of the survivor.

8. No one should be deprived of love without the very best of reasons.

9. No one can love unless he is impelled by the persuasion of love. . . .

11. When made public, love rarely endures. . . .

14. The easy attainment of love makes it of little value; difficulty of attainment makes it prized.

15. Every lover regularly turns pale in the presence of his beloved.

16. When a lover suddenly catches sight of his beloved, his heart palpitates.

17. A new love puts to flight an old one.

18. Good character alone makes any man worthy of love.

19. If love diminishes, it quickly falls and rarely revives.

20. A man in love is always apprehensive.

21. Real jealousy always increases the feeling of love. (2/8)

Andreas' third book seems to recant the first two. Is he imitating Ovid's *Remedies of Love?* No matter how pleasureful human love is, it is at best ephemeral and fraught with suffering, anxiety, and jealousy. Perhaps also a northern and more churchly view is seen in which married romance tends to supplant the adultery of the southern troubadours.

God punishes those who enjoy Venus outside of wedlock. Moreover, this love harms one's neighbor. Also one who neglects the honor of his friend to serve the flesh is unworthy. No sin is more serious than fornication, for it stains both soul and body. Furthermore, love makes a man a slave. It can lead one to penury, for he gives what he has not. While love causes suffering, chastity is a high virtue.

Love leads to crime—murder, adultery, perjury, theft, war,

etc. Fleshly pleasures themselves are not good for men. Love forces men to lose Heaven and suffer on earth. The Devil is really the author of love and lechery. Love breaks up marriages. "A man ought not to love anything in this world as much as the wife to whom he is lawfully bound."

In this section Andreas is not above misogynism. Thus women are: avaricious, slanders, greedy, fickle, dishonest, proud, gossips, loudmouths, wantons.

Whereas in his first two books Andreas shows Walter how to get the fullest delights of the flesh—in the third: "If you abstain from it [love] the heavenly king will be the more favorably disposed to you in every respect."

The Church and Courtly Love

Does Andreas' third book reflect the church's attitude toward courtly love? Bernard of Clairvaux and William of St. Thierry, contemporaries of courtly love, sing of divine love as superior to the love of the troubadours. We shall see more of their songs in the next chapter.

Whereas courtly love is beset with suffering, fear, and anxiety, divine love has none of these. While courtly love is frustrated in trying to seek its beloved, divine love possesses it. And the pleasure that courtly love desires is enjoyed by the soul in divine love.

Besides Bernard's commentaries on the Greatest Song, we have a renewed interest in monastic chastity and newly legislated clerical celibacy. Sometimes chastity is a reaction to a period of free love. Mary, the ideal woman, Queen of Heaven, is served by her loyal and chaste monk-knights and virgins. And she is celebrated in festival and stone. Moreover, the heretical Cathars celebrated their own brand of chastity.

For the church, marriage is a sacrament to be defended against adultery, granted that the medieval noble marriages were not always the happiest.

The love of Bernard is heavenly, courtly love is earthly. Bernard attains the goal, courtly love falls short. Both exhibit restraint—chastity, if you will—but Bernard's is higher and more rewarding.

Even marital passion was looked down upon by some as against man's highest faculty, reason, paralleling the pleas of Reason in the love allegories. We shall see more of the medieval monastic and university love themes in the following chapter.

The Trouvères and the Romances of the North

The troubadours of the South singing their lays of love in the *langue d'oc* are succeeded by the *trouvères* of the North writing in the *langue d'oïl*. The northern romancers were inspired by the southern singers, but also by Ovid and ancient Celtic legends, giving us the Arthurian romances, *Tristan* and *Lancelot*, with courtly love moving from song to narrative.

Eleanor of Aquitaine, granddaughter of the troubadour William IX of Aquitaine, left her southern court of love to marry Louis VII, King of France, at the age of fifteen. Then in 1152, her first marriage annulled, she married Henry, Duke of Normandy, soon to be King of England. And she took her love-singing troubadours along. Eleanor's daughter, Countess Marie of Champagne, also helped spread the romantic spirit.

The *trouvères* of the North seem inferior to the troubadours of the South in mystic wisdom, dealing more with the physical side of love. For example, the starting point of *Lancelot* and *Tristan* is the physical possession of the woman, a sin against courtly love.

Northern romances usually follow five stages: beginning, development, betrothal, ordeal, and union.[12] Almost all medieval romances, not to mention their modern descendants, follow this plan.

Love sometimes begins at first sight; at other times it is gradual. Sometimes a love dart, entering through the eye, pierces the heart. Sometimes there is an immediate mutual love; at others, reciprocity must be won.

Love makes the lover sick. He assumes a pale and wan complexion and he cannot eat or sleep. A certain fear and trembling overcomes him at the sight and thought of her. "God, whence come this fear of a girl, alone, weak, timid, simple, and gentle? . . . Whoever would love, must fear, otherwise he cannot be in love. But he shall fear only her whom he loves, and for her sake brave all the others besides." (Chrétien de Troyes, *Cligés*, 3845 ff)

In the third stage of love, mutual devotion and understanding grow along with companionship and common hopes. But secrecy must be kept to protect them from envy and jealousy.

In the fourth stage comes the test of true love.

> The great lessons of *fine amor* in courtesy, morality, and loyalty are always learned through suffering. And for the most part come after the happiness of plighted troth has established mutual faith and the strong sense of sentimental duty characteristic of true lovers.[13]

In this period, as in their happiness, the lovers mistrust the world. In their separation, a souvenir, a gift, a lock of hair, or any other possession of the beloved is a reminder. The rumored death of the beloved is the greatest test. Another trial is the temptation of other and undesired loves.

In the fifth and last phase the lovers are restored to each other's arms, their love escalated by their long separation.

The romances reflect medieval society, with knights and ladies, courts and jousts, etc. There are two main types of romances. One stresses sentimental love, while the other underlines chivalry. In the first type the union of lovers must overcome all social obstacles, such as discrepancy of rank and wealth, parental opposition, etc. During the period of separation a loveless marriage may be arranged by the father.

Love can be a source of worldly gain—improving one's status.

Indeed a romancer may teach the independence of love, may sympathize with its defiance of social barriers, may exalt its indifference to wealth and position. But when he comes to write the marriage contract for his hero and heroine, he makes even better terms with fortune than the most ambitious parent, unassisted by romance, could desire.[14]

Sometimes in the romances love displaces morality. Thus love has the right of way. Sometimes a jealous husband forces his wife into the arms of her lover, as Archambault and Flamenca. "The problem is how to be a successful, happy lover in spite of opposition. And the solution depends upon the power of love to cope with the ideals of chivalry, whether the end be in marriage or an illegal amour."[15]

Besides the romances that stress love, there is a second kind that accents adventure and chivalry. Hence love is a complement to prowess.

Prowess is the more conspicuous motive, but love, though yielding it the foreground, serves it as incitement and stimulus, furnishing it with a definite goal, and gives it the sentimental refinement which the authors of the society romances always affect.[16]

Often the victorious knight is rewarded with the lady of his desire.

The knight's lady is frequently idealized: physical beauty—blond hair, red and white complexion, gorgeous figure, and a gracious and courtly manner. The hero is a knight of noble deeds and sentiment, a model knight and lover. Qualities: sweet and strong, gentle yet vigorous, courteous and brave, saved from his effeminacy by courage and skill at arms.

And his heroine is his chief stimulus to chivalry and courtesy.

She is, of course, idealized but she is no angel and rarely much of a saint. The glorification of her beauty and sweetness of her social graces, and of her wise and loyal efficiency in the service of love, is not infrequently tempered with a recognition of her tendency to caprice and her genius for duplicity.[17]

Her virtues are worldly and sentimental rather than moral and spiritual.

In fact, her worldlywise tricks rather typify courtly love in contrast to spiritual love.

> In truth, courtly love is, in the final analysis, always of the world worldly. For all his exaltation of his theme, for all his emphasis upon the delicacy, the sweetness, the mysterious strength of the passion that he celebrates as the noblest that can animate a hero, the medieval romancer does not spiritualize love. With him it is throughout erotic and social. However disciplined and refined, however ennobled by Christian ideals, it may be at its best—its ultimate level is material, not spiritual.[18]

Having seen some of the major themes of the northern romancers, let us turn to the leading *trouvère*, Chrétien de Troyes.

Marie, daughter of Eleanor of Aquitaine and King Louis of France, married Count Henry the Liberal of Champagne (1164), continuing her mother's interest in love literature. Troyes, her husband's capital, was a literary center of the time. Andreas was court chaplain there.

One of the most famous of the *trouvères* of Troyes is Chrétien. He was among the first of northern France to write a serious love poem—*Erec and Enide*, uniting the Provençal love theme with Arthurian legends. As Lewis writes: "He stamped upon men's minds indelibly the conception of Arthur's court as the home par excellence of true and noble love."[19]

Chrétien places chivalry in the mythological past, for it seems to be dead by his time. Perhaps chivalry has always been a myth anyway. Chrétien is not entranced with adultery as the southern troubadours were.

Erec, an early work probably written before Marie came to

Troyes, is a story of married love and against the adulterous southern themes. Thus when Erec asks for Enide's hand, she consents and serves as his loyal wife.

The story of Lancelot Chrétien heard from the Countess Marie and he wrote it down for her pleasure. The tale illustrates courtly love as it was introduced into the North by Eleanor and Marie. Thus the love of another man's wife is featured, though Chrétien had little sympathy with the theme, for he never finished it.

This is the secret love of Lancelot and Guinevere, the queen in captivity in the land of Gorre, whence she is rescued by Lancelot. It reflects Ovidian and courtly themes. Lancelot has problems on the way—disgrace, humble ride on a cart, ridicule, wounds. Moreover, the queen is cruel to him. She heard that he hesitated to ride on the cart, so she orders Lancelot to do poorly in the tournament. The submission of Lancelot to Guinevere borders on religious devotion.

Chrétien tells the story and analyzes the motives, using allegory on the Provençal model. Thus Reason and Love debate before Lancelot ascends the humble cart.

About the same time a certain Thomas wrote the *Romance of Tristan*, probably for Queen Eleanor of Aquitaine, now Queen of England. This Pict story of Tristan and Iseult was already familiar to the court. This is a fatal love story, for happy love is not news. As De Rougemont remarks: "Romance only comes into existence where love is fatal, frowned upon and doomed by life itself."[20] People want to hear of frustrations, heartbreaks, disappointments, love triangles. "Is there something fatal to marriage at the very heart of human longing?"

Tristan is a popular myth of adultery. Myth is used to show passion's link with death.

Tristan is sent by King Mark to find Iseult, the girl with the golden hair. He kills the dragon and is nursed by Iseult, the daughter of the queen. While Tristan is taking Iseult back to King Mark, they drink a love potion, with the inevitable results. When Mark finds out, he banishes Tristan. Later, as Tristan is dying, Iseult comes and dies with him.

De Rougemont asks how Tristan can be held up as a model of chivalry when he betrayed his master and the queen.[21] He sees the latter part of the twelfth century as a rivalry between chivalry and the feudal system. Tristan contrasts the two. In the Arthurian romances, the knight, formerly the vassal of his lord, is now the slave of his body. And the authors favor courtly chivalry over against the feudal law of loyalty to the lord.

Donnoi or *domne* is the Provençal name for the vassal relationship between a knight-lover and his lady or *domina*.

It would seem that passion from the love potion would allow Tristan to keep Iseult, but instead he delivers her to Mark, for courtly love does not allow passion to be fulfilled. And at the same time Tristan fulfills his feudal obligation to his lord. Mission accomplished.

Do Tristan and Iseult love each other or do they love love with the catalyst of the love potion? De Rougemont comments: "Tristan loves the awareness that he is loving far more than he loves Iseult the Fair. And Iseult does nothing to hold Tristan. All she needs is her passionate dream."[22]

They seem to prefer absence to presence. Thus the story is sprinkled with obstructions, many partings and reunions of lovers. And the very marriage of Iseult and Mark escalates the love between Iseult and Tristan.

> The love of love itself has concealed a far more awful passion, a desire altogether unfavorable, something that could only be "betrayed" by means of symbols such as that of the drawn sword and that of perilous chastity. . . . In the innermost recesses of their hearts they have been obeying the fatal dictates of a wish for death; they have been in the throes of the active passion of darkness.[23]

The Romance of the Rose is a thirteenth-century romance extremely popular for three hundred years, even rivaling the

8. The love of love itself" (De Rougemont, *Love in the Western World*, 46)

Bible. Written by William of Lorris and Jean de Meun, its allegories offer many interpretations. Some say it is autobiographical, while others see in it a humorous account of the Fall.

The *Romance* tells its story through the Lover's eyes. As Lewis writes: "Any protracted wooing involves a conflict not only between the man and the woman, but between the woman and herself; it is this second conflict which occupies the most interesting scenes of the Romance."[24]

The allegorical garden mirrors the court, the sphere of love's operation. Character personifications can be neutral and apply to either the hero or the heroine, such as Venus and Love; or to the heroine—such as Bailacoil (Friendliness), Franchise, and Pity. Or they can apply to the hero—Hope, Sweet Thought, and Reason. Those kept out of the love garden are: Avarice, Envy, Poverty, Age, Sadness, Hate, Covetise, Papelardie (Hypocrisy).

The portress, Idleness, shows our hero the garden of delight, the god of Love following unseen. He sees the beautiful rose garden reflected in the fountain of love and one special bud which particularly appeals to him. The rosebud is the lady's love. And as he reaches to pluck it, he is struck with the arrow of love. Then the god of Love instructs the Lover of the duties he must perform and the pains he must bear. Love vanishes.

The Lover makes an overture to Rose, but is chased off by Danger. Reason cautions the Lover to abandon Love, but on the advice of Friend, he tries again. Bailacoil once again smiles and leads the Lover within the hedge guarding the garden. Venus prompts a kiss.

Then Confusion, Jealousy, and Malebouche are angry with Bailacoil. The hedge is repaired and a castle built, guarded by Shame, Danger, Fear, and Malebouche with Bailacoil imprisoned inside.

The second part of *The Romance of the Rose* was written forty years later by Jean de Meun, probably at the University of Paris. Whereas William is an allegorist, Jean is more of a satirist with many digressions.

Dreamer is left outside the castle with Reason. Under Friend's advice, and with the aid of the god of Love and his barons, Dreamer assaults the castle. Two aides, Falsemblant and Constrained Abstinence, get rid of Bad Mouth. Venus and Love team together and Nature helps. Venus destroys the castle with a fiery arrow. Bailacoil is rescued and surrenders Rose, and Dreamer awakens.

Jean de Meun mixes his story with numerous digressions on love which may reflect the university milieu in which he writes. Lewis remarks: "What Jean really does is to substitute a third rate literal story for a first rate allegorical story and to confuse the one with the other so that we can enjoy neither."[25]

Reason explains love (4376 ff):

Love, if I think right, is a sickness of thought that takes place between two persons of different sex when they are in close proximity and open to each other. It arises among people from the burning desire, born of disordinate glances, to em-

brace and kiss each other and to have the solace of one
another's body. A lover so burns and is so enraptured that
he thinks of nothing else. He takes no account of bearing
fruit. But strives only for delight.[26]

Reflecting medieval church teaching, Jean says that lying
with a woman should be for the purpose of procreation. "Nature has implanted delight in man because she wants the work-
man to take pleasure in his task in order that he might neither
flee from it, nor hate it." Youth seeks the pleasure alone without
the obligation, but Old Age has remorse. (4477)

Reason mistrusts love, for love is basically irrational.
(4600 ff.) "Hearts drunk with love are too much given over
to misguided acts. You will know this at the end when you
have lost your time and wasted your youth in this sorry pleasure." While Reason pours advice in one ear, Love whispers in
the other. Dreamer admonishes Reason: Love may have its
problems, but it is still better than hate.

There are many loves: friendship, charity, fortune. Universal
love is better than particular love. (5434) "Let him form there
a lasting union in which many participate. You can lawfully
love all those of the world in a general way. Love them all
as much as one, at least with the love of what is common to
all."

But the Lover rejects Reason, for he wants his Rose.
(6901 ff.) Moreover, he twits Reason for referring to testicles,
words which should not come from the mouth of a courteous
girl. Reason responds that they are good things and sources of
life and not just for pleasure.

The second part of the *Romance* sometimes portrays misogynism. Women are greedy, tricky, etc. The Old Woman says
(13265 ff.): Since all men betray women, a woman should
get the jump on them. She should use every device to trap
them, from low-cut gowns to reveal her smooth white chest
to hiding her defects, smiling discreetly, and tears. "But no
man should be disturbed when he sees such tears flowing as

fast as rain. For these tears, these sorrows and lamentations
flow only to trick him." (13367 ff.)

She should be willing to play and go out to be seen and
see and show off her body while she still has young legs. She
should spread her nets wide to snare all. Thus she is bound to
catch a few fish. "How when she hears a lover's request she
should be reluctant to grant him all her love. Nor should she
refuse everything, but try to keep him in a state of balance
between hope and fear." (13663)

Lewis feels that the second part of the *Romance* is not a
turning away from reverence of courtly love and women
to ridicule.

> The truth is that cynicism and idealism about women are
> twin fruits on the same branch—are the positive and nega-
> tive poles of a single thing—and that they may be found
> anywhere in the literature of romantic love, and mixed in
> any proportions.[27]

It seems that Jean is trying to put love in its proper place
rather than hoping to demolish it. "The history of courtly love
from beginning to end may be described as an 'amorous-odious
sonnet,' a scholar's 'love and hatred.'" We have seen the ambivalence of human love in previous authors. Though delightful, human love is but a shadow of divine love.

In the end, though, Dreamer rejects Reason for his beloved
Rose—as he must, for love is not a reasonable thing.

> I rendered thanks among the delicious kisses ten or twenty
> times. First to the god of Love and to Venus, who had aided
> me more than anyone, then to all the barons of the host,
> whose help I pray God never to take away from pure lovers.
> But I didn't remember Reason who gave me a lot of trouble
> for nothing. (21743 ff.)

But even the Dreamer has his Rose only in his reverie.
"Straightway it was day and I awoke." Is courtly love more of
a fantasy than reality? Probably.

Chaucer and Dante

We have seen the development of courtly love from the love songs of the troubadours to the full-blown *Romance of the Rose*. It continued to flourish.

The Romance of the Rose was popular and its themes of gracious eroticism, dreams, allegory, and satire are to be found in subsequent literature.

Geoffrey Chaucer, fourteenth-century English poet of courtly love, translated the *Rose*, which inspired his love lyrics. "In his greatest work we have the courtly conception of love, which Chaucer learned from the French allegory, put into action in poetry which is not allegorical at all."[28] In his *Book of the Duchess* we see a courtly dream modeled on the reverie of the *Rose*, though he does not obtain his desire.

Chaucer's *Parliament of Fowls*, influenced by Dante, does not so much ridicule courtly love as present it as an escape, a truancy from vulgar common sense and from the Ten Commandments. "The truancy is felt to be in some flawed and fragile way a noble thing, the source of every virtue except chastity, the 'flemer' of every vice save one."[29]

Chaucer's *Troilus and Criseyde* was stimulated by Boccaccio's *Il Filostrato* and *The Romance of the Rose*. Troilus is a new Lancelot and his beloved Criseyde is a virtuous and amorous widow.

> By Christian standards forgiveable, by the rules of courtly love, needing no forgiveness. This is all that needs be said of Criseyde's act in granting the rose to Troilus. But her betrayal of him is not so easily dismissed.[30]

When Troilus leaves Criseyde, her sadness leads to her fall, and Diomede becomes her refuge.

> Such a woman has no resistant virtues that should delay her complete degradation when once she is united with a de-

grading lover. The same pliancy which ennobled her as the mistress of Troilus, debases her as the mistress of Diomede.[31]

Her uncle Pandarus is the teacher of love's law, a realist who sees through the hard facts of life showing through the love reverie. He can tease and even laugh at the lovers. On the other hand, he sees the dichotomy between the religion of love and the law of God.

Troilus is the personification of suffering love. He is another Lancelot, ideal lover and warrior, but one of enduring suffering and despair.

The first two books of the romance are happy with the wooing and winning of Criseyde, while the third is the fruition of love, erotic poetry. How can Chaucer write erotic poetry without slipping into Ovidian pornography? Lewis answers.

> The secret lies, I think, in his concreteness. Lust is more abstract than logic. It seeks (hope triumphing over experience) for some purely sexual, hence purely imaginary, conjunction of an impossible maleness with an impossible femaleness.[32]

The poem praises love, but ends with the death of Troilus by Hercules.

Chaucer ends with an appeal to a higher love. Human love is a chancy thing at best.

> O young lusty folk, youths and maids in whom love ever grows up with your age, get you home from worldly vanity! Cast up the eyes of your heart to that God that made you after his image, and think that all this world is but a market-fair, and passes as soon as the sweet flowers. And love him who for pure love, to redeem our souls, first died upon the cross, and rose again, and now sits on high in heaven. He will fail no creature, of that be sure, who will lean his heart wholly on him. And since he is most gentle and best to love, what need to seek feigned loves?

Another fourteenth-century love poem is John Gower's *Confessio Amantis,* the story of the death of love or an old poet's unsuccessful love for a young girl. At last he awakens, reconciling himself to the reality that old age is the cure of love.

The poet meets Venus and is handed over to the priest Genius to confess his transgressions of the code of love. Influence of the *Rose* may be seen here. The priest Genius is really Love itself as a father confessor, so Love betrays the lover. He becomes the lover's deepest heart, telling him the stark realities of life. Love allegories were popular into the sixteenth century, evolving into ever new forms.

Spenser's *Faerie Queene,* especially the third and fourth books, marks a triumph of married love over courtly, perhaps reflecting changes in the love mores of the time. Lewis comments:

> When Britomart, married love, rescues Amoret from this place of death, she is ending five centuries of human experience, predominantly painful. The only thing that Spenser does not know is that Britomart is the daughter of Busirane, that is, married love grew out of courtly love.[33]

Amoret is love begotten in Heaven and raised to natural perfection in the garden and to civil and spiritual perfection in the temple. It was separated from marriage by courtly chivalry and now finally is restored to it by chastity. Is Spenser capitulating to the law of God and church over against the religion of love? Love may have been forced out by the artificial court marriages of medieval times, to return with more freedom of choice in matters of love.

Spenser, Lewis says, gave us the foundation of the romantic marriage which inspired all love literature from Shakespeare to Meredith.[34]

Dante is another great medieval lover, reflecting court, school, and cloister. His love for Beatrice, whose ravishing beauty he had only fleetingly glimpsed, is, at least in the beginning, a courtly love—that is, a love that must remain unrequited. Especially after Beatrice's death, this love permeates his whole life.

She is the inspiration of his love songs. As Gilson writes: "It is the poet's love for the woman whose presence liberates his genius and makes his song burst forth."[35] This is the classical theme of chivalry, namely, the beautiful lady inspiring the knight to valor, in this case with his pen. "Dante's most original contribution to the history of chivalrous love is perhaps the fact that he lived it so intensely."[36]

Beatrice liberated the muse within him. His quick glance of her divine beauty had forced him into a certain transcendence to describe a love that is almost extracorporeal. Her gorgeous body signifies a beauty of a more exalted kind. To love Beatrice is to praise her.

Some say that from *Vita Nuova* to *The Divine Comedy* Dante moves from courtly love to recantation. Then, in a sense, moves further to a love of the resurrected Beatrice. "The noble fusion of sexual and religious experience in the *Comedy* is a different fusion from that of the *Vita Nuova*. In the *Vita Nuova* the religious element has in it elements of parody, even of blasphemy, that are wholly absent in the *Comedy*."[37]

Whereas Dante's love of Beatrice was a part of his passionate adolescence before reason was fully awakened, his love for Donna Gentile in the *Convivio* is rational.

Was there a divine aspect in Dante's love for Beatrice from the beginning? There must have been, to flower so after her death. "Amor is the divine and therefore personal power which drew Dante to Beatrice and thus ultimately, through her, to his vision of God, in which he found himself as the poet of the *Comedy*."[38] The *Comedy* takes Amor from the *Vita Nuova* and puts it in a theological way.

Dante recants courtly love as he faints at the sight of Francesca in Hell. (5) Whereas in the *Vita Nuova* there seems to be a blend of sex and religion, Dante's wish is to be the perfect cavalier. Sexual love is the underlying presupposition of the *Vita Nuova*, but the religious element is more prominent. The religious language of the *Vita Nuova* could be rhetorical. Thus salvation comes through Beatrice's beauty. (19/7–8)

In *Paradise* (18/21) Beatrice has to educate Dante out of his idolatry of her. "Turn thee about, and listen: not in mine eyes alone is paradise." Thus she steps aside to be his equal.

In the *Comedy* the symbols seem to be both literal and allegorical. Thus Beatrice is both the Florentine beauty and the church. She is the inspiration of the poet. But in the *Comedy* she appears in her resurrected body.

Is there a fusion of sex and religious experience in the *Comedy*? Or rather a proper ordering? The sexual mistakes of Francesca and Brunetto are punished, but Dante seems to transcend into a new order. "Certainly Dante's love of Beatrice is spiritualized, but not made incorporeal, but more corporeal."[39]

Beatrice leads Dante to Mary and through Mary to Christ—human and divine and with the divine light a threefold rainbow. Dante's will is controlled completely by that love that moves the sun and stars. Divine love wins in the end. Human love is but its poor image and hazy foreshadowing.

We have seen glimpses of courtly love from the troubadour William of Aquitaine to his granddaughter Eleanor and his great-granddaughter Marie, with her friends Andreas and Chrétien. Then the famous *Romance of the Rose*, which inspired Chaucer and others and finally the Italian lover Dante.

Through them all two streams flow: worldly courtly love and heavenly divine love. Even when courtly love turns into married love in the romances, still a certain sadness, finiteness, and suffering permeates it. It is predestined for death and separation from its inception. *Aimer, c'est mourir un peu.*

Having seen the evolution of medieval courtly love, let us turn now to the monasteries and universities to see other facets of Christian love.

THE REASON FOR LOVING GOD
IS GOD HIMSELF

Bernard, On the Necessity of Loving God, *1*

Medieval Christian Theology of Love

The Christian theology of love evolved slowly from the sixth century on with strong Neo-Platonic nuances. Besides Augustine, whom we have seen, Pseudo-Dionysius (6th cent.) had a great impact on the medieval Christian theology of love, especially through his work *On the Divine Names.* Dionysius teaches that Eros is the unitary force in the universe. Coming down from above, he turns the longing of creatures upwards.

He further identifies the beautiful with the good. The beautiful gets its name (*kalos*) because it calls (*kalein*) all things to itself. As Proclus before him, Dionysius identifies God and Eros:

Eros is the necessary correlate of Being, Good, and Beautiful. Eros is what gives the cosmic process its dynamic nature. If the divine Eros forces were not diffused throughout the universe, it would be impossible to speak of "The Good" or "The Beautiful" since these are constituted essentially by the longing and desire they arouse, that is by Eros. (4/7–17)[1]

Eros is dynamic in descending and ascending, descending in creation and drawing everything in return to its origin.

(4/10) Eros is an ecstasy which forces the lover out of himself and into his beloved. (4/13) With the aid of Eros man can climb the earthly and heavenly ladder to God.

The monk John Climacus (6th–7th cent.) also teaches a ladder to God. But whereas Dionysius' ladder is hierarchical, with the bishop on top and the monk and layman near the bottom, John's stairway is ascetical, with the monk higher up. The four top steps of John's ascent are: *hesychia* (rest), *henosis* (union in prayer), apathy, and agape. In apathy the bridegroom leaps over the wall and lands in the bridal chamber of the royal palace. The very top stage is agape, the inebriation of the soul.

Maximus the Confessor (7th cent.) helped synthesize the two views of Dionysius and John. Thus God becomes man to enable us to practice love, the highest virtue. But first of all one must free himself from earthly desires.

John Scotus Erigena (9th cent.) is also a bridge, translating Dionysius into Latin and developing his views of love. Thus everything is from God and flows back to him. Though God is unmoved, he sets all things in motion by his beauty as a magnet. (*Division of Nature*, 1/74) Love holds everything together, drawing all back to God through the cycle of nature, with divine self-love as the basic form. "If then the Holy Trinity loves itself in us, and in itself, it is assuredly loved by itself in a glorious manner unknown to all created beings." (1/76)

Bernard of Clairvaux

Bernard is the Christian doctor of love of the Middle Ages. His twelfth century is a time of renaissance.[2] The Crusades, the rise of towns and states, Gothic cathedrals, vernacular languages, revival of Latin classics, Roman law, Greek science and philosophy with Arabic nuances, beginnings of the universities, chivalry and courtly love. All of these mark the twelfth century as a time of resurgence.

But it is also a time of conversion and mystical lights. We have already seen the Sufi way and the Kabbalah and Hasidim. Christian mysticism flowered in the monasteries and convents. In 1112 Bernard with four brothers and twenty-five companions entered monastic life at Citeaux, seeking love of God in a more intimate way.

What is the relationship between mystical literature on love and that of the troubadours and *trouvères?* Some feel that courtly love and the mystical grew together. Others say that mystical love may have been a reaction to the profane love of Ovid taught in the schools and courts. Gilson writes: "The flowering of courtly poetry and courtly romance, all this amorous literature in the French tongue, is preceded and accompanied by an abundance of theological speculation."[3]

Divine love is a prevailing *Zeitgeist*, with the Carthusian school under the leadership of Guigo I, the Benedictines and Cistercians with Bernard of Clairvaux and William of St. Thierry, and the Victorines led by Hugh and Richard.

In general, these lovers worked apart from the various popular philosophies of the day. They are more literary stylists trained in Cicero and Augustine than philosophers or dialecticians. Cicero was of particular interest because of his teachings on disinterested friendship and benevolent love.

Citeaux, with its attempt to restore the pristine Benedictine rule, is a center of monastic love. As the young postulant climbs the hill to the monastery, he is mounting to a life of higher love. And he is proving his love by returning to God what he has been freely given—himself. There is no other solid motive for becoming a monk. The attraction of choir, teaching, research, calligraphy, escape from the world, are nothing when compared to the loving self-gift of the monk to God.[4]

The influences on Bernard and William's mystic writings are many: Paul, John, Tertullian, Origen, Augustine, Gregory of Nyssa, Dionysius, the desert fathers, John Cassian, Gregory the Great. But the main catalyst of mysticism is the very monastic tradition itself, going back through Gregory, Benedict, John Cassian, and Evagrius.

Gilson points out several important fonts of Bernard's teachings on love.[5] First of all, there is the apostle John and especially his first letter on union of the soul with God in love.

From Maximus and perhaps from Dionysius comes divine ecstasy (*excessus*), which can never be complete in this life. Maximus and John give Bernard his view of God as charity which God gives to us, restoring our divine image and uniting ourselves to him in ecstasy.

The Benedictine life itself is a central pillar of Bernard's love with its humility and renunciation of will which are the introduction to charity.

The medieval mystic spirit permeated other religious traditions, as we have seen, particularly the Islamic Sufis and the Jewish Kabbalah and Hasidim. How much interaction there was among these streams has yet to be explored. But all three shared a strong mystical love of God.

Bernard not only meditated on love and pursued it during his monastic life, but also preached and wrote about love. For example, in 1125 he wrote a letter on charity to the Carthusians of Grand Chartreuse (L 12). Three years later he added it to his treatise *On the Necessity of Loving God*, Chapters 12–15.

Charity, he writes, is loving the good of our neighbor equally with our own. One who loves his own good or loves it more, loves it unchastely since his love is not for God's sake.

There are three basic types of men. One praises God because he is powerful, the second because he is good to him, and the third because he is good. Only the charity of a son, the last case, is disinterested love. Charity alone "is strong enough to convert a soul from love of self and of the world and direct it to God." (3)[6]

Self-centeredness is the enemy of charity. It is like a dark and private corner where dirt and mold gather. But the law of the Lord is charity which seeks the good of all. This charity is the heart of the unity of the Trinity and this charity is God himself, not just a quality of him. "Charity is rightly called both God and the gift of God, and so charity gives charity, the substantial gives what is an accident." (4)

The servant and the hireling have their own law, ignoring the law of the creator. But they end up in a state of bondage. Charity is the only true freedom. "The law of charity therefore is good and sweet. It is not only lightly and sweetly borne but renders the laws even of servants and hirelings bearable and light." (7) Charity chastens fear and keeps cupidity in line.

Bernard sees four degrees of love. The first is to love oneself for his own sake. The second loves God for man's sake. The third loves God for God's own sake. And in the last, man loves himself for God's sake. "Forgetful of himself, in a wonderful way, as it were, and as though entirely falling away from himself he will advance wholly into God, and thereafter being joined to him he will be one spirit with him." (8) Love of the flesh will be changed into love of the spirit and human affections changed into divine.

About the same time (1125–26) Bernard wrote *On the Grades of Humility and Pride*. All monastic founders saw humility as a necessary foundation for charity. For unless one recognizes his place, how can he be selfless and charitable to others? Benedict gives twelve stages of humility leading to love. (1–2)

Man's search for truth through humility is based on the beatitudes. Meek, merciful, and pure of heart, we realize our own weakness following the example of the humble Christ. As man seeks the truth, he must first recognize his own weakness. Then become sympathetic to his neighbor's weaknesses. And then, with his heart cleansed from evil, he proceeds to purity and love. (3–6)

The Holy Trinity leads the way, with the Son producing humility by joining the Word to human reason, while the Holy Spirit makes love (charity) by sanctifying the human will.

And the Father receives the sanctified soul as his bride. The ascending scale is: humility, charity, and contemplation. (7–9)

Finally Bernard gives the twelve steps of pride divided into three classes, opposing the twelve degrees of humility, beginning with curiosity and levity, extending through presumption and contempt for authority, and ending up with contempt for God.

Perhaps Bernard's greatest work on love is his *On the Necessity of Loving God* (1127–35).[7] First he asks why we should love God at all. "The reason for loving God is God himself. The measure of loving God is to love him beyond measure." Not only does God have a title to our love, but it is also to our advantage. First of all, he gave himself to us, who are undeserving of the gift. "If then in asking the reason why we should love God we seek to know his title to our love, it is chiefly this: because he has loved us first [1 Jn 4/10]." (1) And he proved his love by giving his only Son for us.

Man owes everything to God, all his gifts of body and soul, though sometimes he wrongly attributes these things to himself. But Christians have more incentives to love God than pagans do. For when they see all that God did for them through Jesus crucified and God's charity revealed through him, "they are filled with shame at not paying back even the very little which they are themselves, in return for love and condescension so great." (3)

It is easy to love, if one knows he is loved. The soul sees the life of Christ, his death and resurrection. Reminiscent of his Sermons on the Canticle, Bernard writes: "The heavenly bridegroom rejoices in such fragrance and freely enters often into the bridal chamber of the heart which he has found filled with fruits of this sort and strewn with flowers." The groom comes where he is contemplated. And his bride decorates the bed of her heart with fresh flowers and fruits to attract her groom. The bride finds sleep and rest in her remembrance of the abundance of the sweetness of her groom, who embraces her with his left hand supporting her head and his right arm around her body. (4)

Having received everything from God, the least one can do is to return the gift with love.

> In the first work, he gave me myself; in the second, himself; and when he gave me himself, he restored me to myself again. Given therefore and restored, I owe myself in return for myself and I owe it as a twofold debt. What shall I render to God in return for himself? For even if I were able to give myself back a thousand times, what am I in comparison with God? (5)

This self-gift, or rather the returning to God of his own gifts, is the very essence of the religious life, as we have seen.

Bernard continues:

> My God, my help, I shall love you according to your gift to me, and according to my measure, which is less, to be sure, than justice demands. But clearly not less than I am able to give. For although I cannot give as much as I owe, nor yet can I give beyond what I am able, I shall be able to give more when you deign to give me more, but never according to your worth. (6)

Though we give, not expecting any reward,

> true charity cannot be unprofitable nor is it, however, mercenary. Certainly it seeks its own [1 Cor 13/5]. It is a matter of affection, not a contract: it neither gains nor is gained by a compact. It exerts its influence freely and makes one free. True love finds satisfaction in itself. It has its own reward, but it is the object it loves. (7)

The reward attracts one who has not yet learned to love, but no one rewards someone who does what he desires. Thus who pays a hungry man to eat? So the soul that loves God seeks nothing else but God as the reward of his love.

Lesser goods such as beauty, wealth, honor, etc., never satisfy. Though the wicked endlessly seek to end their desires, yet they flee that which alone can give them rest. The cause of love is God, arranging the occasion, causing the affection, consummating the desire.

Bernard explains the four degrees of love that he had mentioned to the Carthusians, namely, carnal selfish love, loving God for man's sake and for his own sake, and loving himself for God. But this last love is impossible in this life because of man's weakened condition, for he is attached to his body and even after death longs for it. So it is only after his resurrection that he can reach this perfect state. "Now we do not even love ourselves save for his sake. So that he himself is the reward of those who love him, the reward eternal of those who love for all eternity." (10)

Some of Bernard's most penetrating thoughts on love are in his Sermons on the Canticle of Canticles or the Greatest Song. This was originally a collection of Hebrew wedding songs, as we have seen, but adopted by the rabbis and Christian Fathers to signify the love of God and man. Origen and Gregory of Nyssa were Christian commentators. The Jewish Kabbalists and Hasidim sang its praises. And medieval Christian mystics such as Bernard and William of St. Thierry loved it. Certainly it is an ideal song to switch those engrossed in carnal love to divine.

The constant theme of Bernard's sermons is that the love between the soul and God is analogous to that of bride and groom, a common medieval mystic leitmotif.

In Sermon 7, Bernard says: "'Let him kiss me with the kisses of his mouth.' Who is it that speaks these words? It is the bride. Who is the bride? It is the soul thirsting for God."[8] There are many dispositions of men to their superiors. For example, the slave fears his master, the hireling seeks wages from his boss, a disciple gives attention to his teacher, and the son honors his father. But the soul loves God. "If then love is especially befitting to a bride and bridegroom, it is not unfitting that the name of bride is given to the soul which loves. It is a sign of her love that she makes this request." Thus the Canticle is perfectly fitting for Bernard's monks, whose souls are brides of God.

In Sermon 8, Bernard exclaims how the Father loves and embraces his Son and the Son loves his Father. "Now this cognition of mutual love between him who begets and him who is begotten, what is it but a kiss, as deeply mysterious as it is sweet?" (8/1)

Jesus passed this divine kiss on to his church. "That was without a doubt a kiss which he gave them. What? That physical breath? Nay, but the invisible Spirit who was thus communicated by the breathing of the Lord. So by this very action it might be understood that he proceeds from the Son equally as from the Father." (8/2)

There are three ways to love God (Sermon 20), namely, with carnal, rational, and spiritual love. Carnal love of God is the purpose of the Incarnation.

> I can consider that a principal cause why God who is invisible, willed to render himself visible in the flesh and to dwell as a man among men, was to draw, in the first place, to the salutary love of his sacred flesh all the affections of carnal men who were unable to love otherwise than in a carnal manner and so by degrees to draw them to a pure and spiritual affection. (20/6)

Rational love is to love according to faith without deviation from the church, with all one's soul.

> If to this be added a force so great and an assistance so powerful, as that of the Holy Spirit, so that neither troubles nor sufferings, however violent, nor even the fear of death, can ever cause the desertion of the righteousness, then God is loved with all the strength, and that is spiritual love. And I think this name particularly suitable to such love, because of the fulness of the spirit which so particularly distinguishes it. (20/9)

Love unifies.

This song is a song of love. And it is appropriate to fill it with loving speeches, only also this love is of God. Nor does he have it from any other than himself, because he is the source of love. And it is so much the more powerful and vigorous as he and love are but one. But those whom he loves he treats as friends not as servants. From being the master he becomes the friend. . . . Love looks up to no one, but neither does it look down upon any. It regards with equal eye all who are united among themselves in a perfect bond of love. It combines together in its own self the loftiest with the lowest. Nor does it merely make them equals, but makes them to be one. (59/1–2)

God loved us first! "For the Lord emptied himself so that you might know it to be the effect of his great love. That his fulness was poured forth and expanded, that his loftiness was brought down to the level of others, and his unique position associated with them." (64/10)
And the bride loves her groom in return.

The bride, burning inconceivably with holy love, seeks some relief and solace in the ardor which she endures, and in seeking it takes no heed of how she speaks, but urged on by her love, bursts forth with the first words which come to her mouth. And what should she speak except that with which her heart is filled? (67/3)

My beloved is mine and I am his. "There can be no doubt that in this passage is apparent the flame of an ardent and reciprocal love of two persons, one for the other: while in this love appears also the supreme felicity of the one and the marvelous condescension of the other." (67/8)
There are different degrees of love. For example, children have affection for their parents, yet they are often thinking of their heritage. This is an impure love since it is based on the hope of something else.

Love that is pure is not mercenary. It does not draw strength from hope, nor is it weakened by distrust. This is the love which is felt by the bride because all she is is only love. The very being of the bride and her only hope consists in love. In this the bride abounds, with this the bridegroom is content. He seeks nothing else from her. She has nothing but this to give. Then it is that he is bridegroom and she is bride. This belongs exclusively to the wedded pair, and to it none other attains, not even a son. (83/5)

But the bride must love her lover. How could she fail to do otherwise? How can love fail to be returned?

Rightly, then, does she renounce all other affections, and devote herself wholly and entirely to him who is love. Since she can make return to him by a love which is reciprocal for whom she has poured herself forth entirely in love. What would that be in comparison with the everflowing and inexhaustible source of love? Not with equal fulness of resource flows that stream from love and from the creature that loves him, from the soul and from the word, the bridegroom and the bride, the creator and the creature, and the thirsty wayfarer with the fountain that satisfies thirst? (83/6)

Because she is less, she loves less, yet she loves with her whole soul in a spiritual marriage. Yet the soul is both anticipated in loving by her groom and surpassed in love.

Bernard speaks of love also in other sermons. For example, on the three degrees of divine love (Sermon 29)[9] which oppose the three degrees of concupiscence. The three loves as mentioned to Peter (Jn 21/15–17) are to love with tenderness and affection, with prudence and fortitude. To love with one's whole heart is to love with affection, to love with his whole soul is to love with prudence, and to love with all his strength is to love with fortitude.

Love of Christ's incarnation and death brings affectionate love of the heart. "What carnal pleasure can be pleasing to him who finds so much sweetness in the passion of his savior?" But this can lead astray without prudence which expels all vain curiosity. Fortitude makes us able to resist violence and suffer anything for justice.

The Lord questioned Peter about his love.

Was it not natural that he to whose charge the flock was to be committed should be interrogated about his love? For none ought to be appointed to rule others, save such as are inebriated with the wine of charity, so that, forgetful of themselves, they may seek not the things that are their own, but the things that are Jesus Christ's.

William of St. Thierry

William is another great twelfth-century lover, a fellow monk and admirer of Bernard. The first abbot of the Cluniac monastery of St. Thierry, he moved to the Cistercian foundation of Signy (1135). The monastery for William, as it was for Bernard, is a school of divine love, a school opposed to the secular schools and courts where the profane love of Ovid was taught.

William seems to be more inspired by Augustine than Bernard is, especially in the memory's place in the science of love. The love of God is naturally in man's heart, but original sin drives it away. Monastic life tries to bring man's love back to his creator. Through God's grace man can recover the divine likeness in memory, intellect, and will.

In his *On the Contemplation of God* (1119–35),[10] William writes in a prayerful manner reminiscent of Augustine's *Confessions*.

I contemplate by the gift of your grace all the corners and borders of my consciousness. I desire only and especially to see you, that all the boundaries of my land may see the salvation of the Lord our God, that I may love him when I see him, for to love him is to truly live. I say to myself in the languor of my delight: Who loves what he does not see? And how can someone be loveable who cannot be seen? (4)

Love and desire are closely allied.

There is the love of desire and the love of enjoyment. The love of desire sometimes merits vision; and the vision—enjoyment and the enjoyment—the perfection of love. I thank your grace who deigned to speak to the heart of your servant, and who answers up to a certain point his anxious question. I receive and embrace this pledge of the Holy Spirit, and happy I await in this pledge the fulfillment of your promise. This is because I desire to love you and I love to desire you and in this manner I run to grasp him by whom I have been seized. That is, to love you perfectly sometimes, you who loved us first, O beloved and loveable Lord. (8)

Everyone according to his own strength loves and desires to love and the unity of love precludes diversity.

Surely it is the love itself which is loved which from the superabundance and nature of its goodness fills with an identical grace but with an unequal measure, those who love and those who love together, those who enjoy and those who enjoy together. Moreover, this love infuses itself with abandon into the senses of those who love and it makes them capable of possessing itself. It sates them but without cloying. And in this satiety the desire is not diminished, but increased, but without any misery of anxiety. Love it is, they say, which is loved, which from the very torrent of its voluptuousness repels every misery from its lover—either cloying satiety or anxious desire or jealous zeal. . . .

This is glory, these are riches in the house of his blessed lover because present to the desirer is that which he desires and to the lover that which he loves. Therefore, he who desires, always loves to desire. And to the desirer and lover, what he desires and loves you give in abundance, O Lord, so

that neither anxiety afflicts the desirer nor cloying the en-
riched. (11)

The love of God and man is mutual, but quite different.

This is your love by which you love those who love you by
the sweetness of your goodness which you have towards
your creature. O good creator, to inspire in them this desire
of loving you and the love by which they love both to desire
and to love you. You are not influenced towards us or by us,
when you love us. But you are that what you always are.
. . . We, however, are attracted by you, we who can be miserable and not love you. That is to say, to exist and to exist
badly.

To you, however, who are always the same, nothing can
be added if in loving we proceed to you, and nothing is
taken away when we pull away from you. (12)

Man's love can only be for God.

For the love of a rational soul, as said a certain servant of
yours [Bernard, Sermon 20/9, on the Canticle], is a movement or a quiet rest or an end beyond which the appetite of
the will judges there is nothing more to be desired or coveted. He who seeks something better than you, beyond you,
or above you, seeks nothing. For there is nothing better or
sweeter than you. Therefore nothing is gained by withdraw-
ing from you who alone are to be truly loved. And he forni-
cates or debauches himself in alien loves, as I said, having
strange names. For love, as was said, and should be said, is
to you alone, Lord, in whom alone is whoever truly is—
where there is quiet and secure rest. Because to fear God by
the chaste fear of love and to observe his commandments,
this is the whole man [Eccl 12/13]. (14)

God loves us first through Christ.

And whatever he did, whatever he said on earth, even to
insults, even to spit and slaps, even to the cross and grave,

was only your word to us in your Son, by your love pro-
voking and stimulating our love to you. For you knew, God,
creator of souls, that this affection cannot be forced in the
souls of men, but rather should be stimulated.

Therefore, you wanted us to love you, we who could not
justly be saved unless we love you, nor could we love you
unless it proceed from you. Therefore, Lord, as the apostle
of love says to you, and we have already said, you loved us
first and you love first of all your lovers. (17)

The Holy Spirit, the mutual love of the Father and the Son,
proceeds from the Father and the Son and so great is his love
that Father and Son are one substance. "You also love yourself
in us, sending the Holy Spirit into our hearts by the sweetness of
love and by the strength of good will, inspired in us by you,
crying 'Abba, Father' [Gal 4/6]. Thus you make us your lovers,
loving yourself in us." (19)
This love unites our spirits with God.

But when we love you, our spirit is drawn to your Holy
Spirit living in us, by whom we have the charity of God diffused in our hearts. Since your love, the love of the Father
to the Son, the love of the Son to the Father, the Holy Spirit
dwells in us—towards you is what is. That is, your love converts and sanctifies all the captivity of Zion, that is, the affection of our soul. We love you and you love yourself in us
one in you by your unity, that is, by your Holy Spirit whom
you gave to us . . . (23)

We have already seen the popularity of the Shekhinah, God's
Holy Spirit of love, in the medieval Jewish Kabbalah.

William wrote his *Nature and Dignity of Love* (1119–35)[11]
against the popular secular Ovidian love.

The art of arts is the art of loving. Nature itself and God,
nature's author, are its teachers. For love itself is given by
the creator of nature, and unless its natural purity has been

soiled by some adulterous affection, love teaches itself, I say, to its own disciples, to the disciples of God. (1)

As did Augustine, William sees love as a weight. "Love is a power of the soul by a natural weight, bearing it in its place or towards its end. Every creature either spiritual or corporeal has a certain place where it is naturally at home, and a certain natural weight which bears it there." Weights do not necessarily bear down. For fire rises, water falls, as do bodies, while the spirit ascends. So also love bears the soul up to God. (1)

Love grows.

Just as by increase or decrease of life a boy becomes a youth, a youth becomes a man and a man an elder, and according to the changes of qualities, the names of the ages are changed. So according to the progress of virtues the will grows in love, love into charity, and charity into wisdom. (4)

The birth of love was when God stamped his trinitarian image on man, as Augustine says: memory, intellect, and will. (5)

Love is blind.

When love remains blind it still accomplishes that which it does. Though it does not know whence it came or where it is going, it works with its affections as a blind man does with his hands.

He sees neither his hands nor the work he does, and when someone instructs him, he takes him by the hand to instruct in the use rather than the art of the work to be done.

Likewise blind love is formed from without by all the means described above, forced to a certain dignity of life and mores. When by a long apprenticeship the substance of the interior man will become plastic and capable of receiving the print and seal of their form, then it will produce the peaceful fruit of salvation. . . . When love becomes charity, when the soul attains its perfect purity, then I will tell you and point out in detail something else, the divine. (11)

Enlightened love is charity.

Love from God, in God, and to God is charity. In fact, charity is God. God is charity, says John [1 Jn 4/16]. This is a short praise, but it includes everything. For whatever you can say about God, you can say about charity, when you consider it according to the nature of gift and giver. In the giver it is called substance, while in the gift—quality. But for emphasis even the gift of charity is called God. (15)

Love presumes faith and hope. The lover can only love what is believed and hoped. As the body has five senses by which it is joined to the soul, so the soul has five senses by which it is joined to God—"By which charity quickens the soul, that is, carnal love, e.g. of parents, social love, natural love, spiritual love, love of God. Through the five bodily senses the living body is joined to the soul. Through the five spiritual senses by charity the soul is united to God." (18)

William compares the five spiritual and bodily senses with the highest divine love by sight. (19–23) "By the sight of the eyes all the rest of the senses are said to see. Although only the eye sees, we say 'touch and see,' 'taste and see,' etc. So by divine love all the rest are said to be loved which are well-loved." The vision of God which is charity is divided into the two eyes of reason and love. (25)

Love the Lord your God with your whole heart. (Lk 10/27)

Four movements to God are needed in us totally. When the Lord says "With your whole heart" he wants the whole will for himself; "With your whole soul" all love; "With all your strength" he means the virtue of charity; "With your whole mind" the enjoyment of wisdom. First the will moves the soul to God, love advances, charity contemplates and wisdom enjoys.

And the enjoyment is a certain flavor, a divine taste. (33)

Like his friend Bernard, William, too, is preoccupied with the Greatest Song of Solomon, writing and editing several commentaries, including one each made up of quotes from Ambrose and Gregory the Great. Let us look briefly at William's second commentary. (PL, 180/473–546)

The Holy Spirit has given to men a song of spiritual and divine love whose interior affair he describes in images of carnal love. And since only this full love can grasp the divine, carnal love must be led, must migrate into love of the Spirit in order that it may grasp spiritual things (*Expositio*).

O love from which all love is named, even carnal and degenerate love. O holy and sanctifying love, chaste and purifying and vivifying life, open to us your holy song, reveal the mystery of your kiss, the interiority of your whisperings by which you sing your virtues and the delights of your sweetness in the hearts of your sons. (481)

William then comments on the sacred kiss.

"He kisses me with the kiss of his mouth." I saw, she says, over me his bright face, and I perceived the joy of his glance. Nobody comes between, nothing interferes. He kisses me with the kiss of his mouth. Beyond this I cannot bear, nor do I accept the spirit of an alien kiss. All the rest smell to me depraved. But the kiss of my beloved has a divine fragrance. The kiss of a friend is an exterior joining of bodies, but a sign and incentive of interior union. What is shown by mouth is not only a union of bodies, but also from the mutual contact—a spiritual union.

Christ is the spouse of the church, reaching out a kiss from Heaven—as God becomes man. So God offers his kiss to the faithful soul of his spouse, pouring in his love, "attracting her spirit to him and pouring his in her that they may be one spirit." (483)

In Augustinian manner William shows the place of rest of the lover and beloved. "The place of reclining and rest of the spouses is the memory, intellect and love. In these rest the spouses, he pouring in grace, she piously remembering, humbly understanding and ardently loving." (499)

The bride seeks the common love bed.

There she goes, there she conceives, there she is anxious. She wants to love, wants to enjoy, not in the reclining of the will, but in the habit of the mind, when she chooses the flowering bed. In the sense of a soul seeking God, the enjoyment of God can be expected in whom his similitude precedes. Therefore, she says "Our bed." When she says it will be ours, common to you and me, it will breathe holy delights and it will be warmed by mutual love. (508)

The groom's left hand supports his bride's head, while his right hand hugs her body. This is the Holy Spirit.

For it is the Holy Spirit, who is the communion, the charity, the friendship, the hug of the Father and the Son of God. He is everything in the love of the spouses. But there his majesty is of consubstantial nature, here a gift of grace; there dignity, here an honor, but the same Spirit. The hug is begun here but completed there. This abyss calls for the other one. That ecstasy dreams from afar of another which it does not see. This secret pants for another secret, this joy imagines another joy, that sweetness anticipates another sweetness. . . .

Then there will be a full kiss, a perfect hug, when the supporting hand will not be needed but the delights of the groom's right hand will totally envelop the bride all the way to the end of infinite eternity. Then, I say, the kiss will be full, and the hug, too, whose strength is the wisdom of God and the sweetness of the Holy Spirit, the perfect and full enjoyment of divinity and God, all things in all. Faith will not palpitate there, nor hope tremble because full charity in the complete vision of God will exalt all the affections into one effect of enjoying and rejoicing. (520)

Carnal experience is used to explain divine love in the Canticle. The groom seems to be playing with his bride in a wanton manner. Frequently he withdraws himself violently from his beloved to return once again. Sometimes he seems to walk out as if never to come back again, that he may be more ardently pursued. At other times, he goes back to her as if he would never leave, inviting her more sweetly to kisses.

Sometimes he seems to stand on the other side of the wall and to look through the windows, flattering her to excite the desire of his beloved. But he is not totally there. No, he is heard calling and inviting, but from afar. Then as the fire rises in the heart of his beloved, he departs and recedes and is neither seen, nor heard, nor felt. Since the bride cannot hold back her departing lover, she only asks him to return sometimes, saying, "Return, my delight, may you be like a wild goat and a young stag on the mountains of Bethel." (538)

In his *Mirror of Faith* (1144),[12] William describes the important place of the Holy Spirit in divine love. We have seen earlier the importance of this in Jewish mysticism, linking human and divine love. Christian mystics taught the same thing. At first glance the femininity of the Jewish Shekhinah seems to be missing in the Christian Holy Spirit; however, when one sees the human soul or spirit as the bride of God in Christian writings, and the Holy Spirit of love linking the soul with God, perhaps the female aspect is not entirely missing.

One cannot love God unless under the influence of his Holy Spirit. "Since the soul can love nothing which it does not envisage as a good, and since all love is due only to the sovereign good, the soul goes to God with all its love, unless it be deceived by some false good and made captive thereby." (20)

God's love is compared to our natural love as the soul is to the body. Without God's love, ours is dead and cannot attain understanding which God desires. "But when we are truly alive with the love of God, we are made one with the Spirit of God, for the sense of love is more powerful than all the faculties of mind and body."

The Holy Spirit, the substantial will of the Father and Son, draws the will of man to himself in love so that the soul is completely transformed into God. "It is not changed into the divine nature, but into that form of beatitude which, though less than divine, is more than human." (21)

Man's inmost soul cleaves to God, so that it is truly an image of its creator and the likeness of the divine goodness. Man finds himself in the midst of the Trinity, united to God in the charity which unites Father and Son. "Such a grace is more than the mind can grasp, such goodness is unfathomable, to be made holy in the spirit of all holiness, where Father and Son embrace. . . . Sweetness, O deep security for the loving heart."

An enemy of both Bernard and William was Abelard, who certainly was not against love, as his affection for Héloïse attests, but who, as one of the founders of medieval Christian dialectics, placed more stress on reason than on simple belief. Abelard's road to reason was condemned as intellectual pride by Bernard and William. Abelard's theological view of love seems more dialectic despite his human love ecstasies with Héloïse. Bernard's and William's theology of love is more mystical, to be fulfilled in beatitude. However, Abelard says that pure love can only be motivated by divine perfection even to forgoing beatitude.

Gilson writes that after Bernard and William the Cistercian mystic thrust loses steam and turns toward religious moralism.[13] Thus Isaac Stella seeks God through metaphysical speculation. And the eclectic monks of Citeaux, drifting away from the lofty speculation of Bernard, followed the general trend of the times.

Another home of speculative mysticism in the twelfth century is the abbey of the Augustinian canons of St. Victor in Paris, with their two stars, Hugh and Richard. Hugh teaches that contemplation in love anticipates the eternal joys of divine love and presupposes the science which we must acquire in order to transcend to God.

Both Bernard and the Victorines influenced the Franciscan giant Bonaventure, who was also inspired by Augustine, Dionysius, and Francis of Assisi. Originally the whole world pointed to God, says Bonaventure, but when man sinned, the ladder was broken, so he needs the incarnate Christ as a ladder to ascend to God, Father, Word, and Love in mystical union.

Thomas Aquinas

Aquinas (13th cent.) also wrote of love, but in a dialectic manner perhaps more suitable to the university lecture halls than to the monastic cloisters. Also Aquinas showed the inspiration of Aristotle more than the school of Bernard and William, though we find Augustine in both traditions. Thomas' thoughts on love and charity may be found in his *Summa Theologica* (1–2, qq. 26–30).

First of all, there is a natural love even in inanimate things. "For an inanimate thing wants what is in accord with its nature, not through its knowledge of them, but through that possessed by the author of its nature." (*ST*, 1–2/26/1) Though the object does not know why it moves, love does.

In the case of the natural appetite this cause, which might be called "natural love," is a sense of affinity with the object in question. Thus a heavy body's sense of affinity with its natural place arises from its weight, and might be called "natural love." Similarly the terms "sensory love" and "intellectual or rational love," apply to the attachment, the sense of affinity with some good, the feeling of its attractiveness, felt respectively by the sense appetite or the will. (26/1)[14]

Love as a weight we have seen in men like Aristotle, Augustine, and William of St. Thierry. Here natural love, in a sense, resembles Aristotle's cosmic love, with the Prime Mover drawing all things to itself in love.

Natural love for medieval authors is a certain connaturality inclining a thing to its natural place. Thus earth is in the lowest place, water above, then air and fire in the highest places. So bodies fall, water goes downhill, and flames rise.

There is a certain circularity in the appetite and its object (as Aristotle commented in *De Anima*, 3/10):

> First the object works on the appetite, imprinting itself there, as one might say. Then the appetite moves towards the object with the purpose of actually possessing it, so the process ends where it began. The first effect produced in the appetite is love, which is simply a feeling of the object's attractiveness. This feeling gives rise to an appetitive movement towards the object, e.g., desire, and finally this comes to rest in joy. (26/2)

Since love is an affection produced in the appetite by its object, it is a passion. Love is a virtue, then, giving rise to movement toward union with its object.

Aquinas studies love (*amor*) and its correlatives *dilectio*, *caritas*, and *amicitia*. Love (*amor*) includes *dilectio* and *caritas*. *Dilectio*, which refers to a prior choice, lies in the will. Charity adds the nuance that the loved object is highly prized, as the word *caritas* (*carus*) implies.

Two important loves are those of friendship and desire, the love for the one for whom the good is wanted and the good which is wanted. (26/4)

Aquinas sees the good, knowledge, and similarity as causes of love. (27) The good and the beautiful are two aspects of the good. The will rests in the good, while the sensible and intellectual apprehensions rest in the beautiful. This is an object-centered love, but one can only love the good when he knows it and sees a similarity. Similarity can consist of having like qualities or in one having potentiality for another's actuality.

The first of these two kinds of similarity gives rise to the love of friendship or the love of good will. For the fact that two people are alike in having some form means in a sense that they are one form. . . . The result is that the affections of the one are bent upon the other as being one with himself, and he wishes well to the other as to himself. (27/3)

Similis simili congaudet. The second type of similarity is based on desire and is selfish.

Love underlies all the other passions as they move toward their objects and rest in them.

The effects of love (28) include union, mutual indwelling, ecstasy, and jealousy. The first effect is union of the lover and beloved. They are united either in reality or by inclination and feeling. And this union can bring about either selfish good or good for the other. "When one has love of friendship for a person, he wants good things for him as one does for himself. One therefore looks upon him as another self, wishing him well as he does himself." (28/1)

Mutual indwelling is another effect of love, both by knowledge and by desire. When the beloved is absent, the thought and desire of the lover follow. "Perfect love allows but one life to subsist in two. Each speaks of his self and his other self." (28/2)

Ecstasy is an important effect of love. Ecstasy is to be carried outside of oneself either by the cognitive or by the appetitive faculties. For example, the ecstatic can be carried above his normal powers beyond the limits of sense or reason. Ecstasy can be either above or below one's normal state, thus an ecstasy of madness. "Cognitive ecstasy is caused by love dispositively: for as we have seen, love keeps turning a person's mind to thoughts of the beloved and intense preoccupation with one thought withdraws the mind from others. . . ."

Appetitive ecstasy is caused by love directly, either the love of friendship or the love of desire. In the love of desire, the lover is carried out of himself in the sense that he is not content to enjoy what is already in his possession, but is anxious to enjoy something he has not. But since he wants to bring this back to himself, he is not completely or fully carried out of himself.

In love of friendship, however, the ultimate term of the person's feeling is located outside him completely for he wants some good thing for his friend, and works for it, exercising thought and care about his friend's interests for his friend's sake. (28/3)

Jealousy is a common effect of love. (28/4) "Jealousy arises from the intensity of love, for the more intensely an active power is bent upon a given object, the more vigorously does it resist anything opposed to or incompatible with that objective." Love is an active power and so will fight to resist any opposition. Either this jealousy can be selfish, as in the love of desire. Thus I am jealous over a success of another because I do not have it for myself. Or jealousy can also be selfless, as in the love of friendship. Here one is jealous for a friend that no one will hurt him, etc.

In general love is good. (28/5) Why? Because it brings the lover in contact with an appropriate good. But love of a lesser good can harm him. Materially or psychologically love can be harmful if in excess.

There are four proximate effects of love: melting, pleasure, languor, fever. (28/5) "Frigidity or hardness of heart is therefore a state incompatible with love; whereas melting or warmth suggests a certain softness which means that the heart will be quick to let the object loved enter into it." If the beloved object is possessed—joy and pleasure. If not, languor and sadness and feverish desire for possession.

Love is really the cause of every action, for one acts for a certain good which he loves.

Hate is the opposite of love. (29/1) Just as there is a natural love when a thing is in harmony with what is agreeable to it, so there is a natural hate toward alien objects. The same holds true for the sensitive and rational appetites. As the object of love is good, the object of hate is evil. Hate is caused by love in the sense that we hate things that go counter to our loves. (2)

But love is stronger than hate, for hate is caused by love. Moreover, the soul reacts more strongly to good than to evil, though the unpleasantness of something hated can be more keenly felt than the pleasantness of something loved. (3)

Desire and aversion parallel love and hate. (30) Desire is the impulse to move toward the absent object which has aroused the emotion of love. Concupiscence is the desire for the goods of the animal life both in men and in animals. Cupidity is proper to man in acts of passion. The satisfaction of concupiscence is pleasure or delight, while the satisfaction of cupidity is joy.

But one cannot compare the precarious sense pleasures of concupiscence with the stable joys of the mind. Intellectual pleasures are more beloved than physical, writes Aquinas. (31/5) "For there is no one who would not forfeit his bodily sight rather than his intellectual vision." Also sensual objects are seen only partially, whereas the intellect sees the whole.

Is sexual pleasure the enemy of man's noble reason? Conjugal intercourse, though in accord with reason, hinders it. But reason cannot be operative all the time. It needs a rest in sleep or in sex. However, Aquinas feels that before the Fall sex and reason were in perfect accord. (34/1)

Having seen some of Aquinas' thoughts on love, let us now turn to his doctrine of charity. Earlier (1–2/26/1) he said that charity adds to love (amor) the nuance that the loved object is highly prized. Of course, the most highly prized object of love is God.

"Charity is a certain friendship of man for God," writes Thomas. (2–2/23/1) Charity is a virtue, a strength, moving man to God, and it is the most excellent virtue. "Because it touches God himself and remains in him not so that we might obtain something for ourselves." (23/6)

As love motivates all human acts, so charity gives form to the acts of the other virtues, directing them to God.

Following Judaeo-Christian tradition, Aquinas teaches that love is infused by the Holy Spirit, who is the mutual love of the Father and the Son. (24/2) Charity can be increased and be perfect if one habitually places his whole heart in God so that he thinks of nothing or wishes nothing that is contrary to the divine will. (24/8) But sin drives out both love and the Holy Spirit. (24/11–12)

The love of God and neighbor are really one. "The reason for loving our neighbor is God. We ought to love our neighbor because he is in God. Thus it is clear that by the same species of act we love God and neighbor, and because of this habit of charity the act not only includes love of God, but also love of neighbor." (25/1)

Aquinas asks a lot of practical questions about love which probably grew out of student discussions. For example, should we love animals? (25/3) Strictly speaking, one cannot love an animal as a friend except in a metaphorical sense. Also love pertains to beatitude, which animals cannot reach. "However, out of charity we can love irrational creatures as goods which we wish for others; insofar as from charity we wish them to be conserved for the glory of God and the use of man. Thus also God loves them out of charity."

But should man love himself? He should love God and all those things that are proper to God, including himself. (25/4)

How about sinners? (25/6) We should hate in sinners the fact that they are sinners and love in them their capacity for beatitude. We should love the man and not his sin. We should even love our enemies insofar as they are our neighbors, loving all for God's sake. "Since we love our neighbor out of charity for God's sake, the more we love God, the more we show love for our neighbor without unfriendliness impeding our love."

Is it all right to love some people more than others? (26)
We should love God first of all as the cause of our beatitude and our neighbor as participating with us in beatitude.
Man should love himself according to his spiritual nature even
over his neighbor. But may one love some neighbor more than
others? Yes, since the loving God is the principle of love. In
all those in whom this principle is found, the order of loving
is graded according to comparison with this principle. Thus
to the man who is closer to God we wish him greater good
out of charity.

Also those who are close to us we love more.

Those who are conjoined to us more closely are to be loved
more out of charity, because they are loved more intensely,
and because they are loved for many reasons. The intensity
of love is from the closeness of the loved to the lover. . . .
In those things that pertain to nature we ought to love our
own relations more.

And among our own close relatives our father should be loved
more as the active principle of our natural origin, while our
mother is the passive principle.

Should a man love his wife more than his parents? Thomas
cleverly distinguishes: "One's parents should be loved more
than his wife as the principles of his origin, but his wife should
be loved more than his parents by reason of closeness—two
in one flesh."

Love of God and neighbor is the proper act of the virtue
of charity, resulting in spiritual joy. (27, 28)

Though man aims at perfect charity, it cannot be attained
in this life. Man is bound to love God with his whole heart.
But this can be done only insofar as no contrary affection
exists. Being human, men are bound to earth and so cannot
attain perfect charity, which is God himself, here below.

We can lose charity through sin. Since God is the cause of
charity, when one turns away from him, charity goes, too. But

in Heaven this cannot happen and the soul is united to God in perfect charity.[15]

In this chapter we have seen several medieval Christian theologians of love, Bernard and William of the Cistercian school and the Dominican Thomas Aquinas of the University of Paris. Aquinas' friend and fellow student Bonaventure led the Franciscan school of love.

As we have seen in the last several chapters, love permeates the Middle Ages from the Islamic Sufi and the Jewish Kabbalah to the feudal courts, from the cloistered mystics to the university lecture halls.

We shall now turn to the Renaissance and the Reformation. Though faith is often seen as the shibboleth of the Reformation, love plays no less a part.

⋖ XIV ⋗

FAITH WITHOUT LOVE
IS NOT ENOUGH

Martin Luther, Wittenberg Sermons, March 9, 1522

The medieval mystics relentlessly pursued their ascent to God. Early Renaissance authors such as Dante sang its praises. But the Reformation brought a new tradition. Monasticism's ascetical way to God crumbled, to be replaced by the ex-monk Luther's teaching of God's way to man through Christ. Of course, this is an oversimplification, for all the mystic writers have always insisted that their way to God is a free and unmerited gift from God himself.

Instead of man's ascent to God, Luther underlines God's descent to man. Perhaps Luther's own life mirrored his teachings, for he found the monastic ascent to perfection all but impossible. How can a man be an angel? Luther is inspired by the Scriptures, particularly the Psalms and Romans and Augustine's *On the Spirit and the Letter*, stressing man's complete helplessness and dependence on God.[1]

Luther is famous for his teaching of faith in God's loving mercy over justification by works—the law of faith over the law of works. For Luther the foundation of man's fellowship with God is not any self-righteousness or ascesis or holiness, but his sinfulness, the fact that he needs God! Christ comes to us, not we to Christ. "Man is justified not by ascending to

God in *caritas* but solely by receiving in favor God's love, which has descended to us in Christ," writes A. Nygren.[2]

Thus the medieval upward motion through piety, scholasticism, and mysticism is rejected, with eros replaced by agape. Sinful man is unable to seek God through his corrupt reason or through ascesis.

Luther perhaps missed the point of monasticism, which is not so much self-justification as a divine call and self-gift. But without the divine call and grace there can be no self-gift. As Augustine said, we return to God his own gifts.

Luther, though strong on faith in God, was no less emphatic on the works of love that must flow from faith, as we shall see.

Communion of the Saints

First, Luther's teachings on love in his early life up till his condemnation by the Edict of Worms (1521). For example, in 1515–16 he comments on Romans 5/5: "Because the love of God is shed abroad in our hearts." He says we can bear the tribulation of the world only through the love of God which we receive through the Holy Spirit.

Luther's love is not that which man spontaneously gives on his own, but is rather a gift of God to man that enables him to love God.

> It is then this "love of God" alone, this unqualified devotion to God, which creates men of right heart; it alone takes away iniquity; it alone extinguishes the enjoyment of self-righteousness. Because it loves God in and for himself and not what God gives, as the hypocritical moralists think, it does not get exalted when physical and spiritual goods come flowing in.

Nor does it get disappointed when they flow out.[3]

This love of God is charity, says Luther, echoing Aquinas.

It is therefore called charity in difference from the very unfruitful and very low kind of love by which one loves a creature. For "charity" means to love something dearly and preciously or to esteem as precious what one loves. So also to esteem God above everything means to love him with a precious love, that is, with charity. (166)

But to love God for his gifts is to use him, not to enjoy him, an Augustinian nuance. True love of God lives in man's heart so that he is a free son and not a slave.

Augustine's *On the Spirit and the Letter* inspired Luther's teaching on justification. The letter kills, but the spirit gives life. The moral or spiritual interpretation of the Bible deals with love and disposition of heart. We should do what we do out of love of God and not fear of his punishments.

Luther frequently speaks of love of God that supersedes obstacles. Thus he comments on Romans 8/28–39: "We know that to them that love God, he will work together all things for good." To those who are loved by God and love him, the Holy Spirit works all things, even apparent evils, to the good.

The love of God is not a selfish love, writes Luther (Rom 9/3–5). Paul's love was not selfish, for he spent himself for souls though this might seem foolish to some "who regard themselves as holy and who love God with a foolish love, that is, for the sake of their own salvation and eternal rest and for the purpose of avoiding hell, in other words, not for God's sake, but for their own sake." (262) These people think that charity begins at home with their own salvation first, then their neighbor's.

One should submit his will perfectly to God, even if this means condemnation. Christ offered himself to the Father this way in perfect love and God raised him up.

To love oneself does not mean to desire good things for oneself! No! "'To love' means to hate and condemn oneself. To desire something that is bad for one, in accordance with the word of Christ." (263)

Love, moreover, should be genuine (Rom 12/9) and not dissimulated, which is nothing more than artificial love which often cloaks hatred. Thus the cloying subservience of subordinates to their superiors. Others honestly believe that they love till trial and adversity show them up.

Still others fall short of true love either by failing in fraternal correction or even by praising unwittingly the vices of others. This can easily happen in the intense love for a person in whom good and evil are not distinguished. "When we give our love to a person with unreserved assurance and devotion, we are ready and eager to cherish and defend whatever he may happen to think. But we do not ask ourselves how we can recognize what is good or evil in him." (343) Love is blind to the faults of the beloved.

Brotherly love (*philadelphia*) (Rom 12/10) is the hallmark of the Christian. This is a special love, not at all like the love one has for enemies and strangers. Paul also uses *philastorgoi*, that is, to have tender affection for someone.

True love is self-hatred, says Luther. "He, therefore, that hates himself and loves his neighbor, loves himself truly. For then he loves himself outside himself and thus he has divine love for himself as long as he loves himself in his neighbor." (407)

The admonition to love the neighbor as oneself really illustrates a selfish love. "You are wholly bent in on yourself and versed in self-love and you will not be straightened out and made upright unless you cease entirely to love yourself and, forgetting yourself, love only your neighbor." (408)

We are selfish and want to be loved by all. But we can cease being turned in on ourselves and straighten up by doing for everyone else what we wanted selfishly to be done for us.

So the command—love your neighbor as yourself. Jesus does not say: love your neighbor as you love yourself. But rather love your neighbor as yourself, that is, inasmuch as you no longer love yourself. "Nor will it be necessary for you to love yourself as the neighbor inasmuch as by loving your neighbor you already love yourself most truly and all others in turn love you."

In his Heidelberg disputation of 1518 (28), Luther speaks of creative love. "The love of God does not find, but creates, that which is pleasing to it. The love of man comes into being through that which is pleasing to it."

The second part is clear, namely, that human love is determined by its object. It seeks the good for itself according to Aristotle. But:

The love of God which lives in man loves sinners, evil persons, fools, and weaklings in order to make them righteous, good, wise and strong. Rather than seeking its own good, the love of God flows forth and bestows good. Therefore sinners are attractive because they are loved; they are not loved because they are attractive. (LW, 31/57)[4]

The love of Christ came for sinners. "This is the love of the cross, born of the cross which turns in the direction where it does not find good which it may enjoy, but where it may confer good upon the bad and needy person." While man's love shuns sinners, the weak and ill, Christ's love seeks them out.

The mutual love of Christians makes the communion of saints in which all things are held in common—sharing prayers and works and each other's burdens.[5] Community means that Christ's sacrifice of love makes the believers one body, one loaf with it and so with each other. Just as Christ shared all with men, so all his followers should share with each other.[6]

The Blessed Sacrament is the sign of the fellowship of the saints, the communion of the saints. Christ and the saints are one body in common and to excommunicate is to drive out of the community.[7] "This fellowship consists in this, that all the spiritual possessions of Christ and his saints are shared with and become the common property of him who receives this sacrament." (5) Sufferings and sin also become common property and love brings love in return. Just as many grains form the bread and many drops the wine, so the communion of saints is formed of many members, as Ignatius of Antioch taught.

> Christ with all the saints, by his love, takes upon himself our form [Phil 2/7], fights with us against sin, death and all evil. This enkindles in us such love that we take on his form, rely on his righteousness, life and blessedness. And through the interchange of his blessings and our misfortunes, we become one loaf, one bread, one body, one drink, and have all things in common. (14)

In like manner we take on the infirmities of other Christians and all the good we have we share with them. "That is real fellowship and that is the true significance of this sacrament. In this way we are changed into one another and are made into a community by love. Without love there can be no such change." (14)

The Christian brotherhood is founded on the body of Christ. At Luther's time there were many brotherhoods. They seemed to have stemmed from monastic and religious orders, becoming lay sodalities of devotion. In Wittenberg (1520) there were twenty. Members shared in mutual benefits, including prayers and masses for the dead. Many of the sodalities were dedicated to a saint, for example, the Blessed Virgin, St. Anne, or St. Sebastian, or were attached to a religious order.

But some of them had turned into social clubs, and Luther laments their debauchery.

> The brotherhood is also supposed to be a special convocation of good works; instead it has become a collection of money for beer. . . . If a sow were made a patron saint of such a brotherhood, she would not consent.[8]

Luther wants the common brotherhood of the saints based on the Eucharist, with one baptism, one Christ, one sacrament, one food, one body, etc.

> The organized brotherhood shares one roll, one mass, one kind of good works, one festival day, one fee; and as things

are now, their common beer, common gluttony, and common drunkenness. But none of these penetrates so deeply as to produce one spirit, for that is done by Christ's brotherhood alone. (71)

The brotherhood should be based on love.

Love serves freely and without charge, which is why God in return also gives it every blessing, freely and without charge. Since, then, everything must be done in love, if it is to please God at all, the brotherhood too must be a brotherhood in love. It is the nature of that which is done in love, however, not to seek its own, or its own profit, but to seek that of others, and above all that of the community [of saints]. (72)

And the Sacrament is the leaven of love. One becomes certain of the love of the brethren who will stand by him in time of need.

And you in turn take to heart the shortcomings and lapses of all Christians and of the entire community [of saints], [as these occur] in any individual Christian. So that your love goes out to each one and you desire to help everyone, hate no one, suffer with all and pray for all. (72)

Love must be tested.[9] "Love of God proves itself when he smites and afflicts, as was shown in the case of the martyrs and in the suffering of Christ; and love of one's neighbor proves itself when the neighbor offends and seems to deserve hatred." (374)

True love thrives on those who need it. "Bear one another's burdens." (Gal 6/2)

To love means to wish from the heart what is good for the other person, or to seek the other person's advantage. Now if there were no one who errs or falls—that is, no one who needs what is good—when are you going to love, whose good are you going to desire, whose good are you going to seek? (LW, 27/391)

Carnal lust, on the other hand, only wishes for those who will complement its own selfish desires, seeks only its own benefits. These people avoid the foolish, hot-tempered, troublemakers, etc., and seek out the cultured, refined, quiet, and saintly, who are more pleasing to them. "The church was always best when it was living among the worst people. For in bearing their burdens, its love shone with a wonderful glow." (392)

Luther condemns the Bohemians for leaving the Roman church in order to escape evil priests, etc. This is against the unity of love! "For if the bishops or priests, or any persons at all, are wicked, and if you were aglow with real love, you would not flee." (392) Luther felt that he would abandon true love if he left Rome despite its corruption. For love that can bear nothing but benefits is fictitious.

There has been much discussion over Luther's *Communio Sanctorum*. Does *Communio* mean congregation, community (*Gemeinde*), or common participation and sharing (*Gemeinschaft*)?[10] It seems that Luther uses *Communio* in both senses, as a community of holy people and as a common participation, e.g., in the Eucharist. But the second is implied in the first.

Althaus writes:

> The German "Gemeine" used by Luther in the sense of "Community" to translate "Communio" in the Apostles' Creed also expresses a living "give and take" relationship. It is the nature of this gathering or community (Gemeine) that everything is held in common. Whoever belongs to this is a member not only of a group of people, but also of a body. Luther never thinks of the gathering together of the many in the unity of the community without understanding unity in terms of membership in the body and thus as sharing (Gemeinschaft) with one another.[11]

Luther scripturally brought the Communion of the Saints to earth from Heaven. Also he insisted on the equality of all members in the body versus the artificial classes of hierarchy and ascesis.

This is the communion of the saints in which we glory. Whose heart will not be lifted up, even in the midst of great evils, when he believes the very truth, namely, that the blessings of all the saints are his blessings, and his evil is also theirs. . . . Consequently I can actually glory in the blessings of others as though they were my very own. They are truly mine when I am grateful and joyful with the others. It may be that I am base and ugly, while those whom I love and admire are fair and beautiful. By my love I make not only their blessings but their very selves my own. By their honor my shame is now made honorable, my want is supplied by their abundance, and my sins are healed by their merits.[12]

In 1520 Luther made a last attempt at reconciliation with Rome in his *The Freedom of a Christian* (LW, 31/333-77), in which he teaches the freedom of faith through love. Faith becomes active in the free works of love. "The works of the freest service, cheerfully and lovingly done, with which a man willingly serves another without hope of reward; and for himself he is satisfied with the fulness and wealth of his faith." (31/365)

And again: "From faith thus flow love and joy in the Lord, and from love a joyful, willing and free mind that serves one's neighbor willingly and takes no account of gratitude or ingratitude, of praise or blame, of gain or loss." (367) If we recognize the great gifts of God, our hearts will be filled by the Holy Spirit with the love that makes us free, joyful, overcoming tribulation, servants of the neighbor.

Mary freely and lovingly fulfilled the Law, but not in order to be justified and purified. No! "So also our works should be done, not that we may be justified by them, since, being justi-

fied beforehand by faith, we ought to do all things freely and
joyfully for the sake of others." (368) Even secular rulers
should be served out of love as Paul said (Rom 13/1–7), submitting his will to others in the freedom of love.

As from Christ good things have flowed to us, so they should
flow from us to those in need.

> He has so "put on" us and acted for us as if he had been
> what we are. From us they flow on to those who have need
> of them. So that I should lay before God my faith and my
> righteousness that they may cover and intercede for the
> sins of my neighbor which I take upon myself and so labor
> and serve in them as if they were my very own. That is
> what Christ did for us. This is true love and the genuine rule
> of a Christian life. Love is true and genuine where there is
> true and genuine faith.
>
> A Christian lives not in himself but in Christ and in his
> neighbor. Otherwise he is not Christian. He lives in Christ
> through faith, and in his neighbor through love. By faith
> he is caught up beyond himself into God. By love he de-
> scends beneath himself into his neighbor, yet he always re-
> mains in God and in his love [Jn 1/51]. (371)

Faith and Love

Luther continued his faith-love theme during the crisis period between his condemnation at Worms (1521) and his
marriage to the ex-nun Katharina von Bora (1525).

Love is necessary to genuine faith, he writes in his Preface
to the New Testament (1522).

> Christ never gave any other commandment than that of
> love, because he intended that commandment to be the
> test of his disciples and of true believers. For if [good]
> works and love do not blossom forth, it is not genuine faith,
> the gospel has not yet gained a foothold and Christ is not
> yet rightly known.[13]

For Luther faith and love are central. "Faith remains the doer and love remains the deed."[14] Man is a pipeline through which God's goodness flows. He is connected to God by faith and to man by love. Thus the Christian stands between God and his neighbor. There is a parallel between the person and works, doer and deed, faith and love.

Is there a tension between faith and love? Though man is justified by faith, he is still on the road to righteousness to be completed in resurrection. "The duality of faith and love is the expression of a fundamental tension, from which all the antitheses of Luther's thought could be derived and to which they were all linked."[15]

The pull of faith and love is understandable only in the context of justification. There is an inseparable connection between man's relationship to God and his relationship to his neighbor. Thus God encounters the world through man, and faith and love are necessary to each other.[16]

Faith gives the power to works just as a tree bears fruit. Faith is not the power to act which makes good works, but it is the power of the good which makes works good. Without faith the works are still there, but they are dead and not good. "Man must know that he is ultimately—that is, in the sight of God— affirmed, accepted and loved, in order to have freedom to love and to carry out works that are completely real and truly good."[17]

Love needs faith, because only when an ultimate certainty takes away from man his anxious care for himself can love be pure love. And faith does not need love, but brings love with it unasked through its own inner necessity. For faith which is the life-giving work of God in man, cannot exist without human creative life proceeding from it.[18]

In his Wittenberg Sermons (1522) (1) Luther again preaches the necessity of love for genuine faith. He chastises the Wittenbergers for their lack of love, for they have failed to give to one another what God has given to them in faith. They talk a lot about love, but don't do much.

> God does not want hearers and repeaters of words [Jas 1/22], but followers and doers, and this occurs in faith through love. For a faith without love is not enough—rather it is not faith, just as a face seen in a mirror is not a real face, but merely the reflection of a face [1 Cor 13/13]. (LW, 51/71)

In Sermon 7, Luther teaches love as the fruit of the Sacrament. God has poured out his treasures on us. "For God is a glowing furnace of love, reaching even from the earth to the heaven."

> You are willing to take all of God's goods in the sacrament, but you are not willing to pour them out again in love. Nobody extends a helping hand to another. Nobody seriously considers the other person, but everyone looks out for himself and his own gain, insists on his own way, and lets everything else go hang. (LW, 51/95)

Despite all of Luther's encouragement on faith and love, the Wittenbergers have little of it. Surely God will punish them.

In his work *On Secular Authority* (1523), Luther repeats an earlier theme, namely, that Christian love also serves the state.

> He serves the state as he performs all other works of love, which he himself does not need. He visits the sick, not that he may be made well; feeds no one because he himself needs food. So he also serves the state not because he needs it, but because others need it.[19]

Acting in any other way would be contrary to love and set a bad example.

Ebeling remarks: "Both as a Christian person and as a secular person, man has to act on one and the same basis—love. The difference in the way love works in the two cases is due to a difference in the situation, in what has to be done for the sake of one's neighbor."[20]

True Love vs. Crummy Love

After his marriage to Katharina von Bora, Luther continued to teach love but sprinkled with more references to family love. Luther felt that his marriage was an act of charity toward the poor rejected Katharina.

A love problem that bothered Luther is how one can reconcile God's wrath with his love. This had concerned earlier peoples as well who often gave different names to the punishing and loving aspects of God, e.g., Yahweh and Elohim. Luther taught that wrath is not essential to God, but rather is brought about by man's wickedness. (WA, 40^{II}, 343)

Speaking on Psalm 51/1 (1532), he says:

The thought of God's wrath is false even of itself, because God promises mercy; yet this false thought becomes true because you believe it to be true. However, the other thought, that God is gracious to sinners who feel their sins, is simply true and remains so. (LW, 12/322)

Althaus writes:

The message about God's love without wrath does not come as enlightenment but as proclamation; and faith in God's love is constituted not by deeper insight into God but by running a risk and taking a chance on this proclamation.[21]

"It is only in faith in the gospel that the heart can look backward and recognize God's loving intention in his wrathful activity."

In his sermon "On the Sum of the Christian Life" (1532), Luther quotes Paul: "The aim of our charge is love that issues from a pure heart and a good conscience and a sincere faith." Preachers can't improve on that much. "What must be there is what the law really requires, and that is love, and the kind of love that flows like a rivulet, a stream or a spring from a heart which is pure and a good conscience and sincere unfeigned faith." (LW, 51/267)

The sum of the Law is love. "'Love' in German, as everyone knows, means nothing else except to be favorably and affectionately disposed toward a person from the heart and to offer and show him all kindness and friendship."

Luther criticizes those who puff a lot about love but when it comes to practice give it only to those few who are like them.

> But it is a long way from being love when I select a person or two who please me and do what I wish and treat them kindly and favorably and nobody else. This is crummy love [parteken Liebe] which does not issue from a pure heart, but is nothing but a filthy mess. (LW, 51/267)

True love flows from a true heart. God commanded us to love all just as his sun shines and the rains fall on good and evil. "Out of sheer, pure love, of which his heart is full and overflowing, and which he pours out freely over everyone without exception, be he good or bad, worthy or unworthy. This is a real, divine, total, and perfect love, which does not single out one person nor cut and divide itself, but goes out freely to all." (LW, 51/267) This is the universal love of Heaven as found in Mencius and in the Torah.

The other kind of love, which is friendly to those who are nice to us and hates those who are against us, is false love. This is a selfish love. "If you praise and honor that kind of person, he smiles; but if you make a sour face at him or say something he doesn't like to hear, he flares up, begins to scold and curse, and the friendship is over." (268) This sounds like the voice of experience, for Luther was by and large rejected by those whom he criticized.

True love

> should be a flowing love, which pours out from the inside of the heart like a fresh stream that goes on flowing and cannot be stopped or dried up. This love says: I love you, not

because you are good or bad; for I draw my love not from your goodness, as from another's fountain, but from my own little spring, from the word which is grafted in my heart and which bids me to love my neighbor. (269)

Love should issue from a pure heart and a good conscience. "That love should issue from a heart which has a joyful, quiet conscience both toward men and toward God."

Luther pursues his theme of love of neighbor in his sermons on 1 John (4/16 ff.) (1532). "So we know and believe the love God has for us, God is love . . ." Love is a divine thing.

If I were to paint a picture of God, I would so draw him that there would be nothing else in the depth of his divine nature than that fire and passion which is called love for people. Correspondingly, love is such a thing that it is neither human, nor angelic, but rather divine, yes, even God himself. (WA, 36/424)

The Christian is a channel of God's love, as he had said before. Thus Christian love is not from us, but from God, with man as his instrument of divine love. He freely receives God's love and passes it on to his neighbor. Thus God's love makes him a divine man.

How could he now give greater comfort or give love higher praise than that it produces a divine man, who is one cake with him; a man, who, when he loves his neighbor, forgives his ingratitude and vexations, works—if he spurns and plagues him for his kindness—how can he glory that he has acted like a God? (WA, 36/439)

You should therefore not have the kind of love which exists only in your mouth for that is meaningless love; rather you should have that full love which makes your heart joyful so that even when death and judgment come, you will be able to say: "In spite of this I have done this and this for my neighbor." (WA, 36/444)

Love covers sins, Luther says in his sermon "On Soberness and Moderation" (1539). But it is not our love that does it. "No, it is another's love, namely, Christ's love, which has covered my sins, as Peter says in chapter two [1 Pet 2/24]." (LW, 51/297)

Even in the Christian family and neighborly life. "You must have a strong love, which is best able to cover up sins. . . . The Holy Spirit has sanctified you through faith and gives you love, in order that you may bear with the sins of others." (298)

In this chapter we have seen some of Luther's thoughts on love. He bases his theology of love strongly on the Bible, especially Paul and John, and also on Augustine.

Although Luther has little patience with the scholastic view that love is the form of faith, nevertheless he teaches that love is necessary for genuine faith. A faith that is genuine cannot help but issue forth in works of love.

Luther's stress on God's love for us through Christ and through us to our neighbor, forming a community of brotherly love—*Gemeinschaft*—would inspire many of his sons, from Kierkegaard to Bonhoeffer.

Though his central theme was the love of God for men, the mystical love of man for God is far from dead in the Reformation era. In fact, some see the German Reformers as direct descendants of the medieval mystic Meister Eckhart, especially in their interiority and divine sonship, stressing salvation through faith and love.[22]

Ironically some of the Spanish Inquisitors saw in the powerful beatas there a certain Lutheran individualism, preferring the internal road to God over the external even to a disdain of the institutional church.

ᴥᵹ XV ᵻᴥ

O LIVING FLAME OF LOVE
THAT TENDERLY WOUNDS MY SOUL
IN ITS DEEPEST CENTER

John of the Cross, The Living Flame of Love, *1*

The Mystic Stream

We have seen the passionate Sufi love of God, the painful love of the medieval courts, the ascending love of the monks, and the dialectic love of the universities. Luther taught a descending love by which God works through man to his fellow man. Most of these loves in some way influenced the mystics of sixteenth-century Spain.

Perhaps it has been oversimplified that mystical love is ascending, whereas Luther's love is descending. As we have seen, most mystics portray their love as a divine gift. What is mysticism? Why does it arise frequently in millennial times? How is mystic love related to sexual love?

We have seen mystic streams in Taoism, Hinduism, Judaism, Christianity, and Islam. Common elements are: an awakening, purification, illumination, and finally a divine union in spiritual marriage. Mysticism comes in many shapes, from the noetic speculation of Greek *theoria* to the personal union of Narada, Augustine, or Bernard to the natural mysticism of Lao Tzu and Francis.

How is the mystical love of God related to human sexual

love? Is it a sublimation of sex drives found only in celibates, using sexual terms such as spiritual marriage, kisses, hugs, etc., to express their feelings? Is mystical love an example of what Freud calls aim-inhibited love? Or is the divine union rather the eternal model on which the weak and often ephemeral human sexual love is based?

Certain periods seem to be more mystical than others. For example, is it an accident that Gautama Buddha, Lao Tzu, Confucius, and Deutero-Isaiah may have been contemporaries or near contemporaries?

Hillel, Jesus, John the Baptizer, and Paul flourished in the days of Messianic expectation. The fourth and fifth centuries saw Gregory of Nyssa, Augustine, and Pseudo-Dionysius. The millennial Middle Ages inspired Islamic, Jewish, and Christian mystics from Bernard and William to Francis to Mechtild of Magdeburg and Meister Eckhart and Catherine of Siena and Jan van Ruysbroeck.

But the millennial sixteenth century (1,500 years after Christ) found a new wave of mysticism with Ignatius of Loyola, Teresa of Avila, and John of the Cross. If this timetable holds up, the twenty-first century could see a new mystic trend and some see it starting already at the close of the twentieth century.

There were many streams that flowed into Spanish mysticism. One is Arab Sufism, which permeated Spain in the Middle Ages inspiring Ramón Lull (13th–14th cent.)[1] though other mystics, some Christian and perhaps Jewish, may have stimulated him as well.

Lullian traces may be found in Francisco de Osuna, Pedro de Alcántara, Bernardino de Laredo, and Alonzo de Orozco, who touched Teresa of Avila more directly. And the Flemish mystic current of Jan van Ruysbroeck may have swayed the Spanish saints as well.

Spanish secular literature also may have played a part in sixteenth-century mystical writings, as medieval courtly love songs affected the mystics of their time. Hatzfeld writes:

Listening to the lamentations of S. Teresa over the bitterly felt absence of the beloved, one cannot help thinking of the oldest songs of yearning love, in which the girl expresses her longing for the far-away lover on a crusade or elsewhere. These were Galician songs known under the name of the songs for the friend (*Cantigas de Amigo*).[2]

Hatzfeld adds: "The oldest *villancicos* which Teresa imitated so well were recited by the singer (*juglar*) and joined by the choral song and dance of the listeners, as Teresa's *estribillos* preceding and following her glosses were sung and danced by her nuns."[3]

Teresa's theme of dying from the absence of the beloved partner is the motif of the ancient Spanish love poem *Razón de Amor*. The desperate love of Castilian and Sufi literature preceded Teresa.

The divine love, analyzed by Teresa in its yearnings, sufferings and torments, as well as her concept of the beloved as prisoner of the lover might have been impossible without another tradition, that of human love, idealized by the way, and offered for the first time with an exact love psychology in the short novel *Carcel de Amor* (*Prisoner of Love*) by Diego de San Pedro, the "Werther" of the 15th century.[4]

In sixteenth-century Spain mysticism, ecstasy, rapture, stigmata, were the order of the day. The Alumbrados, the enlightened ones (Sufi influence?), were popular. But suspicions arose that had always clouded mysticism. How does one tell a real mystic from a spurious one? In 1544 the Inquisition declared the ecstasies of Magdalena de la Cruz to be false. After the Council of Trent more accusations, autos-da-fé, and burnings ensued.[5]

Teresa of Avila

Teresa was born in 1515 in Avila, where Ferdinand and Isa-
bella had reigned so gloriously. These are adventurous times,
with many of the young hidalgos seeking fame and fortune in
America. Chivalry abounds, with the lonely maids pining for
their absent lovers.

Raised in a pious family, Teresa dreams of the convent and
martyrdom. In 1536 she entered the Carmelite Convent of the
Incarnation in Avila. Though illness forced her to leave for a
while, she returned to the Incarnation and, under the guidance
of her Dominican and Jesuit confessors, pursued a deeper love
of God.

The Council of Trent had recommended the reform of religious orders and the Convent of the Incarnation was in special need of rejuvenation.

Before a picture of the wounded Christ (*Ecce Homo*),
Teresa experiences her second conversion. Since Christ had
suffered so much for her, she prays never to offend him again.
(*Life*, 9/1)[6]

> This was my method of prayer: as I could not make re-
> flections with my understanding, I contrived to picture
> Christ as within me; and I used to find myself the better for
> thinking of those mysteries of his life during which he was
> most lonely. It seems to me that the being alone and
> afflicted, like a person in trouble, must needs permit me to
> come near to him. (9/4)

Thus the soul advances not in understanding or in meditation, but in love, the radical love of Christ. (9/6)

The life of love for Teresa is following God by the way of
prayer, the God who has loved the soul so much.

> O Lord of my soul, and my good, how is it that, when a soul
> is determined to love you—doing all it can, by forsaking all

things in order that it may the better occupy itself with the love of God, it is not your will it should have the joy of ascending at once to the possession of perfect love? (11/1)

For Teresa the soul is a garden (1) and God is its gardener. The garden may be watered by a well, pump, river, or rain. These are like the four degrees of prayer. Thus beginners have to draw water up from the well laboriously. This is active meditation. Gradually the will reduces disturbances and God grants quiet. He elevates the soul by spiritual illumination, leading her to intermittent ecstasies, to union with the divinity.

"The prayer of quiet, then, is a little spark of the true love of himself, which our Lord begins to enkindle in the soul; and his will is, that the soul should understand what this love is by the joy it brings." (15/6) This second stage of prayer is not something that we can get from our own efforts, but a free gift of God.

This spark, then, given of God, however slight it may be, causes a great crackling; and if men do not quench it by their faults, it is the beginning of a great fire, which sends forth . . . the flames of that most vehement love of God which his majesty will have perfect souls to possess. (15/6)

Teresa in her enthusiasm often mixes metaphors freely, thus water and fire in the soul.

The third stage of prayer is union with God. Now the soul finds no pleasure in the world. "Because it has in itself that which gives it a greater satisfaction, greater joys in God, longings for the satisfaction of its longing to have a deeper joy in being with him—this is what the soul seeks." (17/6)

In the fourth stage of prayer there is a union of all the powers of the soul, no thinking, remembering, and feeling, but only delight and enjoyment without understanding—rapture and ecstasy. "O my Lord, how good you are! Blessed be you forever, O my God. Let all creatures praise you who have so loved us that we can truly speak of this communication which you have with souls in this our exile." (18/5) The soul leaps out of itself like a flame out of the fire, yet the flame and the fire are one. (18/4)

Teresa distinguishes between union and rapture, transport, trance, and flight, which seem to be the same as ecstasy. This is a higher stage than union.

> A rapture is absolutely irresistible; whilst union, inasmuch as we are then on our own ground, may be hindered, though that resistance be painful and violent. It is, however, almost always possible. But rapture, for the most part, is irresistible. It comes, in general, as a shock, quick and sharp, before you can collect your thoughts, or help yourself in any way, and you see and feel it as a cloud or as a strong eagle rising upwards and carrying you away on its wings. (20/3)

In this rapture one is literally carried outside of himself, the root meaning of ecstasy. Though Teresa tries to resist these raptures because of a fear of illusions, she is unable to do so.

The powerful love of God sweeps her off her feet and she has a great fear of offending him. "This fear is bound up in exceedingly great love which is acquired anew, and directed to him, who, we see, bears so great a love to a worm so vile." (20/9)

When this temporary rapture ceases, a pain of loneliness ensues. And the soul is, as it were, crucified between Heaven and earth, getting help from neither. (20/14) "The soul sees distinctly that it seeks nothing but God; yet its love dwells not on any attribute of him in particular; it seeks him as he is, and knows not what it seeks." (20/15)

Imagination ceases and the faculties are at rest. Pain suspends them as joy suspends them in union and in trance. The pulse slows, the body stiffens and rises, and the faculties are lost in God. In all of this Teresa insists that God does it. It is not a question of the soul raising herself up to God or of climbing an erotic ladder, but rather of God raising her up, drawing his unworthy bride to himself.

He loved us first.

Whenever we think of Christ, we should remind ourselves of the love that made him bestow so many graces upon us, and also how great that love is which our Lord God has shown us, in giving us such a pledge of the love he bears us; for love draws forth love. . . . If once our Lord grant us this grace of having this love imprinted in our hearts, everything will be easy, and we shall do great things in a very short time, and with very little labor. (22/21)

Though a contemplative at heart, Teresa is also practical! For her contemplative life and her call to reform Carmel cannot be separated. Even while she is planning her reform (1559), the golden spear of God's love pierces her heart.

The pain was so great that it made me moan; and yet so surpassing was the sweetness of this excessive pain, that I could not wish to be rid of it. The soul is satisfied now with nothing less than God. The pain is not bodily but spiritual; though the body has its share of it, even a large one. It is a caressing love so sweet which now takes place between the soul and God, that I pray God of his goodness to make him experience it who may think that I am lying. (29/17)

In 1559 Teresa started her first reformed convent at St. Joseph's of Avila, and Pope Pius IV approved her constitution (1562). In 1567 at the age of fifty-two, Teresa founded her second reformed convent at Medina del Campo. There she met John of the Cross, who was to be a co-founder of the reform and who learned from Teresa and who taught her as he developed his own poetry and theology of the mystical life.

Teresa wanted to restore the primitive vigor of the sons of Elijah on Mount Carmel. Thus all laxness and distractions in the convent must be driven out in order to leave the soul free for God.

Between 1568 and 1571 Teresa founded six more convents, but not without opposition. They say that it is easier to start a new order than to try to reform an old one. Many disappointments, including the imprisonment and torture of John of the Cross, crushed Teresa. Yet despite setbacks or perhaps because of them, she advanced in prayer and love of God. Perhaps her frustrations were a part of her *desnudez*, the stripping necessary for the soul to be open to God.

In her later years Teresa would enjoy a closer union with God in the spiritual marriage.

Teresa's Works of Love

As we have seen in her autobiography, Teresa is a writer, and a good one. She had shown an early bent as a teen-ager, penning a novel, *The Knight of Avila*.

Why did Teresa write about divine love? Is this not arrogance on her part? There is an affinity between mysticism and writing, as John the Apostle, Augustine, Sufi poets, Bernard, and Ramón Lull attest. Are the divine inspirations of the mystics and the enthusiasm of writers and poets somehow allied?

Another interesting note is that most spiritual writings have come down to us from the hand of religious superiors. There are several reasons for this. First, the need of superiors to instruct their subjects in writing. Another reason could be that superiors discouraged through censorship, etc., the writings of their inferiors. Inferiors who are superior have always been a problem in religious life.

Teresa felt that her mystical experience was so delightful that she is driven to tell others about it. She wrote on the good advice of her confessors to aid her to understand her own growth in prayer and contemplation. But she also wrote to help her daughters through the maze of the contemplative life, with its ups and downs, consolations and aridities, and proper relationships with their mystical bridegroom.

In 1562 Teresa wrote *The Way of Perfection* for the nuns

of St. Joseph's of Avila to teach them the best kind of prayer—paraphrasing the "Our Father" and pointing out the social needs of the church and the salvation of souls.

Besides prayer, poverty, rules, and mortification, Teresa teaches love as the very foundation of convent life, a selfless supernatural love.

> O, what an excellent and sincere love does that nun show who sacrifices her own interests in all the virtues and in the perfect observance of the rule. There is more true friendship in this than in all the tender speeches that can be uttered, and which are not, and must not be used in this house; such as "my life, my soul, my darling" and other expressions people use to one another. Keep endearing words for your spouse. You will often be alone with him and will need them all, since his majesty permits their use. However much you may repeat them to him, they will not make you sentimental, and there is no need to address them to anyone else. (7/7)[7]

Teresa warns her nuns against grudges, particular friendships, sibling rivalries, which are against charity. One who truly loves God cares little for the things of this life.

Christ is the bridegroom of our souls.

> Ought we not, my daughters, to rejoice in these perfections of our spouse, and to learn to know him and what our lives should be? In the world, when a girl is going to be married, she knows beforehand who her husband is to be and what are his means and position. And shall not we who are already betrothed, think about our bridegroom before he takes us home on the wedding day?

Who is this man? Who is his father? What riches does he promise? The bride must pray mentally with recollection. (22/5)

Prayer is the bride's meeting with the bridegroom. "I am not asking you to meditate on him, nor to produce great thoughts, nor to feel deep devotion. I only ask you to look at him . . .

If he does not appear beautiful to you, I give you leave never to think of him, although, daughters, he never takes his eyes off you!" (26/3)

O prince of all the earth, you who are indeed my spouse! Are you reduced to such straits, my Lord, my only good, that you are willing to consort with such a miserable comrade as myself? Yet your looks tell me that you find some comfort even in me. (26/5)

The soul that truly loves God, loves all good, seeks all good, protects all good, joins itself to good men and defends them, and embraces all the virtues. It only loves what is true and worth loving. . . . A love for God may be great or small and shows itself according to its strength. If it is weak, it is little seen. And if it is strong, it appears more clearly. But small or great, love for God can never be concealed. (40/2)

This is a real love and any worldly vanities are thieves stealing it away and real love crushes self-love.

We can easily see that it is divine love that should motivate Teresa's convent. The sister is a spouse of Christ, and her loyalty and affection for him motivate her whole life. Any other loves cannot be tolerated.

In 1574 Teresa continues her love theme in her *Concepts of the Love of God*,[8] a commentary on the love songs of Solomon, so popular in Jewish and Christian mystic traditions. Teresa writes for the guidance of her nuns at the Incarnation, with the encouragement of John of the Cross, her confessor.

The Song of Solomon, as we have seen, is a collection of Hebrew love songs. But Jewish and Christian mystics saw in it a reflection of the divine love between God and man. We can read these psalms with bifocals—on one level visioning the erotic images of human love, while on the other level we see the divine lover beckoning.

There had always been a relationship between human and divine intercourse, as we have seen in the Tantric *shakti* yoga of Hinduism or the Jewish Kabbalah. But Christian mystics, as many of their Hindu *bhakti* and Islamic Sufi predecessors, celebrate this union directly with the divinity without the aid of a human partner, though there were exceptions.

It seems that when Teresa explained the Greatest Song to her nuns, they giggled, for they saw only the human level and not the divine. The Song may be hard to understand, but it shows God's love for us. Teresa tells her daughters not to be shocked at the language of their divine lover. For his kiss is the kiss of peace. This is not the false peace of laxity, laziness, worldliness, and riches.

Genuine peace, union with Christ, and love of God come from the prayer of union, the kiss from the divine mouth. "Let him kiss me with the kiss of his mouth."

O holy bride! Let us now ponder over the kiss you ask for, which is that sacred peace that encourages the soul to wage war with the world, while yet preserving perfect confidence and calm within itself. What a happy lot for us to win this grace! It consists in so close a union with God's will that he and the soul are no longer divided. But their will is one—not in words and wishes only, but in deeds as well. (3/1)

The sweet and tender love of God which comes from God dwelling in the soul in the prayer of quiet, the divine breasts.

The whole creature, both body and soul, is enraptured as if some very fragrant ointment, resembling a delicious perfume, had been infused into the very center of the being. . . . So it is with the most sweet love of our God, with the greatest suavity it enters the soul, which feels happy and satisfied, but cannot understand the reason nor how this great good entered it. (4/2)

The soul enjoys a strong and trustful love protected by the shadow of God, which those feel who have kept their love and suffered for him.

The groom brings his bride into his wine cellar, where he sets charity in order within her.

The king does not appear to bring her into the cellar of wine and leave her thirsting, but wishes her to drink and to be inebriated as much as she chooses, and to be intoxicated with all the wines that are in the storehouse of God. Let her enjoy its pleasures, and admire his grandeur, nor fear to lose her life by drinking more than human weakness can bear— Let her die in this paradise of delights! Blest is the death that purchases such a life. (6/4)

Divine inebriation we have seen in the Sufi poems. The spirits of alcohol and other drugs are compared to divine spirits in other cultures as well. One example that comes to mind is the early Christians on Pentecost Sunday, whose enthusiasm some attributed to wine.

Zealous love of God is of two kinds, performing service to God and even asking for crosses in imitation of Christ crucified. This leads to love of neighbor.

I have noticed in certain persons—there are very few of them on account of our sins—that as they advance farther in this prayer and receive more consolations from our Lord, they become more anxious about the happiness and salvation of their neighbor, especially as regards his soul. (7/10)

Teresa's *Interior Castle* (1571),[9] written at the request of Padre Gracián, describes her whole spiritual development from her practice of oral prayer to her mystical marriage.

The soul is a crystal castle with seven mansions or rooms— with Sufi antecedents. The outer mansions are for servants, etc. But as one moves to the interior, there are more exquisite furnishings for more important people. Finally in the innermost mansion the Lord himself lives.

The three outer mansions show the imperfections in the spiritual life, oral prayer, and meditation, while the four inner ones are the life of contemplation, quiet, mystical betrothal, and marriage.[10]

The mansions are concentric around the central dwelling of the Lord. As the soul moves from the outer to the inner, she leaves behind the reptiles and temptations of the first, doubts and battles with demons in the second, for greater security in the third and sweetness, consolation, quiet, and union in advance of the spiritual marriage. (3–5)

Leaving her fear of damnation, the soul feels the love of God increasing. There are no lizards or snakes in the fifth mansion—too close to Solomon's wine cellar. The silkworm must first die so that the butterfly can fly to God; and the dove seeks its place of rest.

The first meeting with her spouse is in the fifth mansion, the prayer of union.

> We might compare the prayer of union to a visit, for it lasts but a little while. There is no longer any question of deliberation, but the soul in a secret manner sees to what a bridegroom it is betrothed. The senses and the faculties could not in a thousand years gain the knowledge thus imparted in a very short time. (5/4/2)

In the sixth mansion, the spiritual betrothal, the soul is wounded with love for its spouse. "The sight it has enjoyed of him is so deeply imprinted on the spirit that its only desire is to behold him again." (6/1/1)

This disappearance of the spouse and increased longing parallels that of the romantic novels.

> The soul is now determined to take no other bridegroom than our Lord, but he disregards its desires for speedy espousals, wishing that the longings should become still more vehement and that this good, which far excels all other benefits, should be purchased at some cost to itself. (6/1/2)

The bride-to-be undergoes her last trials and sufferings, physical and mental, anxiety and fear. But her Lord has not deserted her. He still calls to her, and his cry pierces her like a wound. "It is conscious of having received a delicious wound, but cannot discover how, nor who gave it, yet recognizes it as a most precious grace and hopes the hurt will never heal." (6/2/2) Though present to the soul, the groom does not show himself—a sweet and delightful wound.

God is like a great furnace of love from which a small spark is thrown off into the soul. And the feeling is so delightful that the soul dwells in it. But the spark quickly dies, leaving the soul longing for more.

Locutions, raptures, flights, visions. In betrothal the Lord enraptures the soul, taking her wholly out of herself. To meet her spouse in a state of full consciousness would undoubtedly mean death. The soul returns to herself fully aware of her bliss. (6/4)

In ecstasy, God closes the outer doors and those between the mansions, and he opens the door leading into the seventh mansion, the apartment of the Lord. But the soul is still held back by its imperfection and memory of sin.

In ecstasy the soul is taken out of herself and the body becomes cold. When the rapture ceases, the will is drunk, unable to do anything but love God. All of these favors only escalate the dove's or butterfly's desires. "She sees herself still far away from God, yet with her increased knowledge of his attributes, her longing and her love for him grow even stronger as she learns more fully how this great God and sovereign deserves to be loved." (6/11/1)

Thus inflamed with love, she is pierced by a fiery dart, a thunderbolt reducing the earthly part of her nature to nothing. "At the time one cannot even remember our own existence, for an instant the faculties of the soul are so fettered as to be incapable of any action except the power they retain of increasing our fortune." (6/11/2)

The spiritual marriage for which the soul longs will be consummated in the seventh mansion, the apartment of the Lord. The groom invites his bride into his mansion.

When our Lord is pleased to take pity on the sufferings, both past and present, endured through her longing for him by this soul which he has spiritually taken for his bride, he, before consummating the celestial marriage, brings her into his mansion or presence chamber. (7/1/3)

The Lord's dwelling place in the soul is a second Heaven.

This is not like the former favors when the Lord united the spirit to himself, making it blind and dumb and preventing it from knowing where and how it enjoys this grace.

But now he acts differently. Our pitiful God removes the scales from its eyes, letting it see and understand somewhat of the grace received in a strange and wonderful manner in this mansion by means of intellectual vision. (7/1/8)

The three persons of the Trinity mysteriously reveal themselves, preceded by an illumination like a dazzling cloud. "O my God, how different from merely hearing and believing these words is to realize their truth in this way." (7/1/10)

The spiritual betrothal of the sixth mansion and the spiritual marriage of the seventh mansion differ. "Here God appears in the soul's center, not by an imaginary, but by an intellectual vision far more mystic than those before." (7/2/2) The union of the spiritual marriage is permanent. "He has bound himself to her as firmly as two human beings are joined in wedlock and will never separate himself from her." (7/2/3) Here there is no possibility of separation as in the spiritual betrothal.

Betrothal is like two candles touching, forming one light. But still they can be separated. Spiritual marriage is like rain falling into a river, becoming one with it. Or light coming through two windows and fusing into one inside a room.

"The little butterfly has died with the greatest joy at having found rest at last, and now Christ lives in her." (7/3/1) Now she is so self-forgetful she seems not to exist any more. She is so transfixed that she does not even recognize herself. Rather she seeks now only God's interest.

Also her desire for suffering increases. She loves her ene-

9. "The little butterfly has died with greatest joy at having found her rest" (Teresa of Avila, *The Interior Castle*, 7/3/1)

mies. "She would be glad to forfeit the favors his majesty shows her, if they might be given to her enemies instead, to prevent their offending our Lord." (7/1/4)

Now instead of longing for death in order to enjoy the Lord's presence, the soul wants to live to serve the Lord. Who are the children of this spiritual marriage? They are good works. Teresa is a contemplative in action, reforming her order, building new houses, combating heresy, aiding the missions.

Works are the unmistakable sign which shows these favors come from God, as I told you. It will do me little good to be recollected when alone, making acts of the virtues, planning and promising to do wonders in God's service, if afterwards, when occasion offers, I do just the opposite. (7/4/10)

"Fix your eyes on the crucified one and all will seem easy. If his majesty proved his love for us by such stupendous labors and sufferings, how can we seek to please him by words alone?" Both Mary and Martha serve the Lord—contemplation and deeds. No room for Quietism here.

Teresa's images of marriage, castle, mansions, butterfly and dove, water and garden, candles and sunlight, describe an ineffable experience—a product of the baroque period. Hatzfeld comments:

> The complexity is, however, exactly what fascinates the reader. He forgets his temptation to bring order into the fulness and is carried on by an imagistic creativity which at the same time both clarifies the most mysterious of all human experiences and shows the way to sanctity.[11]

Teresa had a great impact on subsequent asceticism. We shall see her influence on John of the Cross. Francis de Sales read Teresa and used her ideas in his *Treatise on the Love of God*. Mary of the Incarnation, the French Teresa, also read the Spanish mystic, though Mary's style is more psychological or philosophical. The reformed Carmel would carry Teresa's mystic message of love up into modern times.

John of the Cross

Juan de Yepes y Alvarez was born in Medina del Campo, Spain (1542). Having studied under the Jesuits, he joined the Carmelites (1563), taking the name of John of St. Matthias. Then he pursued Thomism at Salamanca and some feel that scholastic realism may have saved him from the dangers of Illuminism and Quietism.[12]

John was attracted to the contemplative life at an early age. In 1567 Teresa of Avila came to Medina del Campo with permission to establish two houses of contemplative Carmelite fathers. While there she met Padre Antonio and John of St.

Matthias, whom she recruited for her plan, rejoicing that she now had a friar and a half. John was a shorty!

The first priory of reformed fathers was founded in 1568 at Duruelo, with the stress on meditation, the old liturgy of the Holy Sepulchre, the cult of the Blessed Virgin, and obedience. John took the name of John of the Cross.

Though John did not have the same bent as Teresa for the active life, he frequently engaged in pastoral work as needed. He had a great devotion to Christ crucified, sketching in art and verse the agonies of the cross, stripping and scourging himself to better feel the pain of the naked Christ under the lash.

As novice master, John taught his charges the way of union with God. Three signs of this union are: meditation becomes impracticable, imagination ceases to work—the soul cannot fix the imagination or the sense on a particular object. It only takes pleasure in being alone with God without any particular speculation.[13]

John is against any excitement of the senses or long discourses during prayer. Also he does not favor ecstasies, for perfection consists in charity. Like Teresa, John teaches the spiritual stripping (*desnudez*) by which the soul surrenders herself to her lover, as a bride offers her bare body to her husband.

Learned in theology, John was made rector of the college at Alcalá in 1571. John feels that theology's task is to aid the soul in its detachment so that it can turn away from itself and fix itself upon God. Though theology is inferior to mystic wisdom, it can be a way leading to it.

The Carmelite general chapter of Piacenza (1575) ordered the Discalced to leave within three days the houses founded without the permission of the general. Meantime John, a Discalced Carmelite, was chaplain at the Incarnation, which Teresa was attempting to reform. After much internal strife, John was captured and imprisoned.

Though John was punished for his intransigence, he always thought himself innocent since he followed the directives of the apostolic visitors. John was imprisoned for nine months, eating bread and water three times a week on the refectory floor and stripped and scourged publicly by the brethren for the length of a "Miserere."

In solitary, John's contemplative life matured through the dark night of the soul and spiritual marriage. He relished the solitude and looked forward to the stripping and whipping in order to be better assimilated into the nude and wounded Christ. This is real *desnudez*. John began writing poetry into which his tortured soul could pour itself.

When at last he escaped, John became prior of El Calvario and confessor to the nuns at Beas, for whom he wrote his *Spiritual Canticle*. He held other responsible positions. But in the end he was turned out of office and there was even talk of ejecting him from the order. John died in 1591 as he wished, *desnudez*, out of office, in a place where he was unknown and preceded by much suffering. Denuded of worldly attachments, his soul flew to meet her bridegroom.

John's Works of Love

John's four major works—*The Ascent of Mount Carmel, The Dark Night of the Soul, Spiritual Canticle,* and *The Living Flame of Love*—were all written in the last fourteen years of his life. All treat of the way to divine union.

The Ascent of Mount Carmel (Beas, 1579–81),[14] is an allegory in which the lover sings of her fortune in having gone out one dark night to join her beloved.

> One dark night,
> Fired with love's urgent longings
> —Ah, the sheer grace!—
> I went out unseen
> My house being now stilled,
>
> In darkness, and secure,
> By the secret ladder, disguised

—Ah, the sheer grace!—
In the darkness and concealment,
My house being now all stilled,

On that glad night,
In secret, for no one saw me,
Nor did I look at anything
With no other light or guide
Than the one that burned in my heart.

This guided me
More surely than the light of noon
To where he waited for
—Him I knew so well—
In a place where no one else appeared.

O guiding night!
O night more lovely than dawn!
O night that has united
The lover with his beloved,
Transforming the beloved in her lover.

Upon my flowering breast
Which I kept wholly for him alone,
There he lay sleeping,
And I caressing him
There in a breeze from the fanning cedars.

When the breeze blew from the turret
Parting his hair,
He wounded my neck
With his gentle hand
Suspending all my senses.

I abandoned and forgot myself,
Laying my face on my beloved,
All other things ceased; I went out from myself,
Leaving my cares
Forgotten among the lilies.

John had experienced the active and passive purifications of the night (*desnudez*) and attained the divine union which is the summit of Mount Carmel. Two nights of purification must be traversed, the sensory and the spiritual, for beginners and the proficient.

John calls it a dark night for three reasons. First, by denial— a night of the senses. Second, the road to union is through faith, the dark night of the intellect. Third, God is as a dark night to man in this life. But there is really only one night.

The first part, the night of the senses, resembles early evening, that time of twilight when things begin to fade from sight. The second part, faith, is completely dark, like midnight. The third part, representing God, is like the very early dawn just before the break of day. (1/2/5)

Man must first of all detach himself from the love of creatures. Why?

For love effects a likeness between the lover and the object loved. . . . He who loves a creature, then, is as low as that creature, and in some way even lower, because love not only equates, but even subjects the lover to the beloved object. By the mere fact, then, that a man loves something, his soul becomes incapable of pure union and transformation in God. For the baseness of a creature is far less capable of the sublimity of the creator than is darkness of light. (1/4/3)

All creatures when compared with God are nothing.

The journey to God leads up the mountain, the obscure habit of faith transcending the intellect.

Like a blind man he must lean on dark faith, accept it for his guide and light, and rest on nothing of what he understands, tastes, feels or imagines. All these perceptions are a darkness that will lead him astray. Faith lies beyond all this understanding, taste, feeling, and imagining. (2/4/2)

John's primacy of faith as a proximate means of divine union remind one of Thomas Aquinas' faith as the beginning of eternal life.[15]

Only faith, hope, and charity can unite the faculties of intellect, memory, and will with God by stripping themselves. "Faith causes darkness and void of understanding in the intellect, hope begets an emptiness of possessions in the memory, and charity produces the nakedness and emptiness of affection and joy in all that is not God." (2/6/2)

The three signs that the soul is ready to move on to the contemplation of God, based on Tauler's Institutions, are: first, little satisfaction in the discursive method; second, the disinclination to fix the imagination or the senses on particular objects.

> The third and surest sign is that a person likes to remain alone in loving awareness of God, without particular considerations, an interior peace and quiet and repose, and without the acts and exercises (at least discursive) of the intellect, memory and will. And that he prefers to remain only in the general, loving awareness and knowledge we mentioned, without any particular knowledge or understanding. (2/13/4)

This seems to be the essence of loving union.

The Dark Night of the Soul,[16] complementing *The Ascent of Mount Carmel,* is written to help people understand the night. Whereas in the *Ascent* the soul reaches perfection through mortification of the appetites and the journey of faith to purify the senses and spirit of all things contrary to perfect faith and love—in the *Dark Night* God purifies the soul passively, bringing its faith and love to the perfection outlined in the *Ascent.*

Divine communication to the soul is the main theme of the *Dark Night.* How can one know when he is in the sensory night? First, there is no satisfaction or consolation from the things of God or man. "Since God puts a soul in this dark night in order to dry up and purge its sensory appetite, he does not allow it to find sweetness or delight in anything." (1/9/2)

The soul worries over its distaste for God. She can neither meditate nor use her imagination. Moreover, God ceases to communicate himself through the senses and discursion and synthesis as he did before. "But he begins to communicate himself through pure spirit by an act of simple contemplation, in which there is no discursive succession of thought." (1/9/8)

Of what use is the dark night with its aridities and voids? It is a means to the knowledge of God and of self. But the knowledge of the night of the senses is not as great as in the night of the spirit.

Purgation of the senses is a gateway to contemplation which leads to purgation of the spirit. (2/2/1) Through this light of contemplation God illumines the soul about its own wretchedness and God's own purity and transcendence.

This dark contemplation of the soul is not only night, but also affliction and torment. God's infused contemplation prepares the soul for its union with him through love by purging and illuminating.

But why call the divine light a dark night? Because divine wisdom exceeds the capacity of the soul and because of the soul's own baseness and impurity, it is dark and painful. (2/5/2) The soul feels imprisoned and abandoned as in a dungeon. But the fruit of this darkness is a strong passion of divine love.

The fire of love penetrates the soul, as natural fire consumes wood. Though the divine love is similar to human love, it is also different.

For this enkindling of love occurs in the spirit and through it the soul in the midst of these dark conflicts feels vividly and keenly that it is being wounded by a strong divine love and it has a certain feeling and foretaste of God. Yet it understands nothing in particular, for as we said, the intellect is darkness. (2/11/1)

The passion of love flares up and the soul begins to share in the union with God. This love is a gift of God. But the soul can only receive its wound of love insofar as its appetites are brought under control.

When the soul is wounded, touched and impassioned, all its strength and its appetites are recollected in this burning of love. How will we be able to understand the movements and impulses of all this strength and these appetites? They are aroused when the soul becomes aware of the fire and wound of this forceful love and still neither possesses it nor gets satisfaction from it, but remains in darkness and doubt. (2/11/5)

"The touch of this divine love and fire so dries up the spirit and so enkindles the soul's longing to slake its thirst for this love that a person will go over these longings a thousand times." (Ps 62/2) (2/11/5) The soul simultaneously desires and suffers with the anxiety of a burning wound. (Job 7/2–4)

A man's anxiety and affliction in this burning of love is more intense because it is doubly increased. First, through the spiritual darknesses in which he is engulfed and which afflict him with doubts and fears. Second, through the love of God which inflames and stimulates and wondrously stirs him with a loving wound. . . . And this is the second way of suffering: with desire and anxiety of love in the innermost parts of the spirit. (2/11/7)

Yet in these dark afflictions the soul feels the consoling divine presence and strength, so that when anxious darkness passes, the soul feels empty and alone. "The reason is that since the strength and efficacy of the dark fire of love which assails it is communicated and impressed upon it passively, the darkness, strength and warmth of love ceases, when the assault terminates." (2/11/7)

Dark contemplation is the secret ladder by which the soul conducts itself in the night. The wisdom of love is secret.

The ladder of divine love begins with the soul sick in an advantageous way. The bride searches unceasingly for her lover. The soul is prompted to perform works of love. Solitude gives courage. There is a habitual yet unwearisome suffering, an impatient desire and longing for God. The soul runs to God and experiences many touches in him. In an ardent boldness, the soul is impelled to lay hold of the beloved without letting him go. The soul burns gently. And finally she is assimilated perfectly to God completely because of her clear vision of God in Heaven.

Inspired by the Song of Solomon as were so many of the mystics from earliest times, John wrote the first three stanzas of his *Spiritual Canticle*[17] while in prison at Toledo, finishing it at Granada (1582–84). Scheme: an anxious loving search for the beloved, the first encounter, spiritual espousal, spiritual marriage, and desire for perfect union in glory.

The bride searches for her beloved in the mountains (1–12), learning from him, but not yet satisfied.

Reveal your presence
And may the vision of your beauty be my death;
For the sickness of love
Is not cured
Except by your very presence and image.

O springlike crystal!
If only, on your silvered-over face,
You would suddenly form
The eyes I have desired,
Which I bear sketched deep within my heart. (11–12)

Though the bride sees her beloved, creatures try to lure her away. (13–21)

Withdraw them, Beloved,
I am taking flight!
Return, dove.
The wounded stag

Is in sight on the hill
Cooled by the breeze of your flight.

My Beloved is in the mountains
And lonely wooded valleys
Strange islands,
And resounding rivers,
The whistling of love—stirring breezes. (13–14)

At last—union with the beloved. (22–35)

The bride has entered
The sweet garden of her desire,
And she rests in delight,
Laying her neck
On the gentle arms of her Beloved. (22)

There he gave me his breast;
There he taught me a sweet living knowledge;
And I gave myself to him,
Keeping nothing back;
There I promised to be his bride. (27)

The small white dove
Has returned to the ark with an olive branch;
And now the turtle dove
Has found its longed-for mate
By the green river banks. (34)

The bride desires to go with her beloved to the mountain to the vision of his beauty in glory. (36–40)

Let us rejoice, Beloved,
And let us go forth to behold ourselves in your beauty
To the mountain and to the hill,
To where the pure water flows,
And further, deep into the thicket. (36)

There you will show me
What my soul has been seeking,

And then you will give me,
You, my life, will give me there
What you gave on that other day. (38)

John's verses show the soul's struggle through purgation, illumination, and union of the spiritual marriage.

In his *Living Flame of Love*,[18] written for Doña Ana del Mercado y Penalosa of Granada (1584), plus a commentary later, John writes of a very intimate and qualified union and transformation of the soul in God. As wood penetrated by fire leaps out into flame, so the soul is not only transformed by the fire of love, but actually produces in itself a living flame.

The soul cries in its affectionate union with God.

O living flame of love
That tenderly wounds my soul
In its deepest center! Since
Now you are not oppressive,
Now consummate! If it be your will,
Tear through the veil of this sweet encounter.

O sweet cautery
O delightful wound!
O gentle hand! O delicate touch
That tastes of eternal life
And pays every debt!
In killing, you changed death to life.

O lamps of fire!
In whose splendors
The deep caverns of feeling,
Once obscure and blind
Now give forth, so rarely, so exquisitely,
Both warmth and light to their beloved.

How gently and lovingly
You wake in my heart,
Where in secret you dwell alone;

And in your sweet breathing
Filled with good and glory,
How tenderly you swell my heart with love. (1–4)

This metamorphosis of the soul is the spiritual marriage—
a total merging into the beloved—a divine union through the
likeness of love beyond which the bride cannot pass in this
life. Both the cognitive and the affective activity of the soul
become divine—its likeness and participation in God's life.
Does God act through the soul? Rather he elevates the soul.
God, tending toward himself, moves the soul to himself.

This is a habitual union in the substance of the soul, in
Heaven permanent and on earth temporary. This is the glowing ember, the actual transformation, leaping flame. Actually
few reach this perfect union because they do not make room
for it.

We have seen two outstanding Renaissance mystics, Teresa
and John. This is a mystical time, an apocalyptic time, of
reformation, of inquisition and auto-da-fé. This is a time of
renewal of the arts, knowledge explosion, vernacular, national-
ism, foundations and reformations of religious orders, and the
exploration of new continents. Probably only the latter half
of the twentieth century has come close to paralleling it.

Teresa and John are brother and sister in the mystical world.
Both are for reform and contemplation. But John is a trained
theologian and poet, while Teresa writes in images. Teresa
combines action with contemplation, founding houses, rules,
etc., whereas John feels more at home in contemplation.

Both suffer on the road to union, stripped by God of earthly
desires and self-love, open to the embraces of the beloved.
Both write so that others may benefit from their experience.
And both use the divine-marriage analogy of Solomon's Song.

The lessons of Teresa and John took their rightful place in
Spanish literature and serve as guides to future generations
in the difficult road to divine love. Though their descriptions

fall far short of reality, nevertheless Teresa and John give good glimpses into the depth of divine love and union.

Did Teresa and John write only for nuns and priests? Is this union and mystical marriage possible also for a layman or laywoman outside of cloister walls? Both feel that the contemplative way may be followed by laymen. For example, Teresa addresses herself to laymen (*Interior Castle*, 3/2/12), and she speaks to the problems of lay life. Also John writes his *Flame* for the widow Doña Ana and his *Ascent* for laymen. (Prol., 8)

Is the mystical way of love open to all or only the chosen few? If it is a call to perfection, then none can be excluded. But is the mystical road easier to follow in a religious life of poverty, chastity, and obedience, with fewer worldly distractions? Is the *desnudez* from the world and family life a necessary prerequisite for mystical union with the beloved? Certainly it is a help in this direction.

The Spanish mystics give us insights not only into the theology of love but also into its psychology. Teresa especially is a master psychologist of the spiritual life, though some of her methods might seem a bit primitive at first glance.

Is Teresa's mystical marriage to her divine lover a sublimation of sex at a time when male lovers were in short supply due to their adventurous voyages to the New World? Teresa would never accept a nun who would not make a good wife. No frustrated old maids for her! No smooth young flesh for man and wrinkled old body for God!

⋅⋖ XVI ⋗⋅

THE STATE OF LOVE CONSISTS IN
A FLOWING OVER OF THE EGO-LIBIDO
TO THE OBJECT

Sigmund Freud, On Narcissism, *121*

Freud, Youth and Times

We have seen many views of love, from the sensual Indian *kama* to the altruistic love of the *bodhisattva* to the mystical marriage of Teresa of Avila.

In the late nineteenth and early twentieth centuries a more scientific view of love—in many ways opposed to the divine love of mystical contemplation—was popular. This is the scientific psychology of love. We have seen some love psychologists, including Plato, Ovid, Augustine, Ibn al-Arabi, and Andreas Capellanus. But nineteenth-century materialism and positivism would try to make the psychology of love more of a science than an art.

Whereas the Enlightenment boasted that man's reason was capable of fathoming all truth, the English Empiricists and French Encyclopedists opened up an investigation of reason itself. B. Stoodley comments: "Reason doffed the garb of the seer and donned the humble garb of the scientist."[1] Theories of natural selection and biological determinism led the way, with a view that they might lead to man's improvement. But by the end of the nineteenth century this was doubted.

Sigmund Freud grew up in this period of disenchantment and both nineteenth-century biological determinism and twentieth-century sociological determinism would affect his thought.

Freud was born in 1856 in Freiberg, Moravia, of a Jewish family—five girls and three boys. Young Sigmund was greatly attached to his mother and had conflicts with his father (Oedipus?). When his young brother Julius died at the age of eight months, Freud felt deep remorse, since he may have wished to get rid of the rival for his mother's affections.

Early friends and enemies may have laid the groundwork for Freud's later theories of love. Certainly the Christian ideal of loving one's enemies never appealed to him.

Both Judaism and anti-Semitism were important factors in Freud's youth. He came from a strong Jewish family which lived in a world of alienation. Eventually four of his sisters would die cruel deaths in Nazi concentration camps. The sense of alienation of a Jew living in a hostile Christian world could not but impress the young Sigmund, as it had Karl Marx before him. Yet traumatic though the bitter anti-Semitism was, nevertheless it sets the Jew apart, for if he were not of a superior people he would never be persecuted.

From his hatred of anti-Semitism and the long Jewish tradition of study, plus a positive view of sex uninhibited by taboo and restriction, Freud was able to develop a free form of the psychology of love.

The young Freud was an excellent student, working under Ernst Wilhelm von Brücke at the Psychological Institute in Vienna. He became an outstanding physician and his theme of the close relationship of body and mind reflects the Jewish tradition of the unity of man.

Stages of Development

Although Freud's early biological themes mirror his medical training, he soon sensed an influence from outside of man in his interpersonal experience. In his early period Freud felt that mental phenomena might be related to somatic states. Thus anxiety would be a subcortical expenditure of libido quantum.[2] But he soon realized that the large variety of mental experiences could not be matched by similar somatic conditions and he even felt that the mind could influence the soma.

Freud next tried a more sophisticated conceptualization of mental experiences with the unconscious, preconscious, and conscious. "In other words, he shifted his theory from the somatic or objective field to the mental or subjective field."[3] But he never completely gave up somatic causation of mental phenomena.

Now he sees a mutual effectivity of mind and body. For example, sexual excitation finds its mental representation in a mental system known as the Unconscious. Freud still feels that the dynamics of mental processes are essentially related to the accumulation and discharge of somatic tensions. Yet in his *Interpretation of Dreams* (1900) Freud sees no clear relationship between the Unconscious and somatic sexual excitation.

In his second stage, Freud develops the ego to help explain the outgoingness of human activity. Thus self-preserving instincts are removed from the Unconscious and placed in the ego as the basis of object cathexes. "Freud introduced a component of libidinal energy into the ego by the assumption that the sexual instinct 'supported itself upon' the self-preservative instincts."[4] Consequently, there must be a constant demand for libidinal energy, which in turn requires a continuous condition of sexual excitation (erotogenicity).

Freud's libidinal theory dominated his second period. Thus: "Personality process is to be explained largely by the behavior of energy arising out of somatic excitation and flowing either in the direction of anaclytic object-cathexis or into ego-cathexis."[5] And he reduces both Unconscious and ego to quantitative libidinal factors. But the ego ideal would spell an end to Freud's libidinal theory.

In his third stage (*Beyond the Pleasure Principle*, 1920) Freud asks what is the instinctual basis of the ego-ideal type of motivation, leading to repetition-compulsion and life and death instincts. In this period he is more socially conscious, reflecting the social interests of the era. He reduces all social groups to one main type—a primal patriarchal family, with his own interpretation of mythology and anthropology.

Eros, the outgoing, altruistic behavior of the individual, is also found in society, the moral person. Freud feels that the outgoingness of the individual is based on another eros, the cultural system and the individual's experience of this.

The formulation of a coherent ego which is a whole, not just a body ego or libidinal ego, but also an experiential ego, depends on internal dynamics and environmental forces as well. Aim-inhibited instincts now take on a more social aspect.

Social eros opens up the field of interpersonal relations since they influence personality dynamics and they supplant others that limit social influence, such as the castration and Oedipus complexes. The true source of eros now is not the biological organism, but society. So pseudo-anthropology and aim-inhibited instincts are rendered obsolete.

Freud's aim now is to explain the relationship between the organism and its social environment and so is similar to that of social science. So the threefold development of Freud's thought: somatic, topographical, and social.

Theories of Love

Freud stresses sexuality in his psychology and persists in reducing energy to sexual energy. This reminds one of some of the theories on sexual energy of the Hindu Tantric tradition. A basic criticism of Freud, as with Tantra, is that he over-stresses sex. His sexual theories also seem to have developed through three stages.

Freud sees life as dualistic: love-hunger, ego-sex, life-death, love-hate. In his practice he had seen the good and evil mixed in man. Like Dr. Ovid, Freud sees proper love as a key to health, while improper love leads to illness.

Freud says two currents unify in love. The first is the affection of a small child for his parents and family. This is based on self-preservation. The tiny baby smiles to please his protectors. But there are also sexual nuances here. Thus even at its beginning, sexual love has a basis in narcissism, namely, self-preservation. At the age of puberty these instincts are joined by the powerful sensual element. ("On the Universal Tendency to Debasement in the Sphere of Love," 1912) (SE, 11/111-12)[6]

Freud sees the paradox of love, as so many had before him. Thus if love is to thrive, it must be frustrated. And if it comes too easy, it loses value. The pain and passion sung of by poets and mystics is essential to love. "An obstacle is required to heighten libido, and where natural resistances to satisfaction have not been sufficient, men have at all times erected conventional ones so as to be able to enjoy love." (SE, 11/187-88)

Far from destroying love, asceticism makes it more valuable. Thus the chastity practiced by monks and nuns does not despise love but makes it all the more valuable. Moreover, sexual energies can be channeled into other useful areas—love of neighbor, the needy, the poor, children, orphans, the abandoned.

Freud saw early that man's ego-libido is opposed to the sexual instinct. Later, with his clinical experience of megalomania, he detected the importance of narcissism, the return of love energy to the ego in lieu of an outside agent. Ego-libido and object-libido are opposed, so that as one increases, the other decreases.

The highest phase of development of which object-libido is capable, is seen in the state of being in love, when the subject seems to give up his own personality in favor of an object-cathexis; while we have the opposite condition in the paranoic's phantasy of "the end of the world." (*On Narcissism*, 1914) (SE, 14/76)

A certain degree of self-love and self-preservation is necessary. In pain and in sleep one withdraws into oneself. But there has to be a balance with object-libido, a balance between narcissism and attaching oneself anaclytically to one who mothers or cares for us, one upon whom we can lean.

Parents' love for their children is typically naricissistic—as any teacher can readily attest. The child is a part of the mother or father, so any criticism of their child is taken as a personal insult. Here megalomania and overevaluation of the love object is typical. (SE, 14/91) But the child usually knows that he does not measure up to Mama's ego ideal. In fact, sometimes the child will totally reject the ego ideal.

Being in love is a self-lowering, so that one can become a love object for another person and thus have his ego-libido restored. "I am nothing." "No, you are something." Thus in normal adult love, object-libido and ego-libido coincide. (SE, 14/98–100) "The state of love consists in a flowing over of ego-libido to the object. It has the power to remove repressions and re-instate perversions. It exalts the sexual object to a sexual ideal." (SE, 14/121)

Love is ambivalent, as we have seen, and seems to thrive best in a state of frustration. It reminds one of the alternating current of electricity, attracting and repelling. Of course, for

10. "The state of love consists in a flowing over of the ego-libido to the object" (Freud, *On Narcissism*, 121)

love to exist at all there must be a basic antithesis: subject-object, active-passive, pleasure-pain. Other priorities are: love-hate, self-love and other-love, love-hate and indifference. (*Instincts and Their Vicissitudes*, 1915) (SE, 14/134)[7]

Freud limits love almost exclusively to sex, eliminating it from the scope of self-preservation. (SE, 14/137) Thus: "Love is derived from the capacity of the ego to satisfy some of its instinctual impulses autoerotically by obtaining organ-pleasure." (SE, 14/138–39)

Love starts out as narcissism and then moves to objects which are outside of the self or ego, but which have been incorporated into the extended ego insofar as the ego seeks them as objects of pleasure. As man develops, this love becomes identified with sex.

> As the first of these [sexual] aims we recognize the phase of incorporating or devouring—a type of love which is consistent with abolishing the object's separate existence and which may therefore be described as ambivalent. (SE, 14/139)

Thus the well-known relationship between love and the desire to eat the beloved. "I could eat you up!" Some see this significance in the eating of the body of Christ in the Christian Eucharistic love banquet.

At a higher stage, this is an urge for mastery over the subject, even to injury and annihilation. "Love in this form and at this preliminary stage is hardly to be distinguished from hate in its attitude toward the object. Not until the genital organization is established does love become the opposite of hate." (SE, 14/139)

Hate is older than love, since it reflects the primordial rejection of external objects by the ego, and is closely allied with self-preservation.

The complexity of love and its ambivalence ultimately led Freud to concepts of hate and death. This death-destructive force can be directed either to outside objects or to the inside self. And it can become a social force in war. ("The Disillusionment of War," 1915)

Love can perhaps best be described in its absence in mourning and melancholy. (*Mourning and Melancholy,* 1917) (SE, 14) Melancholy embraces dejection, loss of interest in the outside world, incapacity to love, lowering of self-regard, and deserving of punishment. With one exception, loss of self-esteem, these same characteristics are found in grief and mourning.

When faced with the reality that its love object no longer exists, the mourning ego must withdraw its affection and libido attachments. Once this pain is complete, the ego is free again.

Melancholy is often related to an unconscious loss of a love object, whereas in mourning it is conscious. Also in melancholy there is a deep feeling of worthlessness, a rejection of life—even to suicide. Perhaps this low self-esteem is justified, though often exaggerated—but with little sense of shame. Often the self-reproach is really reproach against a loved object which has been transplanted to the ego. For example, a woman's criticism of her husband is laid on herself.

The occasions giving rise to melancholy for the most part extend beyond the clear case of a loss by death and include all those situations of being wounded, hurt, neglected, out of favor, or disappointed, which can import opposite feelings of love and hate into the relationship or reinforce an already existing ambivalence. (SE, 14/251)

Thus love and hate combined are transferred to self in melancholia. Suicide is a redirecting of murderous impulses against self.

Beyond the Pleasure Principle (1920) begins the third stage of Freud's thought, as we have seen, moving from the biological and topological or regional study of love to a more social dimension.

Freud's *Group Psychology* (1921) contrasts with his earlier individual psychology. Only rarely can the individual be considered apart from others. For example, love is usually of another person, even though the beloved may be considered an extension of the ego.

Group psychology sees the individual as a member of a race and so under the influence of the social instinct, herd instinct, or group mind. This begins with the family.

What about love and the group? "The nucleus of what we mean by love naturally consists . . . in sexual love with sexual union as its aim." (SE, 18/90–91) Yet we cannot separate from this other types of love, namely, self-love, love for parents and children, friendship and love for all men.

In relations between the sexes these instincts force their way towards sexual union. But in other circumstances they are diverted from this aim or are prevented from reaching it, though always preserving enough of their original nature to keep their identity recognizable. (SE, 18/90–91)

Thus desire of proximity and self-sacrifice are common in these other types of love as well.

In both church and army, two artificial groups, the chief is often bound to the group by love as a father figure and also the mutual love of the brethren. And when these libidinal ties are broken, panic (*Angst*) ensues. Moreover, the so-called love religions are frequently intolerant toward those outside.

As we have seen, all love is ambivalent and combined with feelings of hate. This is also true of groups and nations. Thus rivalries and wars between families, clans, nations, races. Basically this is group narcissism.

But the group tends to repress individual narcissisms.

Such a limitation of narcissism can, according to our theoretical views, only be produced by one factor, a libidinal tie with other people. Love for oneself knows only one barrier—love for others, love for objects. . . . And in the development of mankind as a whole, just as in individuals, love alone acts as the civilizing factor in the sense that it brings a change from egoism to altruism. (SE, 19/102)

Being in love can be a lot like hypnosis, where "the ego becomes more and more unassuming and modest, and the object more and more sublime and precious, until at last it gets possession of the entire self-love of the ego, whose self-sacrifice thus follows as a natural consequence." (SE, 18/113) The object has taken the place of the ego ideal. Is there a parallel in groups?

"A primary group of this kind is a number of individuals who have substituted one and the same object for their ego-ideal and have consequently identified themselves with one another in their ego." (SE, 18/116) Libidinal unity in political and religious groups may be explained in this way. Augustine in his *City of God* had seen love as the moving force in groups.

Is the herd instinct the result of a fear of being alone? Man has a herd instinct to form group relationships in which he is united to the leader and to each of his brethren. But what is the relationship of individual, sexual male-female love to group love? It would seem that the two are incompatible.

Two people coming together for the purpose of sexual satisfaction, insofar as they seek solitude, are making a demonstration against the herd instinct, the group feeling. The more they are in love, the more completely they suffice for each other. (SE, 18/140)

Freud feels that "being in love" is a late development and so is its opposition to group ties. Philo had pointed this out concerning the Essenes in his *Apology* for the Jews.[8] Thus artificial groups such as church, army, monastery, fraternity, business, have little place for individual male-female love.

So *de jure* or *de facto* celibacy or continence plays a strong part in the history of these groups. Thus the vow of chastity in a religious order which dictates that when a member marries he or she must leave the order. Priestly celibacy is perhaps based more on the fraternity of the presbyters than on any other factor, with remote origins, possibly, in the continence of the Jewish Haburah, a fraternity of scholars.[9] Freud feels that homosexual love is more compatible with groups. Hence the danger of it in armies, prisons, or even cloisters.

Love must mature for the individual to mature. (*The Ego and the Id*, 1923) (SE, 19/13–66) The object of love—whether the mother's breast or the father ideal, friend or girl, or even self—must appear lovable.

The small baby is, in a sense, nonsocial or perhaps presocial, with his love energy general and out of focus. Gradually he develops sympathy and empathy for others.

> In Freudian terms, a man is sexually mature if he has absorbed and transcended his Oedipal and narcissistic levels, has come to terms with his natural oral and anal tendencies, and genetically focused his needs. . . . That man who can wholeheartedly love a woman of about his own age without disesteeming either her or himself, who can give and take in love openly and honestly with neither fetishistic pride nor anxious love, is relatively mature.[10]

Mature love unites ego and object into one. "At the height of being in love the boundary between ego and object threatens to melt away. Against all the evidence of his senses, a man who is in love declares that 'I' and 'You' are one and is prepared to behave as if it were a fact." (*Civilization and Its Discontents*, 1930) (SE, 21/66)

Love and work, *lieben und arbeiten*, eros and *ananke̅*, are the twofold pillars of life and of the human civilization. (SE, 21/101)

Love in the family also operates in an extended manner throughout civilization both as sexual love and as aim-inhibited affection.

People give the name "love" to the relation between a man and a woman whose genital needs have led them to found a family; but they also give the name "love" to the positive feelings between parents and children, and between brothers and sisters of a family, although we are obliged to describe this as aim-inhibited love or "affection." (SE, 21/102–03)

Both of these loves extend outside the family: genital love forms new families, while aim-inhibited love makes friendships, which are especially valuable since they avoid the exclusivity of sexual love.

But love and civilization can be at odds—with love defying the community and the community laying down restrictions. Thus the reluctance of families to give up a member to marriage or to the wider service of the community or church.

There is hate as well as love in society. Hating and loving seem to be a part of man. War, crime, hate, sadism, death, are everywhere and seem to rush civilization to its destruction. Is there erotic pleasure in war? We know the sexual symbolism of swords, spears, and guns. Perhaps Freud was right in explaining man's urge to war as sexually oriented.

Eventually it emerges without any sexual purpose, in the blindest form of destructiveness. We cannot fail to recognize that the satisfaction of the instinct is accompanied by an extraordinarily high degree of narcissistic enjoyment, owing to its presenting the ego with a fulfillment of the latter's old wishes for omnipotence. (SE, 21/121)

Religious Love

Freud, as we have seen, is a product of his materialistic and positivistic times and so could not take religion too seriously. He sees the Jewish God more as a Darwinian father figure, and religion in general as an illusion, a neurosis based on early totems and taboos.

Outlining the mythological basis of his theory of religion in his *Totem and Taboo* (1912–13), Freud says that past mythological events in primordial groups affect man today. The individual's development parallels that of society. Ontogeny recapitulates phylogeny.

Taboo itself is ambivalent, meaning both something sacred and something forbidden. The blocking off of the taboo by external law causes frustration and anxiety even in later ages when the original source of the anxiety is long forgotten.

As Freud associates neurotic behavior with taboo, so he correlates obsessive-compulsive behavior with religion. The link between taboo and religion is the totem. Religions, says Freud, are basically totemic groups united around a totem and taboo celebrated in totemic feasts in which the horde and totem are united. "The sacrificing community, the god and the sacrificial animal were of the same blood, and members of one clan." (SE, 13/136)

This blood covenant with God has been compared to a marriage bond, especially in Hebrew literature. Thus a love covenant; and the totemic feast is a marriage banquet.

In most totemic rites there is an approach-avoidance conflict which could become neurotic. For Christians, Christ is the totem and his death the totemic sacrifice and the Eucharist the totemic meal, according to Freud.

The Oedipus complex plus totem and taboo combine in

Freud's God, based on Darwin's patriarchal primitive horde. The sons admired, yet feared, their father's power. When they killed him in order to get his power and women, remorse came and they enforced the father's taboos, honoring him as a god.

Freud sees both Moses and Jesus as anti-types of the primordial father. Freud's concept of divinity, based on imagination, myth, and underdeveloped anthropology, leaves much to be desired. Some say that he shapes the myths to fit his theories, as when he asserts that Moses was killed by the Israelites in the same manner that his patriarchal archetype was murdered by his sons.

Leaving aside the myths, let us examine some of Freud's other observations on religion. First, love is basic to religion. For example, it is love of Christ and mutual love of the Christians for each other that is the foundation of the Christian church. (*Group Psychology*, Pt. 5) (SE, 18/93 ff.)

> Every Christian loves Christ as his ideal and feels himself united with all other Christians by the tie of identification. But the church requires more of him. He has also to identify himself with Christ and love all other Christians as Christ loved them. (Pt. 12) (SE, 18/134)

In both points the church requires that the group libido be supplemented. "One can be a good Christian and yet be far from the idea of putting oneself in Christ's place and of having like him an all-embracing love for mankind." This distribution of libido in the group is the basis of Christianity's claim to a higher ethic, according to Freud.

On the one hand, Freud sees religion as a manifestation of neurosis, and yet, on the other hand, he admits that it can alleviate neurosis.

> Even those who do not regret the disappearance of religious illusions from the civilized world of today will admit that so long as they were in force, they offered those who

were bound to them the most powerful protection against
the danger of neurosis. Nor is it hard to discern in all the
ties with mystico-religious and philosophico-religious sects
and communities the manifestation of distorted cures of all
kinds of neuroses. (Pt. 12) (SE, 18/142)

Freud feels that this phenomenon is bound up with a contrast
between direct sexual tendencies and aim-inhibited ones.

As we have seen earlier, Freud admits the value of aim-
inhibited love, especially when sublimated into works for the
benefit of mankind. At least indirectly this is an argument in
favor of religious celibacy, which seems to be aim-inhibited
love, according to Freud's terms. However, if divine love is
the prime purpose of man, then sexual love is the real aim-
inhibited love and not vice versa.

In *The Ego and the Id*, Freud identifies the ego ideal as
the basis of religion.

Insofar as it is a substitute for the longing for a father, it
contains the germ from which all religions have evolved.
The self-judgment which declares that the ego falls short
of its ideal produces the sense of worthlessness with which
the religious believer attests his longing. (Pt. 3) (SE, 14/37)

Freud feels that religion, morality, and social sense were originally the same thing.

The Future of an Illusion (1927) (SE, 21) epitomizes
Freud's views of religion. Religious truth, he writes, is handed
down from earliest times and is not open to challenge. But,
in scientific fashion, he asks for proofs for religious phenomena.

How about the appeal to inner experience of the mystics?
"If the truth of religious doctrines is dependent on an inner
experience which bears witness to that truth, what is one to do
about the many people who do not have this rare experience?"
(SE, 21/28) Many experiences are not universal, yet they are,
nevertheless, real. We have seen Teresa of Avila's response. She
prayed that those skeptics who doubted her experiences would

receive them, even if she had to give up her own delights and offer them to the doubters.

Yet Freud would admit the influence of religious truths, despite their lack of proof. "In past times, religious ideas, in spite of their incontrovertible lack of authenticity, have exercised the strongest possible influence on mankind." (SE, 21/29) Freud calls religious truths illusions. These are not false delusions, but rather nearly impossible wishes. For example, the desire for a Messiah who would come to initiate the golden age. (SE, 21/31)

Though religion has made contributions to civilization, Freud feels that it has not succeeded enough.

> It is doubtful whether men were in general happier at a time when religious doctrines held unrestricted sway. More moral they certainly were not. . . . If the achievements of religion in respect to man's happiness, susceptibility to culture and moral control, are no better than this, the question cannot but arise, whether we are not overrating its necessity for mankind, and whether we do wisely in basing our cultural demands on it. (SE, 21/37–38)

Religion frequently teaches love of God. But Freud sees the direction of love toward an invisible and unrealizable ideal as, at best, a neurotic defense. In loving God we are expected to have a universal love and not stop at particulars.

> A small number are able by their constitution to find happiness along the path of love. But far-reaching mental changes in the function of love are necessary before this can happen. These people make themselves independent of their object's acquiescence by displacing what they mainly value from being loved into loving. They protect themselves against the loss of the object by directing their love not to single objects, but to all men alike.
>
> And they avoid the uncertainties and disappointments of genital love by turning away from its sexual aims and trans-

forming the instinct into an impulse with an inhibited aim. What they bring about in themselves in this way is a state of evenly suspended, steadfast, affectionate feeling which has little external resemblance anymore to the stormy agitation of genital love, from which it is, nevertheless, derived. (*Civilization and Its Discontents*) (SE, 21/101–02)

This ideal universal love is found in the saints.

But Freud questions universal love, for one should not throw away his love on the undeserving. "If I love someone, he should deserve it in some way. . . . He deserves it if he is so like me in important ways that I can love myself in him. And he deserves it if he is so much more perfect than myself that I can love my ideal of my own self in him." (SE, 21/101–02)

Should I love a stranger? "Indeed, I should be wrong to do so, for my love is valued by all my own people as a sign of my preferring them. And it is an injustice to them, if I put a stranger on a par with them." (101–02) Also if I spread out my love too much, each one gets only a tiny share.

On the other hand, a stranger is worthy of hate, for not only has he no love for me, but he even tries to harm me. Freud rephrases the love commandment. "Love your neighbor as he loves you." This commercial love seems to reflect the xenophobia of the ghetto.

What would Freud say about the sexual language of the mystics in describing their experiences of divine love? And what about their self-flagellations and other seemingly masochistic practices? Is this aim-inhibited love? A sublimation of the sex instinct? Are the mystic virgins really frustrated human lovers who seek an imaginary rapture with their invisible yet steadfast divine spouse in lieu of an absent human partner?

All the mystics maintain that divine love is far superior to ephemeral human love. Rather than divine love as a sublimation of frustrated human love, perhaps it is the other way around, with human love modeled on the divine.

Teresa of Avila saw the danger of frustrated virgins seeking solace in the convents. So she would accept only those candidates who were desirable as human brides. No rejects for the divine spouse.

Freud never experienced mystical love, though it played a strong part in medieval and Renaissance Judaism. And some Hasidic giants, such as Martin Buber, were his contemporaries. Perhaps Freud's materialistic and scientific bent had little place for it.

Response

Freud pioneered in the clinical science of love. Perhaps if he found out anything, he discovered that love is unscientific, irrational, defying analysis. It is best described in poem, song, myth, or legend. But love cannot be analyzed in a test tube or limited to a clinic or a couch. Even Freud mixed his science with myth.

Freud's clinical experience taught him that religion can be a sign of neurosis or repression-compulsion. But perhaps in dealing with the mentally ill he was not familiar enough with those in whom religion is a normal path to maturity. As we have seen, he admitted that religion can give value to people's lives and even aid them to avoid the pitfalls of neuroses. Also he recognized the value of aim-inhibited love. Religion can be pathological in a pathological person. But so is everything else in his life—work, love, play, etc.

If religion is purely an escape which man uses to avoid reality—trouble! But what is reality? If God is reality, then man should flee to this eternal reality from his ephemeral tinsel world.

Let us now see some of Freud's fellow psychiatrists' views of love. First C. G. Jung.[11] Jung claims that Freud does not understand religious experience, as in his *The Future of an Illusion*. Freud of necessity confined his studies to sick minds rather than looking to the whole man and what makes him healthy.

Jung sees the value of religion with its symbols, morals,

rites, etc. Science is an attempt to understand the psyche from the outside. "Just as religious gnosis is a prodigious attempt of the human mind to derive knowledge of the cosmos from within."[12]

Jung says that sexuality is only one of the biological instincts, albeit an important one.

> The kind of sexuality described by Freud is that unmistakable sexual obsession which shows itself whenever a patient has reached the point where he needs to be forced or tempted out of a wrong attitude or situation. It is an overemphasized sexuality piled up behind a dam. And it shrinks at once to normal proportions as soon as the way to development is opened.[13]

Jung's positive view of religion, experience cannot deny or disguise in Oedipus complexes or superegos. Initiation rites attest to man's constant renewal of spirit reflecting divine procreation and the fatherhood of God.

Erich Fromm, another prominent modern psychiatrist, writes of love more as an art than a science. In his *Art of Loving*[14] he criticizes Freud for teaching of love as either an expression or a sublimation of the sex instinct, rather than discerning sexual desire as one of the many manifestations of the need for love and union. Further, Freud's patriarchalism overstresses the masculinity of sex, with the woman appearing as a castrated male.

> My criticism of Freud is not that he overemphasized sex, but his failure to understand sex deeply enough. He took the first step in discovering the significance of interpersonal passions. In accordance with his philosophic premises he explained them physiologically. In the further development of psychoanalysis it is necessary to correct and deepen Freud's concept by translating his insights from the physiological into the biological and existential. (31–32)

There are many types of love. Brotherly love is a love of equals. Motherly love is for the helpless. In contrast, erotic love for union and fusion with one person is exclusive and in it the stranger is transformed into an intimate person. "Erotic love, if it is love, has one premise, that I love from the essence of my being—and experience the other person in the essence of his or her being." (47) Love is not just feeling, but decision, judgment, and promise.

What about self-love? Is it necessarily narcissism or selfish or immature? "The affirmation of one's own life, happiness, growth, freedom is rooted in one's capacity to love, i.e., in care, respect, responsibility and knowledge. If an individual is able to love productively, he loves himself, too. If he can only love others, he cannot love at all." (50)

The selfish man is unable to love. "Selfishness and self-love, far from being identical, are actually opposites. The selfish person does not love himself too much, but too little. In fact, he hates himself." (51) Freud holds that these people are narcissistic, taking love from others and turning it to self, while Fromm asserts that the selfish man cannot love himself either.

The love of God is the highest type of love, for God is the highest good. Man needs to overcome separateness to achieve divine union. Each man or civilization has its own view of what God is—mother, father, polytheist, monotheist. In Western tradition, love of God is essentially the same as belief in God, whereas in Eastern religions and mysteries, love of God is an intense feeling of oneness linked with the expression of this love in every living act. (67–68) "One thing is certain: the nature of his love of God corresponds to the nature of his love for men. And, furthermore, the real quality of his love for God and man is often unconscious—covered up and rationalized by a more mature thought of what love is." (69)

From his practice, Fromm detects a great void of love in the modern world. Like Buber, Marcel, and many others, Fromm feels that the impersonal "I-It" is more characteristic of today's world of business, politics, military, education, etc., than the personal "I-Thou." Computerized supercorporations and conglomerates, supergovernments and megalo-universities, have helped to depersonalize society. Today man is more identified with his function—accountant, engineer, teacher, doctor, etc. Thus identity crises arise when his function becomes obsolete. Teamwork and conformity are the order of the day in the big corporations. But, as we have seen, this is only a pseudo-unity and cannot overcome man's lonely alienation and separateness.

Fromm points out two approaches which have aided the disintegration of love in Western society, namely, love as mutual sexual satisfaction and love as teamwork and a haven from loneliness. (79) And along with the disintegration of the love of man comes the dissolution of the love of God. Many modern men are either practical or theoretical atheists or have reverted back to an infantile dependence on an anthropomorphic God without any attempt to transform their lives according to God's principles. (88)

The art of loving requires discipline, concentration, patience, supreme concern, sensitivity. It should not be narcissistic, but objective, reasonable, humble, faithful, courageous, active, and dynamic. In a word, Paul's "Love is patient, kind," etc.

We have seen some varied views of love through the eyes of modern psychiatrists. But, as Jung says, each psychiatrist starts out with his own presuppositions—Freud atheistic and Jung theistic. Freud taking a negative view of divine love, while Jung and Fromm see in it a positive value.

These men have made valuable contributions to the study of love, yet in their research something eludes them, for love tends to be transcendent, unscientific, and even irrational—more proper to poets and troubadours and mystics than to clinical scientists with their white coats, couches, and note pads.

This is not to say that love in its irrationality cannot lead to perversions which may need professional counseling. But whether we can fit love into definite scientific categories seems doubtful. Though this is not to say that certain dimensions and patterns cannot be seen in love throughout the ages. Nevertheless, love is still more of an art than an exact science.

৺XVII৯

EPILOGUE

Varieties of Love

We have seen many varieties of love, from ancient teachers such as Lao Tzu and Siddhartha Gautama to modern psychiatrists such as Freud, Jung, and Fromm. We have studied human love from the paternal concern of Confucian rulers to the self-effacing love of the *bodhisattva* to the teacher-student love of Plato, from the unrequited love of the medieval troubadour to the scientific love of Freud.

Divine love is also found in most cultures, from the Way of Heaven of the Chinese, upon which all love is based, to the ecstatic *bhakti* love of Shiva or Krishna in India to Israel's sometimes unfaithful love of her divine spouse Yahweh and the Christian agape love of Jesus Christ. Augustine teaches a divine love with Neo-Platonic nuances in which the soul rises to meet its beloved.

Many mystics see the human love of husband and wife reflecting the divine hierogamy. For example, the Jewish prophets taught Israel as the bride of Yahweh. Paul, the apostle of Christ, writes that the union of husband and wife should be modeled on the mystical marriage of Christ and his bride, the church.

Medieval Hindu writings attributed to Narada compare the *bhakti* love of divine union with human love between mother and child, friends, husband and wife. The Sufi mystics passionately paint their love of God, as do the Christian ecstatics from Bernard of Clairvaux to Teresa of Avila. Medieval Jewish Kabbalists sing of marriage as a celebration of the wedding of Yahweh and his beloved Shekhinah.

Those who seek divine union often forgo human physical sexual love. Although human love reflects divine, it is a weak image at best. Human love is temporary and risky by its very nature, while divine love is steady and eternal. One who feels the shortness and chanciness of human love may be driven to seek new human loves to replace the old, or else fly into the arms of a divine lover.

Of course, divine love presupposes a belief in the transcendent or in God. Hindu *bhakti* centers on Krishna, or Rama, or on the impersonal "That." The Hebrews loved Yahweh, the Christians, Christ, and the Moslems, Allah.

But what about atheists? The *Rig Veda* finds the gods to be later creatures. And modern atheists such as Freud describe God as a mythological father figure and divine love as an illusion.

Divine love, like human love, is experiential. And just as one who is an orphan and who has never experienced human love often cannot conceive of it as possible, so one who has never felt or appreciated divine love cannot perceive it as a reality and so will tend to accuse the mystics of illusions or imaginings.

Human Love Today

All the mystics tell us that human love reflects and depends on divine love. Human marriage celebrates the nuptials of the gods. When this is no longer true, human love falls back on its own strength and weakness. It becomes a temporal thing, chancy at best.

The three main ingredients—sex, love, and marriage—often overlap and are frequently considered interchangeable. Sex includes many relationships between male and female, from thoughts to looks, touches, and intercourse.

Sex and love are not necessarily the same thing. For example, a man can have sexual relations with a prostitute without loving her in any way whatsoever. Love seems to include more of a self-giving than a seeking after bodily pleasure with little thought of the partner. The average person experiences thousands of orgasms in a lifetime. How many of these are love and how many are selfish pleasure?

Love and marriage are not the same thing either. In fact, the medieval troubadours felt that the two were incompatible. Today those who insist that love has to be absolutely free say that the restrictions and obligations of matrimony make true love impossible.

Harry Stack Sullivan, a modern psychiatrist, sees love as a mutual satisfaction.[1] "When the satisfaction or the security of another person becomes as significant as one's own satisfaction or security, then the state of love exists." This seems to be mutual support, companionship, acceptance, but is it love?

Strong sexual feelings, needing and wanting to be loved, need for approval, all of these plus a certain peer and parental pressure mix with romantic fantasy in the courtship stage before the disillusionment of marriage.

Is love necessary for marriage? W. Lederer and D. Jackson respond: "A working marriage may be achieved if both parties feel that they are better off together than they would have been separately. They may not be ecstatically happy, and they may not be 'in love' but they are not lonely and they do have areas of shared contentment."[2]

Sexual mores through the ages seem to move from Manicheanism to libertinism. Some have compared the human race to a drunk who falls off a horse, promptly gets up, mounts the horse again, and falls off the other side. Perhaps this is an exaggeration, but it seems hard for man either individually or collectively to walk a moderate road in sexual matters. Thus in certain periods celibacy and virginity are highly prized; in others they are despised.

Michael Zeik comments in his review of *Sex: Thoughts for*

Contemporary Christians: "Surely 20th century western man, having turned his back on Victorian inhibition, has come down on his knees to Dionysius. In our own times we have seen in drama, literature, movies and advertisements, the apotheosis of orgasm."[3]

Rollo May, a modern psychiatrist, says that as external anxiety over sex decreases as the shackles and the clothes of Victorianism are stripped off, internal anxieties increase.[4] As more books of sex instruction and "how to" manuals in the science of love-making pour off the press, as pornography becomes more commonplace, as sex becomes common and everyday rather than a longed-for delight, the spontaneous pleasure of love-making decreases and loneliness, boredom, and depersonalization increase.

As the Victorians sought love without sex, moderns pursue sex without love. Too much sex is worse than not enough. All love traditions tell us that restraint escalates pleasure and promiscuity leads to a jaded impotence, which forces one to perversions in order to seek a stimulus that will produce the physical thrill once more in the faded sexual mechanisms. Worn out from sexual games, more and more are turning to drugs for kicks. The sight of a sexually used-up movie star killing herself with an overdose of drugs is rather ordinary today. Moreover, sexual impotence is a growing problem in modern society.

According to recent statistics,[5] the Playboy Foundation claims that 75 percent of single women under 25 have had sexual intercourse, while Kinsey's studies twenty years earlier, *Sexual Behavior in the Human Female* (1953), showed that only 33 percent had experienced the sexual union.

The Playboy survey asserts that 50 percent of today's college men have had sexual intercourse by the age of 17, twice as many as noted in the Kinsey report, *Sexual Behavior in the Human Male* (1948). And 32 percent of the married men under 25 had committed adultery, whereas 24 percent of the married women of the same age had indulged. Some respond that the

Playboy survey appeals to sexy people who are more than willing to brag about their bedroom capers. The same criticism was leveled at the Kinsey report twenty years ago.

Those who make sex a business, including pornographers, strippers, prostitutes, masseuses, key-club operators, etc., were making millions until a recent Supreme Court decision dumped them in the lap of local courts.

Marriage is in trouble today, with from one out of two to one out of four ending up in the divorce courts, depending on customs and mores of the place. Many reasons are given. Birth control and abortion make the couple freer. In the past children have been a binding influence in marriage. Affluence makes consecutive or simultaneous polygamy fiscally feasible. People are living longer today and thus can look forward to a long boring time together after the kids are raised. Many psychiatrists say that middle-aged people pick younger partners in their perpetual search for youth.[6]

The divorce rate in the United States in 1972 was 4.3 per 1,000 population, involving 800,000 children, while the marriage rate was about 10.6.[7] No-fault divorce laws make marriage splits easier in many states.

The highest divorce rate—three times the overall rate—is found among the under-25s. It seems that some pregnant girls who find abortion repugnant marry the father of their child for the sake of the legitimization, with the divorce agreed upon ahead of time. Also peer and parental pressures force young marriages, as we have seen.

All of this seems to underline the transience and risk of sexual experience. It is not at all the same as love. And even where real love exists, it has time for an enemy.

The restrictions of marriage and the risks of divorce have prompted many young couples to live together unwed. Many of these are childless, using birth control and abortion to keep the arrangement as free as possible.

This brings up the question of children. In Roman times marriage was decreed by law to be for the sake of bringing up children. And some say that children were stressed because there was a trend away from this which was weakening the empire. Marriage for the sake of children has been the traditional view of Christianity, born during those times. The child is the overflow of the mutual love of the parents. The sexual union apart from this is truncated, to say the least.[8] Today, with children either limited or denied through birth control or abortion, the resulting frustrations of the love instincts to expand the personality may prove harmful. Love between two people exclusively is not enough. By its nature it is expansive, outgoing. It must diffuse itself into others, children, grandchildren, etc.

Today many propose abortion rather than have the child be born not wanted. On the other hand, thousands of childless couples cannot adopt. In the past, things evened out, with orphans often being adopted by selfless couples. It is most certainly false that the aborted children are not wanted. It is true that they are not wanted by their mothers, but it is not true that they are not wanted by anyone.

Perhaps it might be good to mention something here about the modern love-fantasy object in the United States, namely, the Playboy bunny. The bunny ideal bears out what happens when human love tries to go it on its own without the aid of divine love. The love fantasy must constantly change; it must be eternally young, shapely, sexy, pretty, etc.

Playboy Clubs keep a constant check on their girls to make sure that they present the ideal of immature love fantasy. Four times a year the bunnies are meticulously scrutinized to see if they have transgressed the laws of sexual fantasy. If sagging breasts, potbellies, droopy bottoms, or crepy thighs are detected, out they go. The love object has to be constantly changing, ever fresh. This is why they like to change the girls around and constantly replace the old girls with younger, smoother, firmer bodies.[9]

When human love is removed from the divine hierogamy, it cannot last. When it is based on looks, health, wealth, it is bound to wane. Face lifts can be done only so many times. Modern plastic surgeons are laughing all the way to the bank as they cash in on the search for the eternally young body.

Finally, as the medieval Kabbalists taught, when God's Shekhinah departs from marriage and love, it cannot last, for infidelity is incompatible with divine love.

Divine Love Today

If human love is in trouble in many ways today, where does divine love stand? Divine love, as we have seen, can be shown in exterior devotion or in interior contemplation and union with God.

One reason human love is in trouble today is that it is divorced from its divine prototype. We have seen that traditionally marriage is a celebration of the divine hierogamy, and where it is separated, it is as significant as a bath removed from the sacred initiation rites.

Unless there is a deep mystical meaning in marriage, it can become lonely and frustrating. Also when old love partners are cast off for new, rather than being a source of love, matrimony becomes a font of hate and hurt for all.

Externally are there any signs that divine love is increasing or decreasing today? Ironically the Christian devotion to the loving Jesus in his Sacred Heart has waned. This might indicate a falling off of divine love in the Christian milieu.

Monastic and religious life in many traditions signifies a marriage to the transcendent, a wholehearted love of God and the neighbor. With the drop in vocations to the religious life and increasing defections, this form of divine love life seems to be on the decline today in some areas.

Also there arose a strong movement against religious celibacy in the 1960's, with priests and nuns in the Roman Catholic tradition marrying at a fast rate. Yet as continence escalates human love and promiscuity destroys it, so celibacy can enhance marriage. Basically the religious celibate is married to God or to the transcendent and so a witness to all the divine hierogamies on which human marriage is modeled.

Freud thought that some might seek the celibate road as an escape from the risks and vagaries of human sexual love. But, on the other hand, he also admits the power and energy that can flow from the sublimation of what he calls aim-inhibited love.

On the positive side, we find an increase in interiority today, with a seeking of divine union or union with the transcendent through meditation. Perhaps there is less exterior devotion through statues and worship today, but more of a trend toward inwardness. And a melding of Eastern and Western traditions here.

Conclusion

We have tried to glimpse many varieties of love. Certain great lovers we barely touched. But we have tried to see some of the major trends in human and divine love and to show their relationships. Influences are often hard to trace. Some are clear, such as Plato's inspiration of Augustine or the Sufi impressions on the medieval troubadours.

Others are children of *Zeitgeist* enthusiasm, such as Jewish, Islamic, and Christian mystics of the Middle Ages. Mystic ages come and go and tend to follow millennial trends. As we near the millennial twenty-first century, the mystic way of divine love seems to be on the increase.

One thing that strikes us as we look through world literature is that love is universal, both human and divine. No successful cult or culture has been built on hate, although some hate and persecute those outside. Sometimes divine love is not of a personal god, but rather a striving for a certain transcendence which often takes on divine aspects.

Both human and divine love are ideals. Man often falls far

short in his daily life, but love is his foundation stone to which he must come back. And when his love errs he must redirect it to its proper object, wife, children, God.

As Dr. Eryximachus and Dr. Ovid taught, proper love leads to health and improper love causes sickness of mind and body. This is why modern medicine and psychology are so preoccupied with love. Teach a man or woman how to love selflessly and you have a healthy person. Improper loves must be corrected to return once again to health.

It is our hope that in these pages we may have contributed a bit to the dialogue on love in an age when many have lost the meaning of true love and immersed themselves in its periphery of sexuality.

NOTES

CHAPTER I. WHEN ALL THE PEOPLE IN THE WORLD LOVE EACH OTHER, THEN THE STRONG WILL NOT OVERPOWER THE WEAK (Mo Tzu)

1. Confucius, *The Sacred Books of Confucius and Other Confucian Classics*, C. W. Chai, ed. and tr. (New York: University Books, 1965), p. 4.
2. Confucian quotes, unless otherwise noted, are from *The Sacred Books of Confucius and Other Confucian Classics*.
3. Lin Yutang, ed., *The Wisdom of China and India* (New York: Random House, 1942), p. 795.
4. Ibid., p. 804.
5. Following quotes from *The Four Books*, J. Legge, tr. (New York: Paragon, 1966).

CHAPTER II. THE SAGE PUTS HIS OWN PERSON LAST AND YET IT IS FOUND IN THE FOREMOST PLACE (*Tao Te Ching, 7*)

1. See N. Smart, *The Religious Experience of Mankind* (New York: Scribners, 1969), p. 157.
2. Ibid., p. 158.
3. E. Morgan, *Tao, the Great Luminant* (Taipei: Ch'eng-Wen, 1966), pp. xxi ff.
4. R. Baird and A. Bloom, *Indian and Far Eastern Religious Traditions* (New York: Harper & Row, 1972), p. 189.
5. *Chuang Tzu: Basic Writings*, B. Watson, tr. (New York: Columbia University Press, 1964), pp. 112–13.
6. Morgan, op. cit., p. xxvii.

7. *Tao Te Ching*, 67, adapted from J. Legge, ed., *The Texts of Taoism* (New York: Dover, 1962), I, 110.
8. *Tao Te Ching*, G.-F. Feng and J. English, trs. (New York: Random House, 1972).
9. Baird and Bloom, op. cit., p. 152.

CHAPTER III. WHEN HE (BODHISATTVA) EXERTS HIMSELF FOR THE GOOD OF OTHERS, HE SHOULD BE FILLED WITH LOVE AND LOVE ALONE WITHOUT ANY ADMIXTURE OF SELF-INTEREST (Arycura, *Arya-Curas, Jataka-Mala*, 4/24)

1. Sermon on Abuse in *Sutra of the 42 Sections* (1st cent. A.D.), in Lin Yutang, *The Wisdom of China and India* (New York: Random House, 1942), pp. 362–63.
2. From J. B. Alphonso-Karkala, ed., *An Anthology of Indian Literature* (New York: Penguin, 1971), p. 302.
3. Lin Yutang, op. cit., pp. 544–45.
4. E. Conze, ed., *Buddhist Texts Through the Ages* (New York: Harper & Row, 1964), pp. 127–28.
5. *Ashtasahasrika*, 20/371–73, in Conze, op. cit., p. 129.
6. See H. Dayal, *The Bodhisattva Doctrine in Buddhist Sanskrit Literature* (London: Routledge, 1932) (Delhi, Banarsidas, 1970), p. 14.
7. Ibid., p. 46.
8. Ibid., p. 47.
9. C. Hamilton, ed., *Buddhism: A Religion of Infinite Compassion* (New York: Bobbs-Merrill, 1952), p. 108.
10. Dayal, op. cit., p. 61.
11. Ibid., p. 179.
12. D. T. Suzuki, tr. (London, Routledge, 1968), p. 211.
13. Conze, op. cit., pp. 131–32.
14. Ibid., pp. 136–37.
15. Ibid., pp. 285–86.
16. Dayal, op. cit., p. 181.
17. Ibid., p. 192.
18. *The Perfection of Wisdom*, E. J. Thomas, tr. (London: Murray, 1952), pp. 86–90.
19. Hamilton, op. cit., p. 111.
20. Ibid., p. 125.

CHAPTER IV. THOSE WHO DESIRE TO TRANSCEND ALL LIMITATIONS AND BONDAGES MUST ACCEPT SUPREME LOVE AS THE HIGHEST GOAL (Narada, *Way of Divine Love,* 33)

1. *Kama* quotes from *Kama Sutra* (New York: Capricorn Books, 1963), section, chapter, and page.
2. See T. W. Organ, *The Hindu Quest for the Perfection of Man* (Athens, Ohio: Ohio University Press, 1970), p. 244.
3. See J. B. Alphonso-Karkala, ed., *An Anthology of Indian Literature* (New York: Penguin, 1971), p. 295.
4. See *The Laws of Manu,* G. Bühler, tr. (New York: Dover, 1969) (SBE, 25).
5. Patanjali, *Yoga Sutra* (2nd cent. B.C.), 2/28, 30; B. D. Basu, ed. (Allahabad: Vasu, 1924), pp. 155 ff.
6. *Atharva Veda,* 11/8/32; 10/2/31.
7. Organ, op. cit., p. 145.
8. S. Radhakrishna, ed., *The Principal Upanishads* (London: Allen & Unwin, 1968), p. 262.
9. See M. Dhavamony, *The Love of God According to Saiva Siddhanta* (Oxford: Oxford University Press, 1971), p. 13.
10. Ibid., p. 43.
11. Ibid., p. 96.
12. *Bhagavad Gita As It Is,* A. C. Prabhupada, tr. (New York: Collier, 1972), p. 576. *Gita* quotes from here.
13. See E. Deutsch, ed., *Bhagavad Gita* (New York: Holt, Rinehart and Winston, 1968), p. 168.
14. Hollywood, Calif.: Vedanta Press, 1971. Quotes from here.
15. *The Wisdom of God, Srimad Bhagavatam,* Swami Prabhavanda, tr. (New York: Capricorn Books, 1968), p. 50. Quotes from here.
16. Organ, op. cit., p. 274.
17. Ibid., p. 275.
18. See *In Praise of Krishna: Songs from the Bengali,* E. Dimock and D. Levertov, trs. (Garden City, N.Y.: Doubleday, 1967), p. xviii.
19. W. G. Archer, *The Loves of Krishna in Indian Painting and Poetry* (New York: Macmillan, 1957), p. 82.
20. Ibid., p. 87.
21. Organ, op. cit., p. 281.
22. Dhavamony, op. cit., p. 140.
23. Ibid., p. 143.
24. Ibid., p. 149.

25. Dhavamony, op. cit., p. 162.
26. Ibid., p. 164.
27. Ibid., p. 166.
28. Ibid., p. 167.
29. See ibid., pp. 342–43.
30. See Organ, op. cit., p. 319.
31. Ibid., p. 321.
32. Ibid., p. 323.
33. A. Bharati, *The Tantric Tradition* (Garden City, N.Y.: Doubleday, 1970), pp. 296–97.
34. *Tibetan Yoga and Secret Doctrines* (New York: Oxford University Press, 1967), pp. 28–29.

CHAPTER V. LOVE IS OF IMMORTALITY (Plato, *Symposium*, 207)

1. *Agape and Eros* (London: SPCK, 1937), I, 127.
2. Ibid., p. 129.
3. *Plato,* in Loeb Classical Library (LCL) (Cambridge, Mass.: Harvard University Press, 1957). Plato's quotes from here.
4. See J. Mohler, *The School of Jesus* (New York: Alba House, 1973), pp. 93 ff.
5. *Love: Plato, the Bible and Freud* (Englewood Cliffs, N.J.: Prentice-Hall, 1964), p. 35.
6. *Plato and the Individual* (London: Methuen, 1964), pp. 90–91.
7. See J. Pieper, *Love and Inspiration: A Study of Plato's Phaedrus* (London: Faber and Faber, 1964), pp. 20–22.
8. Ibid., p. 50.
9. Ibid., p. 76.
10. Ibid., p. 82.
11. Ibid., p. 89.
12. See T. Gould, *Platonic Love* (New York: Free Press of Glencoe, 1963), pp. 125 ff.
13. Ibid., p. 138.
14. Ibid., p. 139.
15. Ibid.
16. See also *Nichomachean Ethics,* chs. 8 and 9.

CHAPTER VI. YOU SHALL LOVE THE LORD YOUR GOD WITH ALL YOUR HEART, AND WITH ALL YOUR SOUL, AND WITH ALL YOUR MIGHT (Deuteronomy 6/5)

1. D. Williams, *The Spirit and Forms of Love* (New York: Harper & Row, 1968), p. 20.
2. Bible quotes from *The Oxford Annotated Bible, RSV* (New York: Oxford University Press, 1965). National Council of Churches of Christ in U.S.A., Division of Christian Education.
3. See also Dt. 6/14–15.
4. For the exposure of adultresses in Hebrew tradition, see L. Epstein, *Sex Laws and Customs in Judaism* (New York: KTAV, 1967), p. 31. Repentant whores in early Christianity were sometimes found wandering naked in the desert, emulating the remorseful Israel. The most famous is Mary of Egypt.
5. See C. Montefiore and H. Loewe, eds., *A Rabbinic Anthology* (New York: Jewish Pub., 1963), p. 277. Rabbinical quotes from here.

CHAPTER VII. GOD IS LOVE (1 John 4/8)

1. A. Nygren, *Agape and Eros* (London: SPCK, 1937), I, 54.
2. D. Morgan, *Love: Plato, the Bible and Freud,* (Englewood Cliffs, N.J.: Prentice-Hall, 1964), p. 69.
3. D. Williams, *The Spirit and Forms of Love* (New York: Harper & Row, 1968), p. 36.
4. Ibid., p. 37.
5. Nygren, op. cit., p. 63.
6. See J. Mohler, *The School of Jesus* (New York: Alba House, 1973), pp. 19 ff.
7. Nygren, op. cit., pp. 158 ff.

CHAPTER VIII. LOVE IS A KIND OF WARFARE (Ovid, *The Art of Love,* 2/511)

1. E. K. Rand, *Ovid and His Influence* (New York: Longmans, 1928), p. 9.
2. H. F. Frankel, *Ovid: A Poet Between Two Worlds* (Berkeley: University of California Press, 1956), p. 9.

3. *Amores*, G. Showerman, tr. (London: Heinemann, 1947) (LCL).
4. *The Art of Love*, J. H. Mozley, tr. (New York: Putnam, 1929) (LCL).
5. J. H. Mozley, tr. (New York: Putnam, 1929) (LCL).
6. See Rand, op. cit., pp. 120 ff.
7. Ibid., p. 144.
8. Ibid., p. 153.

CHAPTER IX. LATE HAVE I LOVED YOU (Augustine, *Confessions*, 10/27/38)

1. See A. Nygren, *Agape and Eros* (London: SPCK, 1937), I, 22 ff.
2. For further Augustinian views on sex, see: "On the Good of Widowhood" (401), "On the Good of Marriage" (414), "On Marriage and Concupiscence" (419–20).
3. *Morals of the Catholic Church* (MCC), 3–4, in W. Oates, ed., *The Basic Writings of St. Augustine* (New York: Random House, 1948), p. 323.
4. See also *Confessions*, 13/9/10; *The City of God*, 11/28.
5. *The Confessions of St. Augustine*, J. Ryan, tr. (Garden City, N.Y.: Doubleday, 1960).
6. See also *On Catechizing*, 4/7.
7. *The City of God*, G. Walsh et al., trs. (Garden City, N.Y.: Doubleday, 1962), p. 321.
8. E. Gilson, *The Christian Philosophy of St. Augustine* (New York: Random House, 1960), p. 172.
9. Ibid., p. 333. See also Augustine's Commentary on Psalm 99/4.
10. See J. Mohler, *The Heresy of Monasticism* (New York: Alba House, 1971), passim.

CHAPTER X. IT IS THE FLAME OF LOVE THAT FIRED ME (Rumi, *Mathnawi*)

1. *The Koran*, M. Z. Khan, tr. (New York: Praeger, 1971).
2. A. J. Arberry, *Sufism: An Account of the Mystics of Islam* (London: Allen & Unwin, 1968), p. 21.
3. *Kharraz Kitab al-Sidq*, p. 6, 40; Arberry, op. cit., p. 27.
4. Hujwiri, *Kashf al-Mahjub*, p. 283; Arberry, op. cit., p. 29.
5. See J. Mohler, *The Heresy of Monasticism* (New York: Alba House, 1971), pp. 100 ff.

6. 'Attar, *Tadhkirat al-Auliya*, I, 66; Arberry, op. cit., p. 42.

7. R. A. Nicholson, "Mysticism," in T. Arnold and A. Guillaume, eds., *The Legacy of Islam* (Oxford: Oxford University Press, 1931), pp. 213–14.

8. Suhrawardi, '*Awarif al-Ma'arif*, Ihya 4, pp. 343, 358; *Readings from the Mystics of Islam* (RMI), M. Smith, tr. (London: Luzac and Co., 1950), No. 7.

9. See Mohler, op. cit.

10. Arberry, op. cit., p. 45.

11. Abu Nu'aim, Hilya 8, p. 17; Arberry, op. cit., p. 53.

12. For possible Hindu influence on Abul Yazid and other Sufis, see R. C. Zaehner, *Hindu and Muslim Mysticism* (New York: Schocken, 1969), pp. 92 ff. For possible Buddhist ancestry by way of the Manichees, see D. M. Lang, *The Wisdom of Balahvar* (London: Allen & Unwin, 1957), pp. 24–29.

13. Kalabadhi, *Al-Ta 'Arruf*, p. 87; Arberry, op. cit., pp. 62–63.

14. Abu Nu'aim, Hilya 9, p. 342; Arberry, op. cit., p. 68.

15. See Arberry, op. cit., pp. 74 ff.

16. See Mohler, op. cit., pp. 64–67.

17. "Deliverance from Error, 4/126, in W. M. Watt, ed., *The Faith and Practice of al-Ghazali* (London: Allen & Unwin, 1967), p. 557.

18. *Readings from the Mystics of Islam*, p. 6.

19. I. Shah, ed., *The Way of the Sufi* (London: Jonathan Cape, 1968), p. 80.

20. Ibid., p. 79.

21. From A. Ansari, *The Persian Mystics*, S. J. Singh, tr. (London, Murray, 1951), pp. 28, 30, 57–59.

22. See Arberry, op. cit., pp. 113 f.

23. Ibid., p. 115.

24. *Mystical Poems of Rumi*, A. Arberry, tr. (Chicago: University of Chicago Press, 1968), pp. 48–49, No. 54.

25. *The Mathnawi of Jalal-ud-din Rumi*, R. A. Nicholson, tr. (London: Cambridge University Press, 1934), 5/1242–56.

26. In Ibn Said's *The Pennants*, from *Moorish Poetry*, A. J. Arberry, tr. (London: Cambridge University Press, 1953), p. 2.

27. R. A. Nicholson, *A Literary History of the Arabs* (London: Cambridge University Press, 1953), p. 426.

28. Ibn Hazm, *The Ring of the Dove*, A. J. Arberry, tr. (London: Luzac and Co., 1953), p. 25.

29. R. Briffault, *The Troubadours* (Bloomington: University of Indiana Press, 1965), p. 29.

30. Ibid., pp. 48–49.

31. See Mohler, op. cit., passim.

32. See J. Trimingham, *The Sufi Orders of Islam* (Oxford: Oxford University Press, 1971), pp. 166 ff.

33. Abu Said in R. A. Nicholson, *Studies in Islamic Mysticism* (London: Cambridge University Press, 1921), p. 46.

34. Trimingham, op. cit., p. 200.

CHAPTER XI. THROUGH HIS UNION WITH THE SHEKHINAH HE HAS BECOME MALE AND FEMALE (*Zohar*, 1/49b)

1. H. Gersh, *The Sacred Books of the Jews* (New York: Stein and Day, 1968), p. 197.

2. Ibid., pp. 199–200.

3. I. Zinberg, *A History of Jewish Literature*, Vol. I: *The Arabic-Spanish Period* (Cleveland: Case Western Reserve, 1972), p. 13.

4. Ibid., p. 15.

5. Ibid., p. 53.

6. R. Patai, *The Hebrew Goddess* (New York: KTAV, 1967), p. 124.

7. Philo, *On Drunkenness*, 8/30; *On the Cherubim*, 14/49.

8. Patai, op. cit., p. 115.

9. Ibid., p. 55.

10. See G. G. Scholem, *On the Kabbalah and Its Symbolism* (New York: Schocken, 1965), pp. 88 ff.

11. G. G. Scholem, *Major Trends in Jewish Mysticism* (New York: Schocken, 1971), p. 20.

12. Scholem, *On the Kabbalah*, p. 94.

13. Ibid., p. 103.

14. Gersh, op. cit., p. 313.

15. See J. Mohler, *The Origin and Evolution of the Priesthood* (New York: Alba House, 1970), p. 59.

16. Scholem, *On the Kabbalah*, p. 108.

17. *The Zohar*, H. Sperling and M. Simon, trs. (5 vols.; London: Soncino Press, 1931).

18. Patai, op. cit., p. 181.

19. Ibid., p. 205.

20. Ibid., p. 243.

21. *On the Kabbalah*, p. 119.

22. Ibid., p. 130.

23. Ibid., p. 138; *Zohar*, 1/8a; 3/98a.

24. Patai, op. cit., pp. 246 ff.

25. Philo, *The Making of the World*, 100; *Special Laws*, 2/56–58.

26. Patai, op. cit., p. 258.
27. Ibid.; *Zohar*, 2/63b.
28. Patai, op. cit., p. 263.
29. Ibid., p. 264.
30. Ibid., pp. 195 f.
31. See J. Mohler, *The Heresy of Monasticism* (New York, 1971), pp. 20 f., 84; *The School of Jesus* (New York: Alba House, 1973), pp. 9 f.
32. See Scholem, *Major Trends in Jewish Mysticism*, pp. 80 ff.
33. Ibid., p. 92.
34. Eleazar of Worms, *Sefer Rokeah*, f. 1b–9a; Scholem, *Major Trends in Jewish Mysticism*, p. 95.
35. *Medieval Jewish Mysticism: Book of the Pious* (Northbrook, Ill.: Whitehall, 1971), p. 11.
36. Ibid., p. 12.
37. Scholem, *Major Trends in Jewish Mysticism*, p. 96.
38. Ibid., p. 96.
39. Ibid., p. 98.
40. Ibid., p. 108.

CHAPTER XII. LOVE IS A CERTAIN INBORN SUFFERING (Andreas Capellanus, *The Art of Courtly Love*, 1/1)

1. C. S. Lewis, *The Allegory of Love* (Oxford: Oxford University Press, 1951), p. 11.
2. Ibid., p. 13.
3. See D. de Rougemont, *Love in the Western World* (New York: Random House, 1956), pp. 81 ff.
4. Lewis, op. cit., p. 21.
5. See J. Wilhelm, *Seven Troubadours: The Creators of Modern Verse* (University Park: Pennsylvania State University Press, 1970), pp. 15 ff.
6. Ibid., pp. 14–15.
7. Ibid., p. 18.
8. Ibid., p. 39.
9. Ibid., pp. 43–44.
10. Ibid., pp. 66–70.
11. Quotes from Andreas Capellanus, *The Art of Courtly Love* (New York: Columbia University Press, 1941).
12. See S. Barrow, *Medieval Society Romances* (New York: Columbia University Press, 1924), pp. 10 ff.

13. Barrow, op. cit., p. 18.
14. Ibid., p. 47.
15. Ibid., p. 57.
16. Ibid., p. 60.
17. Ibid., p. 92.
18. Ibid., p. 67.
19. Lewis, op. cit., p. 23.
20. De Rougemont, op. cit., pp. 15, 17.
21. Ibid., p. 31.
22. Ibid., p. 41.
23. Ibid., p. 46.
24. Lewis, op. cit., p. 116.
25. Ibid., p. 141.
26. G. de Lorris and J. de Meun, *The Romance of the Rose*, C. Dahlberg, tr. (Princeton: Princeton University Press, 1971).
27. Lewis, op. cit., p. 144.
28. Ibid., p. 167.
29. Ibid., p. 172.
30. Ibid., p. 183.
31. Ibid., p. 187.
32. Ibid., p. 196.
33. Ibid., p. 340.
34. Ibid., p. 360.
35. E. Gilson, *Dante and Philosophy* (New York: Harper & Row, 1963), p. 59.
36. Ibid., p. 61.
37. C. Hardie, "Dante and the Tradition of Courtly Love," in *Patterns of Love and Courtesy*, V. Lawlor, ed. (London: Arnold, 1966), p. 28.
38. Ibid., p. 34.
39. Ibid., p. 43.

CHAPTER XIII. THE REASON FOR LOVING GOD IS GOD HIMSELF
(Bernard, *On the Necessity of Loving God*, 1)

1. See A. Nygren, *Agape and Eros* (London: SPCK, 1937), I, 581 ff.
2. See E. Gilson, *The Mystical Theology of St. Bernard* (London: Sheed and Ward, 1940), pp. 1 ff.
3. Ibid., p. 2.

4. See J. Mohler, *The Heresy of Monasticism* (New York: Alba House, 1971), passim.
5. Gilson, op. cit., pp. 21 ff.
6. Quotes from A. Pegis, ed., *The Wisdom of Catholicism* (New York: Random House, 1949), pp. 260 ff.
7. Ibid., pp. 230 ff.
8. *Canticle Sermons,* S. Eales, tr. (London, 1895).
9. Bernard of Clairvaux, *Sermons* (Dublin, 1925), III, 496 ff.
10. Guillaume de Saint Thierry, *Deux Traités de l'Amour de Dieu,* M.-M. Davy, ed. Translated from the Latin by James A. Mohler, S.J. (Paris: Vrin, 1953), pp. 22 ff.
11. Ibid., pp. 70 ff.
12. London: Mobray, 1959.
13. *The History of Christian Philosophy in the Middle Ages* (New York: Random House, 1955), pp. 167 f.
14. St. Thomas Aquinas, *Summa Theologica,* Vol. 19 (New York: Blackfriars, 1964).
15. See *Disputed Question on Charity,* 10–13.

CHAPTER XIV. FAITH WITHOUT LOVE IS NOT ENOUGH (Martin Luther, Wittenberg Sermons, March 9, 1522)

1. See J. Mohler, *Dimensions of Faith* (Chicago: Loyola University Press, 1969), pp. 70 ff.
2. *Agape and Eros* (London: SPCK, 1937), I, 477.
3. Luther, *Lectures on Romans* (LCC 15), W. Pauck, tr. (Philadelphia: Westminster, 1961), p. 162.
4. *Luther's Works* (LW), J. Pelikan and H. Lehmann, eds. (Philadelphia and St. Louis: Fortress and Concordia, 1955).
5. *Short Form of the Ten Commandments* (1520) and *Little Prayer Book* (1522).
6. *Explanation of the 95 Theses,* 37 (1518).
7. *Blessed Sacrament of the Body of Christ,* 4 (1519) (LW, 35/50 f).
8. Ibid., (LW, 35/68).
9. *Commentary on Galatians* (5/22–23) (1519) (LW, 27/373–74).
10. P. Althaus, *The Theology of Martin Luther* (Philadelphia: Fortress Press, 1966), pp. 294 ff.
11. Ibid., pp. 296–97.
12. *14 Consolations,* 6 (1520) (LW, 42/161–62).
13. M. Luther, *Selections from His Writings,* J. Dillenberger, ed. (Garden City, N.Y.: Doubleday, 1961), p. 18.

14. *M. Luthers Werke*, Kritische Gesamtausgabe (Weimar, 1883–1903) (WA, 17/2; 97/7–11) (1525).

15. B. Ebeling, *Luther: An Introduction to His Thought* (Philadelphia: Fortress Press, 1964), p. 164.

16. Ibid., p. 165.

17. Ibid., p. 169.

18. Ibid., pp. 170–71.

19. M. Luther, *Selections from His Writings*, p. 373.

20. Ebeling, op. cit., p. 208.

21. Althaus, op. cit., pp. 172, 173.

22. See R. Blakney, *Meister Eckhart* (New York: Harper & Row, 1957), p. xxi.

CHAPTER XV. O LIVING FLAME OF LOVE THAT TENDERLY WOUNDS MY SOUL IN ITS DEEPEST CENTER (John of the Cross, *The Living Flame of Love*, 1)

1. See H. A. Hatzfeld, *Santa Teresa de Avila* (New York: Twayne, 1969), pp. 138 ff. See also M. T. Olabarrieta, *The Influence of Ramon Lull on the Style of the Early Spanish Mystics and Santa Teresa* (Washington: Catholic University of America Press, 1963).

2. Hatzfeld, op. cit., pp. 147–48.

3. Ibid., p. 148.

4. Ibid., p. 153.

5. See H. C. Lea, *Chapters from the Religious History of Spain Connected with the Inquisition* (New York: Franklin Press, 1967), pp. 213–421.

6. Teresa of Jesus, *Life: Maxims and Foundation*, J. J. Burke, ed. (New York, 1911).

7. *The Way of Perfection*, Benedictines of Stanbrook Abbey, trs.; B. Zimmerman, ed. (London: Baker, 1925).

8. In *Minor Works of St. Teresa*, Benedictines of Stanbrook Abbey, trs.; B. Zimmerman, ed. (London: Baker, 1913).

9. *The Interior Castle*, Benedictines of Stanbrook Abbey, trs.; B. Zimmerman, ed. (London: Baker, 1921).

10. See Hatzfeld, op. cit., pp. 42 ff.

11. Ibid., p. 61.

12. Fr. Bruno, *St. John of the Cross* (New York: Sheed and Ward, 1936), p. 42.

13. Ibid., p. 100.

14. *The Collected Works of St. John of the Cross*, K. Kavanaugh and O. Rodriguez, trs. (London: Nelson, 1963), pp. 68–69.
15. See J. Mohler, *The Beginning of Eternal Life: The Dynamic Faith of Thomas Aquinas, Origins and Interpretation* (New York: Philosophical Library, 1968).
16. *Collected Works*, pp. 295 ff.
17. Ibid., pp. 410–15.
18. Ibid., pp. 578–79.

CHAPTER XVI. THE STATE OF LOVE CONSISTS IN A FLOWING OVER OF THE EGO-LIBIDO TO THE OBJECT (Sigmund Freud, *On Narcissism,* 121)

1. B. Stoodley, *The Concepts of Sigmund Freud* (Glencoe, Ill.: Free Press, 1959), p. ix.
2. See ibid., pp. 236 ff.
3. Ibid., p. 237.
4. Ibid., p. 239.
5. Ibid.
6. *Standard Edition of the Complete Psychological Works of Sigmund Freud* (SE) S. Strachey and A. Freud, eds. (London: Hogarth Press and Institute of Psycho-Analysis, 1964).
7. See also D. Morgan, *Love: Plato, the Bible and Freud* (Englewood Cliffs, N.J.: Prentice-Hall, 1964), pp. 142–43.
8. See J. Mohler, *The Heresy of Monasticism* (New York, 1971), pp. 20–21. Also see Plato's *Republic*, Book 5.
9. See J. Mohler, *The School of Jesus* (New York: Alba House, 1973), chs. 1 and 2.
10. Morgan, op. cit., pp. 151, 153.
11. See C. G. Jung, "Freud and Jung: Contrasts," in *Freud and Psychoanalysis* (New York: Pantheon, 1961), pp. 333–40.
12. Ibid., p. 337.
13. Ibid., p. 338.
14. New York: Bantam, 1963, p. 30. Further quotes from here.

CHAPTER XVII. EPILOGUE

1. Quoted in W. Lederer and D. Jackson, "Do People Really Love?" *Reader's Digest,* January 1974, p. 65 (earlier in *Family Circle,* Au-

gust 1973). Quote from H. Sullivan, *The Mirages of Marriage* (New York: Norton, 1968).

2. "Do People Really Love?" p. 66.

3. Review of *Sex: Thoughts for Contemporary Christians*, M. Taylor, ed. (Garden City, N.Y.: Doubleday, 1972), in *Commonweal*, June 30, 1972, pp. 363–65.

4. "Reflections on the New Puritanism," in *Sex: Thoughts for Contemporary Christians*, pp. 169–82.

5. See "The Sex Poll, 1973," *Time*, October 1, 1973, pp. 63–64. Also R. Sorensen, *Adolescent Sexuality in Contemporary America* (Cleveland: World, 1972).

6. See E. Bergler, *The Revolt of the Middle-Aged Man* (New York: Grosset and Dunlap, 1957).

7. See "What Is Killing Our Marriages?" *Reader's Digest*, June 1973, pp. 152 ff.

8. In Hinduism marital intercourse, *garbhadhana*, is the first prenatal sacrament (*samskara*) of the *child* not of the parents. Parents are agents of the child.

9. See "Drooping Cottontails," *Time*, November 26, 1973, p. 133.

SELECTED BIBLIOGRAPHY

I. CONFUCIANISM

Chan, W. T. *A Source Book of Chinese Philosophy*. Princeton, 1965.
The Chinese Classics. 7 vols. J. Legge, tr. Hong Kong, 1961.
Confucius. *The Sacred Books of Confucius and Other Confucian Classics*. C. W. Chai, ed. and tr. New York, 1965.
Creel, H. G. *Confucius: The Man and the Myth*. London, 1954.
Dobson, W. A. *Mencius*. Toronto, 1963.
The Four Books. J. Legge, tr. New York, 1966.
The I Ching. C. Baynes, tr. Princeton, 1968.
Lin Yutang. *The Wisdom of China and India*. New York, 1942.
Liu Wu-Ch'i. *A Short History of Confucian Philosophy*. London, 1955.
Smith, D. G. *Chinese Religions*. New York, 1971.
Steel, J. *The I-Li or Book of Etiquette and Ceremonial*. Taipei, 1965.
Wright, A. F., ed. *The Confucian Persuasion*. Stanford, 1960.

II. TAOISM

Chan, W. T. *The Way of Lao Tzu*. New York, 1963.
Chuang Tzu: Basic Writings. B. Watson, tr. New York, 1964.
Chung-Yuan, C. *Creativity and Taoism*. New York, 1962.
Creel, H. *What Is Taoism?* New York, 1962.
Day, C. B. *The Philosophers of China*, London, 1962.
Fung Yu-Lan. *The Spirit of Chinese Philosophy*. London, 1947.
Giles, H. A. *Chuang Tzu: Taoist Philosopher and Chinese Mystic*. London, 1961.
Graham, A. C. *The Book of Lieh Tzu*. London, 1960.
Herbert, E. *A Taoist Notebook*. London, 1955.
Lao Tzu. *Tao Te Ching*. G.-F. Feng and J. English, trs. New York, 1972.

Lin Yutang. *The Wisdom of Lao Tzu*. New York, 1948.
Merton, T. *The Way of Chuang Tzu*. New York, 1965.
Morgan, E. *Tao, the Great Luminant*. Taipei, 1966.
The Texts of Taoism. "Sacred Books of the East" (SBE). Vol. 40. 1942.

III. MAHAYANA BUDDHISM

Ch'en, K. *Buddhism in China*. Princeton, 1964.
Conze, E. *Buddhism: Its Essence and Development*. New York, 1959.
——, ed. *Buddhist Texts Through the Ages*. New York, 1964.
——, ed. *Buddhist Wisdom Books* (*Diamond Sutra, Heart Sutra*). New York, 1972.
Cowell, E., ed. *Buddhist Mahayana Texts* (SBE, 49). New York, 1969.
Dayal, H. *The Bodhisattva Doctrine in Buddhist Sanskrit Literature*, London, 1932; Delhi, 1970.
Grousset, R. *In the Footsteps of the Buddha*. New York, 1971.
Hamilton, C., ed. *Buddhism: A Religion of Infinite Compassion*. New York, 1952.
The Lankavatara Sutra: A Mahayana Text. D. T. Suzuki, tr. London, 1968.
The Perfection of Wisdom: The Career of Predestined Buddhas. E. J. Thomas, tr. London, 1952.
Santideva. *The Path of Light* (*Bodhi-Charyavatara*). L. D. Barnett, tr. London, 1959.
Soothill, W., and Hodous, L. *A Dictionary of Chinese Buddhist Terms*. Taipei, 1970.
Suzuki, B. J. *Mahayana Buddhism*. London, 1959.
Suzuki, D. T. *On Indian Mahayana Buddhism*. New York, 1968.
Wright, A. F. *Buddhism in Chinese History*. Stanford, 1965.
Zurcher, E. *The Buddhist Conquest of China*. New York, 1959.

IV. HINDUISM

Archer, W. G. *The Loves of Krishna in Indian Painting and Poetry*. New York, 1957.
Badarayana. *The Vedanta Sutras*. G. Thibaut, tr. New York, 1962. (SBE 34.)
The Beginnings of Indian Philosophy. Edgerton, R., tr. London, 1965.
Bhagavad Gita. E. Deutsch, tr. New York, 1968.
Bharati, A. *The Tantric Tradition*. Garden City, N.Y., 1970.

The Dhammapada. P. Lal, tr. New York, 1967.

Dhavamony, M. *The Love of God According to Saiva Siddhanta.* Oxford, 1971.

Hindu Scriptures. R. Zaehner, tr. New York, 1966.

In Praise of Krishna: Songs from the Bengali. E. Dimock and D. Leverton, trs. Garden City, N.Y., 1967.

Johnson, C., ed. *Vedanta.* New York, 1971.

The Marabharata. G. V. Narasimhan, tr. New York, 1965.

Moore, C., ed. *The Indian Mind.* Honolulu, 1967.

Organ, T. W. *The Hindu Quest for the Perfection of Man.* Athens, Ohio, 1970.

Prabhavananda, S. *The Spiritual Heritage of India.* London, 1962.

Raju, P. T. *The Philosophical Tradition of India.* London, 1971.

Speaking of Shiva. A. Ramanuja, tr. New York, 1974.

Srimad Bhagavatam: The Wisdom of God. S. Prabhavananda, tr. New York, 1968.

The Upanishads. S. Hikhilananda, tr. New York, 1963.

Vatsyayana. *The Kama Sutra.* R. Burton and F. Arbuthnot, trs. New York, 1963.

V. PLATO

Feibleman, J. K. *Religious Platonism.* Westport, Conn., 1971.

Friedlander, P. *Plato: An Introduction.* New York, 1964.

Gould, T. *Platonic Love.* New York, 1963.

Jaeger, W. *Paedeia.* Berlin, 1944.

Kramer, H. J. *Arete bei Platon und Aristotles.* Amsterdam, 1967.

McKeon, R., ed. *Introduction to Aristotle.* New York, 1967.

Morgan, D. *Love: Plato, the Bible and Freud.* Englewood Cliffs, N.J.: 1964.

Nygren, A. *Agape and Eros.* London, 1937.

Pieper, J. *Love and Inspiration: A Study of Plato's Phaedrus.* London, 1964.

Plato. *Works,* especially *Symposium* and *Phaedrus,* LCL.

———. *Great Dialogues.* W. H. Rouse, tr. New York, 1964.

Rankin, H. *Plato and the Individual.* London, 1964.

Robin, L. *La Théorie Platonicienne de l'Amour.* Paris, 1964.

Sinaiko, H. *Love, Knowledge and Discourse in Plato.* Chicago, 1965.

Taylor, A. E. *Plato.* New York, 1911.

———. *Platonism and Its Influence.* New York, 1963.

VI. and VII.   THE BIBLE

Chamberlain, D. B. *How Jesus Loved*. Del-Mar, Cal., 1971.

Cole, W. *Sex, Love and the Bible*. New York, 1959.

Epstein, L. *Sex Laws and Customs in Judaism*. New York, 1967.

Feuillet, A. *Le Mystère de l'Amour Divin dans la Théologie Johannique*. Paris, 1972.

Furnish, V. P. *The Love Command in the New Testament*. Nashville, 1972.

Johnston, G. *The Spirit-Paraclete in the Gospel of John*. Cambridge, 1970.

McKenzie, J. "Love." *Dictionary of the Bible*. New York, 1965.

Mohler, J. *Dimensions of Faith*. Chicago, 1969.

Montefiore, C., and Loewe, H., eds. *A Rabbinic Anthology*. New York, 1963.

Morgan, D. *Love: Plato, the Bible and Freud*. Englewood Cliffs, N.J., 1964.

Outka, G. *Agape: An Ethical Analysis*. New Haven, 1972.

The Oxford Annotated Bible. New York, 1965.

Patai, R. *Sex and Family in the Bible and the Middle East*. Garden City, N.Y., 1959.

Spicq, C. *Agape in the New Testament*. St. Louis, 1963–67.

Williams, D. *The Spirit and Forms of Love*. New York, 1968.

VIII.   OVID

Frankel, H. F., *Ovid: A Poet Between Two Worlds*. Berkeley, Calif., 1956.

Otis, B. *Ovid as an Epic Poet*. Cambridge, 1966.

Ovid. *Works*, LCL.

Rand, E. K. *Ovid and His Influence*. New York, 1928.

Wilkinson, L. P. *Ovid Recalled*. Cambridge, 1955.

IX.   AUGUSTINE

Augustine. *Works*, PL, ACW, FOC, NPNF.

Battenhouse, R. *A Companion to the Study of Augustine*. New York, 1955.

Brown, P. *Augustine of Hippo*. Berkeley, Calif., 1967.

Burnaby, J. *Amor Dei*. London, 1938.

Callahan, J. F. *Augustine and the Greek Philosophers*. Villanova, 1967.

Chapman, E. *St. Augustine's Philosophy of Beauty*. New York, 1939.

D'Arcy, M. *St. Augustine*. New York, 1957.

Gilson, E. *The Christian Philosophy of St. Augustine*. New York, 1960.

Marrou, H. *St. Augustine*. New York, n.d.

Mohler, J. *The Heresy of Monasticism*. New York, 1971.

Oates, W., ed. *The Basic Writings of St. Augustine*. New York, 1948.

O'Brien, E. *The Essential Plotinus*. New York, 1964.

Pope, H. *St. Augustine of Hippo*. Garden City, N.Y., 1961.

Pryzwara, E. *An Augustine Synthesis*. New York, 1936.

X. THE SUFI

Abu Bakr Sirajed-din. *The Book of Certainty*. New York, 1970.

Abu'l-Ala. *The Diwan of Abu'l-Ala*. H. Baerlein, ed. London, 1948.

Ansari, A., *The Persian Mystics*. S. J. Singh, tr. London, 1951.

Arberry, A. J. *Aspects of Islamic Civilization*. Ann Arbor, 1967.

———. *Sufism: An Account of the Mystics of Islam*. London, 1968.

'Attar, Farid al-din. *Muslim Saints and Mystics (Tadhkirat al-Auliya)*. A. J. Arberry, tr. London, 1966.

Avicenna on Theology. A. J. Arberry, tr. London, 1951.

Bell, R. *The Origin of Islam in Its Christian Environment*. London, 1968.

Brown, J. P. *The Darvishes*. London, 1968.

Guillaume, A. *The Traditions of Islam*. Beirut, 1966.

Ibn Gabirol (Avicebron). *The Fountain of Life*. London, 1963.

Ibn Hazm. *The Ring of the Dove*. A. J. Arberry, tr. London, 1953.

Ibn Said. *The Pennants*, in *Moorish Poetry*. A. J. Arberry, tr. Cambridge, 1953.

The Koran. M. Z. Khan, tr. New York, 1970.

Manual of Hadith. M. Muhammad, tr. Lahore, n.d.

Massignon, L. *Passion de al-Hallaj*. Paris, 1929.

Mohammed, *The Sayings of Mohammed*. Al-Suhrawardy, tr. London, 1954.

Nicholson, R. A. *Studies in Islamic Mysticism*. Cambridge, 1921.

———. *A Literary History of the Arabs*. Cambridge, 1953.

———. *Studies in Islamic Poetry*. Cambridge, 1969.

Nykl, A. R. *Hispano-Arabic Poetry and Its Relationship with the Old Provençal Troubadours*. Baltimore, 1946.

Omar Khayyam. A. J. Arberry, tr. London, 1952.

Rahman, F. *Islam*. Garden City, N.Y., 1968.
Readings from the Mystics of Islam. M. Smith, tr. London, 1950.
Shah, I. *Reflections*. New York, 1974.
———. *Caravan of Dreams*. New York, 1974.
———. *Thinkers of the East*. New York, 1974.
———, ed. *The Way of the Sufi*. London, 1968.
Trimingham, J. S. *The Sufi Orders of Islam*. Oxford, 1971.
Watt, W. M., ed. *The Faith and Practice of al-Ghazali*. London, 1967.

XI. THE KABBALAH

Albertson, E. *Understanding the Kabbalah*. Los Angeles, 1973.
Baer, R. *Philo's Use of the Categories Male and Female*. Leiden, 1970.
Barnett, R., ed. *The Sephardic Heritage: Essays on the History and Cultural Contribution of the Jews of Spain and Portugal*. Vol. I: *The Jews in Spain and Portugal Before and After the Expulsion of 1492*. New York, 1972.
Blau, J. L. *The Christian Interpretation of the Cabala in the Renaissance*. Port Washington, N.Y., 1971.
Gersh, H. *The Sacred Books of the Jews*. New York, 1968.
Hebraic Literature: Readings from the Talmud, Midrashim and Kabbala. Washington, D.C., 1901.
Husik, I. *A History of Medieval Jewish Philosophy*. New York, 1966.
Jacobs, L. *Hasidic Prayer*. New York, 1973.
Judah Ben Samuel, He-Hasid (d. 1212). *Medieval Jewish Mysticism: The Book of the Pious*. S. A. Singer, ed. Northfield, Ill., 1971.
Margolis, M., and Marx, A. *A History of the Jewish People*. Cleveland, 1963.
Mathers, S. L. M. *Kabbalah Unveiled, Kabbala Denudata*. London, 1926.
Mintz, J. R. *Legends of the Hasidim*. Chicago, 1968.
Newman, L., ed. *The Hasidic Anthology*. New York, 1968.
Patai, R. *The Hebrew Goddess*. New York, 1967.
Scholem, G. *On The Kabbalah and Its Symbolism*. New York, 1965.
———. *Major Trends in Jewish Mysticism*. New York, 1971.
Shaya, L. *The Universal Meaning of the Kabbalah*. New York, 1974.
Suares, C. *The Song of Songs: The Canonical Song of Solomon Deciphered According to the Original Code of the Qabala*. Berkeley, Calif., 1972.
Weiner, H. *9 1/2 Mystics: The Kabbala Today*. New York, 1969.
Zinberg, I. *A History of Jewish Literature*. Cleveland, 1972.
The Zohar. H. Sperling and M. Simon, trs. 5 vols.; London, 1931.
Zohar: The Book of Splendor. G. Scholem, ed. New York, 1949.

XII. COURTLY LOVE

Andreas Capellanus. *The Art of Courtly Love*. New York, 1941.

Barrow, S. *Medieval Society Romances*. New York, 1924.

Bezzola, R. *Les Origines et la Formation de la Littérature Courtoise en Occident*. 3 vols.; Paris, 1960.

Boccaccio, G. *Filostrato*. N. Griffin and A. Mytick, trs. Philadelphia, 1929.

Briffault, R. *The Troubadours*. Bloomington, Ind., 1965.

Chaucer, R. *The Complete Poetic Works*. J. Tatlock and P. Mackayes, eds. New York, 1940.

Dante. *The Divine Comedy*. J. B. Fletcher, tr. New York, 1933.

———. *Dante Theologian: The Divine Comedy*. P. Cummins, tr. St. Louis, 1948.

———. *La Vita Nuova*. B. Reynolds, tr. Baltimore, 1969.

De Nomy, A. J. *The Heresy of Courtly Love*. New York, 1947.

———. *An Inquiry into the Origins of Courtly Love*. Medieval Studies 6. Toronto.

Fleming, A. *The Troubadours of Provence*. Glasgow, 1952.

Foster, K. *The Mind of Love: Dante*. London, 1958.

———. *Courtly Love and Christianity*. London, 1963.

Fowler, E. *Spenser and the Courts of Love*. Menasha, Wisc., 1921.

Gilson, E. *Dante and Philosophy*. New York, 1963.

Gower, J. *Confessio Amantis*. H. Morley, ed. London, 1889.

Igly, F. *Troubadours et Trouvères*. Paris, 1960.

Kirby, T. A. *Chaucer's Troilus: A Study in Courtly Love*. Gloucester, 1958.

Lawlor, J., ed. *Patterns of Love and Courtesy: Essays in Memory of C. S. Lewis*. London, 1966.

Lewis, C. S. *The Allegory of Love: A Study of Medieval Tradition*. Oxford, 1936.

———. *The Four Loves*. New York, 1956.

Lorris, G. de, and Meun, J. de. *The Romance of the Rose*. C. Dahlberg, tr. Princeton, 1971.

Newman, F. X., ed. *The Meaning of Courtly Love*. Albany, 1969.

Rougemont, D. de. *Love in the Western World*. New York, 1940.

Spenser, E. *The Faerie Queene*. 2 vols.; London, 1937.

Thomas of Britain. *The Romance of Tristan and Ysult*. R. Loomis, ed. New York, 1951.

Weigand, H. J. *Three Chapters on Courtly Love in Arthurian France and Germany*. Chapel Hill, N.C., 1956.

Wilhelm, J. *Seven Troubadours*. University Park, Pa., 1970.

XIII. MONASTERY AND UNIVERSITY

Aquinas, T. *Opera.* Leonine Ed. Rome, 1822–1948.
——. *Summa Theologica.* New York, 1964.
——. *Basic Writings of St. Thomas Aquinas.* A. Pegis, ed. New York, 1945.
Bernard of Clairvaux. *Opera.* Rome, 1957.
——. *Works.* Cistercian Fathers. Washington, D.C., 1969.
——. *Sermons.* 3 vols.; Dublin, 1925.
——. *86 Sermons on the Song of Solomon.* London, 1895.
Bonaventure. *The Enkindling of Love: or The Triple Way.* Paterson, N.J., 1956.
——. *The Mind's Road to God.* New York, 1953.
Chenu, M.-D. *Toward Understanding St. Thomas.* Chicago, 1963.
D'Arcy, M. *The Mind and Heart of Love.* New York, 1947.
Faraon, M. *The Metaphysical and Psychological Principles of Love.* Dubuque, 1952.
Francis of Assisi. *Writings.* B. Fahy, tr. Chicago, 1964.
Gilson, E. *Wisdom and Love in St. Thomas Aquinas.* Milwaukee, 1951.
——. *The History of Christian Philosophy in the Middle Ages.* New York, 1955.
——. *The Christian Philosophy of St. Thomas Aquinas.* New York, 1956.
Graham, A. *The Love of God.* Garden City, N.Y., 1962.
Luddy, A. *The Life and Teachings of St. Bernard.* Dublin, 1927.
Mohler, J. *The Beginning of Eternal Life: The Dynamic Faith of Thomas Aquinas, Origins and Interpretation.* New York, 1968.
——. *The Heresy of Monasticism.* New York, 1971.
Pegis, A., ed. *The Wisdom of Catholicism.* New York, 1949.
Rousselot, P. *Pour l'Histoire du Problème de l'Amour au Moyen Age.* Munster, 1908.
William of St. Thierry. *Deux Traités de l'Amour de Dieu.* Paris, 1953.
——. *La Contemplation de Dieu.* Paris, SC 61, 1968.
——. *Théologie et Mystique de Guillaume de St. Thierry: La Connaissance de Dieu.* M.-M. Davy, ed. Paris, 1954.
——. *Works.* Cistercian Fathers. Washington, D.C., 1969.

XIV. LUTHER

Althaus, P. *The Theology of Martin Luther.* Philadelphia, 1966.
Bainton, R. *The Age of Reformation.* Princeton, 1956.

——. *Here I Stand*. Cleveland, 1960.

——. *The Reformation of the 16th Century*. Boston, 1956.

Ebeling, B. *Luther: An Introduction to His Thought*. Philadelphia, 1970.

Gerrish, B. *Grace and Reason*. Oxford, 1962.

Hermann, W., ed. *The Communion of the Christian with God: Described on the Basis of Luther's Statements*. Philadelphia, 1971.

Luther, M. *Werke*. Weimar, 1883–1903. (WA)

——. *Luther's Works*. J. Pelikan and H. Lehmann, eds. Philadelphia and St. Louis, 1955. (LW)

——. *Selections from His Writings*. J. Dillenberger, ed. Garden City, N.Y., 1961.

——. *A Compend of Luther's Theology*. H. Kerr, ed. Philadelphia, 1943.

——. *Selected Writings of Martin Luther*. T. Tappert, ed. 4 vols.; Philadelphia, 1967.

——. *Lectures on Romans*. W. Pauck, tr. Philadelphia, 1961. (LCC 15)

XV. TERESA AND JOHN

Auclair, M. *Teresa of Avila*. Garden City, N.Y., 1959.

Benedictines of Stanbrook Abbey. *The Medieval Mystic Tradition and St. John of the Cross*. London, 1954.

Bruno, Fr. *St. John of the Cross*. New York, 1936.

Dicken, E. W. T. *The Crucible of Love: A Study of the Mysticism of St. Teresa of Jesus and St. John of the Cross*. New York, 1963.

Hatzfeld, H. A. *Santa Teresa de Avila*. New York, 1969.

John of the Cross. *Vida y Obras*. Madrid, 1960.

——. *Collected Works*. K. Kavanaugh and O. Rodriguez, trs. New York, 1964.

——. *The Mystical Doctrine of St. John of the Cross*. R. A. J. Stewart, ed. New York, 1936.

Peers, E. A. *Behind That Wall: An Introduction to Some Classics of the Interior Life*. New York, 1948.

Peterson, R. T. *The Art of Ecstasy: Teresa, Bernini and Crashaw*. New York, 1970.

Raymond Lully. *The Tree of Love*. E. A. Peers, tr. London, 1926.

Teresa of Jesus. *Obras Completas*. Madrid, 1961.

——. *Life: Maxims and Foundation*. J. J. Burke, ed. New York, 1911.

——. *Works*. Benedictines of Stanbrook Abbey, trs.; B. Zimmerman, ed. London, 1906.

——. *Works*. E. A. Peers, ed. 3 vols.; London, 1944–46.

XVI. FREUD

Costigan, G. *Sigmund Freud.* New York, 1965.

Dempsey, P. *Freud, Psychoanalysis and Catholicism.* Cork, 1965.

Freud, S. *The Standard Edition of the Complete Psychological Works of Sigmund Freud* (SE). S. Strachey and A. Freud, eds. London, 1964.

——. *The Basic Writings of Sigmund Freud.* New York, 1938.

——. *A General Selection from the Works of Sigmund Freud.* J. Richman and C. Brenner, eds. Garden City, N.Y., 1957.

Fromm, E. *The Art of Loving.* New York, 1963.

——. *Psychoanalysis and Religion.* New Haven, 1971.

Jung, C. G. *Modern Man in Search of His Soul.* New York, 1933.

——. *The Integration of the Personality.* New York, 1939.

——. *Freud and Psychoanalysis.* New York, 1961.

——. *Psychological Reflections: An Anthology.* J. Jacobi, ed. New York, 1961.

Lee, R. S. *Freud and Christianity.* New York, 1943.

Morgan, D. "Freudian Love." *Love: Plato, the Bible and Freud.* Englewood Cliffs, N.J., 1964.

Mowrer, O. H. *The Crisis of Psychiatry and Religion.* Princeton, 1961.

Mullally, P. *Oedipus: Myth and Complex.* New York, 1948.

Philip, H. *Freud and Religious Belief.* New York, 1956.

Ricoeur, P. *The Atheism of Freudian Analysis: Is God Dead?* Concilium 16. New York, 1966.

Stoodley, B. *The Concepts of Sigmund Freud.* Glencoe, Ill., 1959.

Zilboorg, G. *Freud and Religion.* New York, 1958.

XVII. EPILOGUE

Bergler, E. *The Revolt of the Middle-Aged Man.* New York, 1957.

Bird, J. and L. *Sex, Love and the Person.* New York, 1967.

D'Arcy, M. C. *The Mind and the Heart of Love.* New York, 1947.

Darst, D., et al. *Sexuality on the Island Earth.* New York, 1970.

Dedek, J. *Contemporary Sexual Morality.* New York, 1971.

Evoy, J., and O'Keefe, M. *The Man and the Woman: Psychology of Human Love.* New York, 1968.

Fromme, A. *The Ability to Love.* New York, 1965.

Guitton, J. *Essay on Human Love.* New York, 1951.

Kinsey, A. *Sexual Behavior in the Human Male*. Philadelphia, 1948.

——. *Sexual Behavior in the Human Female*. Philadelphia, 1953.

Lepp, I. *The Psychology of Loving*. Baltimore, 1963.

May, R. *Love and Will*. New York, 1969.

Oraison, M. *The Human Mystery of Sex*. New York, 1967.

——. *The Harmony of the Couple*. Notre Dame, Ind., 1967.

——. *Being Together*. Garden City, N.Y., 1971.

Packard, V. *The Sexual Wilderness*. New York, 1968.

Pennington, C. *Liberated Love*. Philadelphia, 1972.

Rougemont, D. de. *Love Declared*. Boston, 1964.

Ryan, J. and M. *Love and Sexuality: A Christian Approach*. New York, 1967.

Schillebeeckx, E. *Celibacy*. New York, 1968.

Sorensen, R. *Adolescent Sexuality in Contemporary America*. Cleveland, 1972.

Suenens, J. J. *Love and Control*. Westminster, 1965.

Sullivan, H. S. *The Mirages of Marriage*. New York, 1968.

Taylor, M., ed. *Sex: Thoughts for Contemporary Christians*. New York, 1972.

Thurian, M. *Marriage and Celibacy*. London, 1959.

INDEX